THE GLORIOUS GAME

Also by Alex Fynn (with Lynton Guest)

The Secret Life of Football
Heroes and Villains
Out of Time
For Love or Money

Dream On (with H. Davidson)

Cantona on Cantona (with Eric Cantona)

The Great Divide (with Olivia Blair)

Also by Kevin Whitcher

Gunning for the Double

THE GLORIOUS GAME

Arsène Wenger, Arsenal and the Quest for Success

Alex Fynn and Kevin Whitcher

ORION

First published in Great Britain in 2003 by Orion
an imprint of Orion Books Ltd
Orion House, 5 Upper St Martin's Lane, London WC2H 9EA

A CIP catalogue record for this book is available
from the British Library

ISBN 0 75286 040 2

Typeset by Selwood Systems, Midsomer Norton

Printed and bound in Great Britain by
Butler & Tanner Ltd, Frome and London

Contents

To Arnold Dein, who never failed to lift my spirits

Alex Fynn

Acknowledgements

Without the assistance of many willing hands this book could not have been written. A debt of gratitude is owed to Arsène and Annie Wenger for permitting the intrusion into their home life and the consideration they showed. Similarly, thanks are due to David Dein, Peter Hill-Wood, Liam Brady, Bob Wilson, Alan Smith and Jürgen Klinsmann who gave willingly of their time and for the insights they provided. The players were less forthcoming and most of their observations were acquired through their press conferences, although Robert Pires must be singled out for his time, kindness and illuminating answers (and Patrick Barclay for allowing his interview to be shared).

Greville Waterman must be thanked for his nagging that there was a book to be written on the subject matter and that one mustn't slope off gracefully into retirement before doing so. Liam Doyle, Alex Phillips, Mark Whitford, John and Matt Simmons read some of the early chapters while Gary Jacob, Kevin McCarra and Brian Dawes ploughed through the lot. In addition Leonard Ross, David Churchill and Brian Capper read some of the proofs. All made constructive comments which were invariably taken on board, for which many thanks, particularly to Gary, Kevin and Brian.

Being able to call on the services of the much-maligned media was a boon and at different times Ed Newman and Martin Lipton came to the rescue, generously providing transcripts for some important interviews. In addition the knowledge of experts like Henry Winter, Amy Lawrence, Xavier Rivoire, Richard Clarke and, of course, Kevin McCarra illuminated some dark corners.

Friends and family who provided much necessary support

included Jason Tomas, Gary Mabbutt, David Bissmire, Mike Francis, Steve Ashford, Bernard Azulay, Kevin Collins, Marc Ollington, Adam Velasco, Richard Grace, David Stern and last and by no means least Jay Lindsay and Rhoda Fynn.

Other invaluable sources of information included arsenal-world.co.uk, arseweb.com, anr.uk.com and arsenal.com and of course *The Gooner*. Of the less specific websites, the *Guardian*, *Times* and *Telegraph* were always good value as were *L'Equipe*, *France Football* and TF1's *Telefoot* programme. The Chicken Shed Theatre Company should also be mentioned for unwittingly hosting many of the co-authors' meetings.

And, of course, we are grateful to special agent David Luxton for getting us the gig and to Ian Preece, editor extraordinaire, for his faith in the project and invaluable contribution at all times.

Nothing But The Truth

After the first Premiership and FA Cup double in 1998 Arsenal manager, Arsène Wenger, was en route to Amsterdam to meet up with his friend and the Highbury club's vice-chairman David Dein to attend the Champions League final between Real Madrid and Juventus. Arriving first at the hotel Dein thought he should register for both of them. On Arsène Wenger's form under 'Occupation' he wrote 'Miracle Worker'. He pushed it across to the desk clerk who nodded in agreement.

The problem with greatness is that everyone expects you to do even better next time. In 2003 such was the outstanding quality of their early season play that Arsenal were a foregone conclusion to reach the last four of the Champions League, if not in the view of most pundits to contest the final at the very least. With Manchester United off the pace the Premiership was regarded as a race already run, the cliché that the league is a marathon and not a sprint lost in the hyperbole. Yet at the season's end – which in terms of trophies only had the FA Cup to compensate for a runners-up place in the league and a failure to reach even the knockout stages in Europe's premier competition – voices were raised and fingers pointed at the tactics, selection policy and in particular the inadequacies of the defence.

Of course, like all good fallacies there was some truth in the assertion that Arsenal had blown it. Yet the larger truth was lost in a fog of disappointment and rapprochement. This was another season of high fulfilment. Period.

In Arsène Wenger's six full seasons the record of two Premierships, three FA Cups, four league runners-up places, and two further Cup Final appearances was by any rational criterion a staggering success. Moreover it had all been achieved for the total net cost of £28 million – less than the fee paid by Manchester United for Rio Ferdinand – highlighting the scale of the accomplishment.

Before carping, Arsenal fans in particular might like to know that there was a chance that *Le Technicien Alsacien* might have alighted from France at the other end of the Seven Sisters Road. The fact that he didn't, consigned their neighbours to a solitary trophy – the paltry League Cup – to show for the pain and suffering that was inflicted on them during the Wenger years. The instability that accompanied the changes in the Spurs' boardroom and the manager's seat, with each new incumbent endeavouring to leave his own imprint, has brought them mid-table mediocrity as the sum total of all their efforts. This scant reward has cost Tottenham £53 million, almost twice what it cost Arsenal to achieve their success.

It is a nightmare tale of what might have been had not David Dein and his co-directors been able to persuade Arsène Wenger to come to Highbury. And yet as season 2002–03 draws to a conclusion it is Arsenal who face a critical watershed in their history.

Accepting that they need much greater matchday revenue than the 38,500 capacity that Highbury can provide if they are to keep Manchester United – with their 67,700 stadium – in their sights, the commitment to build their own state-of-the-art edifice at Ashburton Grove has seen a healthy profit almost overnight transformed into a thumping great loss.

Beset by planning, construction and financial problems the house-warming party has had to be postponed until after the manager's contract expires in 2005. He must wonder how much longer he has to wait before he can anticipate tackling his rivals with more weapons at his disposal. United's head start means they will never be caught; their position as the world's richest club is likely to remain unchallenged, at least domestically. Arsenal the football club are in danger of losing their way.

Fortunately there are many players who will be enticed by the club's reputation as one of the leading exponents of the glorious game and it is only a Zidane or Henry who nowadays can write his own contract. It is a testimony to *la patte de Wenger* (the stamp of Wenger) that his star attacker puts equanimity and job satisfaction above the probability that greater financial rewards and a better chance of honours could be had elsewhere at one of the mega Latin clubs. While life is on the side of the big battalions, the future for Arsenal remains in the balance.

While the administrators juggle with the figures it must never be forgotten that to have a successful business you must first have a successful team, that the playing side of the club must be protected and prioritised. Stars like Henry are jewels. They bring sheer pleasure to millions and the team they comprise, orchestrated by a 'miracle worker', is so good it belongs to all of us. This is their story . . . so far.

Chapter One

Arsène Before Arsenal

Dining companions in a plush Monte Carlo rendezvous, they were an odd couple that looked like fish out of water. The tall, slim Caucasian schoolmasterish figure and the nervous young black athlete. In fact the youth was so bemused – it was definitely the first time he had been taken out to dinner, probably the first time he had ever set foot in a restaurant, certainly one of such renown – that completely tongue-tied, his companion had to order for him.

Almost a decade later, in 1995, at a glittering ceremony in Milan to pay homage to the great and the good, the most prestigious award – the FIFA Footballer of the Year – of the world's most popular sport was bestowed on George Weah. The player coaxed his former coach out of the applauding audience to share his moment with him, an all too rare magnanimous gesture in a sport that had evolved into show business. Arsène Wenger shyly joined his protégé on stage. It was the most public recognition of a singular skill that had spotted and nurtured a raw talent and set it along the road to being acknowledged as the best footballer on the planet. Dismissed by Monaco and currently at work in unfashionable Japan, there was obviously something special, a *je ne sais quoi* regarding the unassuming French coach.

Some years later, his coaching credentials established beyond question, he was asked at a charity function about his largely unknown career as a player. He surprised his audience initially by telling them, 'I was the best ... in my village (dramatic pause) ... it was a very small village.'

Arsène was brought up in Dusenheim near Strasbourg. His family ran a restaurant which the local football club used as its headquarters, so his earliest memories were centred around the team, the selection meetings, the pre-match preparations and the post-match bonhomie. Football played a vital role in the everyday existence of his family and even if his parents hadn't instilled a love of the game, his environment would have made it impossible not to have caught the bug and been infected for life.

He revelled in playing the game, although his best years were spent in the French lower divisions with Mutzig, Vauban and Mulhouse for whom, in 1975, he once scored four goals in a Division Two league match and was promptly dubbed 'the Gunter Netzer of Mulhouse', after the renowned German playmaker of the time. He became a media fad when, after joining First Division Strasbourg to look after *le centre de formation* – the youth academy – injuries to the first choice defenders enabled him to make his first-team debut as a *libero* – sweeper – at the age of twenty-nine. His professional career comprised a mere handful of games including a single European outing when Strasbourg were overwhelmed by Duisbourg 4–0. All the same, he recalls the time fondly and says, 'I didn't have the quality to carve out a good career as a player, it is as simple as that,' although 'there was a certain frustration as a player. I was super-passionate from an early age. Perhaps missing something as a player has served me as a coach. It enabled me to invest more as a coach than if I had been fulfilled as a player.'

Of the decision to follow this path, he said, 'I became a coach because I loved doing it. It was a very natural progression.' Two years later he moved to Cannes to take the job of assistant coach, before graduating to the top job at Nancy in 1984. It was a return to his roots. Nancy's director of football was the legendary Michel Platini's father, Aldo, and Nancy were the club where Michel began his playing career. It is a quirk of fate that the club should give a start to both France's greatest ever player and arguably the greatest ever French manager. (Aimé Jaquet might have won the World Cup but he didn't discover or develop the players.)

Arsène Wenger certainly learned his trade the hard way, with Nancy suffering relegation from the top flight in 1987. 'It was a good lesson,' he says, 'because it's better to start with dis-appointment so when you win it's easy. I began as a coach with difficult years.' With greater resources, it seems certain he could have avoided the drop and indeed this was acknowledged by the club. Of that time, Wenger says, 'There were no exceptional players. Nancy offered me a five-year contract with the keys to the club, to do everything. I had the choice of moving to Paris St Germain or Monaco, and Aldo Platini told me, "You must work at a big club", and he had taken me to Nancy in the first place. It looked like Monaco had potential.' So Monaco it was.

The advent of Wenger had immediate impact, taking the club to the league title in his first season. Newcomers Glenn Hoddle and Mark Hateley (the former finally departing Tottenham Hotspur after nearly twenty years), augmented seasoned French internationals: goalkeeper Jean-Luc Ettori and defenders Manuel Amoros and Patrick Battiston. Monaco led the table from the second day of the 1987–88 season and remained there until its end, an incredible feat given that Wenger was a thirty-eight-year-old coach with only three years' experience at this level.

Winning *le championat* was a triumph against the odds not just for the club, but for the coach. Wenger was a young man whose playing CV would hardly have endeared any great respect from those participants in the semi-final of the 1982 World Cup. Although tall, he hardly cut an intimidating figure. He looked as if he really should be instructing schoolkids instead of directing a group of athletes in the ways of winning. His success in gaining the esteem of his seen-it-all-before charges was in some ways as significant to his career as coaching them to the title. It was a virtue that would stand him in good stead when he would be called upon to repeat it in the even more hostile environment of the English Premiership.

Monaco's triumph caught the bigger guns of Marseille, Bordeaux and Paris St Germain by surprise, these sides concentrating on each other on the assumption that the relative minnows leading the table would eventually run out of steam. Coming from a poor club where defence was the priority, Wenger found that with some money to spend for the first time, his team could play a more expansive game. He was particularly fortunate in this respect with the purchase of Glenn Hoddle from Tottenham, as the midfield maestro established himself as the most influential player in France, almost from his first game. But if complacency facilitated Monaco's triumph, Bernard Tapie and company took the necessary steps to prevent a repeat occurrence.

Over the next five seasons, Monaco were runners-up twice and never finished outside of the top three. Yet they could not repeat their title triumph, chiefly because of the improbity in the French game, specifically that instigated by Marseille under their charismatic president – millionaire businessman, local socialist MP and future government minister, Bernard Tapie. Wenger has adopted a philosophical air about that period, but still feels thwarted. 'French football was corrupt and it stopped us winning the title. It is very difficult to explain the (then) prevailing atmosphere,' he says. Money was talking and essentially it was in the hands of ambitious presidents who were prepared to cut corners. The rivalry at that time was almost a duopoly between Marseille and Bordeaux and presidents of these clubs were subsequently found guilty of fraud. Key administrators at both also ended up in jail. Wenger recalls, 'Marseille, Bordeaux and Paris St Germain had much more financial power than us, so it was a miracle to be at the top every year. I think we could have won the title one or two more times but it was a bad time for French football.'

In 1993, a few days before the Champions League final that saw Marseille beat Milan 1–0 to become the first French club to lift the European Cup, they beat Valenciennes by the same score in a vital league match. Marseille were trying to retain their domestic crown while Valenciennes needed points to avoid relegation. Three Valenciennes players: Christophe Robert, Jacques Glassmann and Argentinian World Cup winner Jorge Burruchaga, were each offered £30,000 if they didn't 'exert' themselves. Subsequently it was proved that Robert and Burruchaga initially agreed to go along with the deal, with some of the cash being discovered buried in the garden of Robert's aunt. Among the brazen Marseille directors implicated was Bernard Tapie. In a bizarre attempt to get himself off the hook, he tried to get the now ex-Valenciennes coach Boro Primorac to carry the can. The ploy failed. Marseille were found guilty of bribery, stripped of the French title, demoted to Division Two, and expelled from the European Cup. The incident drew Primorac and Wenger closer as Arsène took Boro with him to Japan and today they are still together. Primorac works as a technical assistant, watching opposition sides, checking prospective players and coaching the first team.

One sphere in which Marseille could not influence Monaco's fortunes were their campaigns in Europe. As league champions they entered the European Cup in 1988–89, and progressed to the quarter-finals courtesy of a 6–2 aggregate demolition of Club Brugge in which Glenn Hoddle shone. It was an unusual position for the club to find itself, as Wenger says, 'It is important to put Monaco's European record into context. Before I arrived they never progressed in the competition beyond the end of the year.' In March 1989, they found themselves in the last eight, where they came up against the Turkish side Galatasaray, but without the injured Hoddle. 'We lost to Galatasaray in a very aggressive tie in Cologne.' The match was Galatasaray's 'home' leg as they could not play the game in Istanbul because of crowd trouble in a previous round. 'It was a hostile environment because there are millions of Turkish people living in Germany who for once could see their club. That was my biggest disappointment as a coach up to that point. Although you can see it as an achievement because everyone at the club was happy as Monaco had poor results in recent years. But for me it was a big let-down.'

Under Wenger, Monaco continued to do well in European competitions, always reaching the last eight. In 1991–92, as French Cup holders, they made a breakthrough reaching the final of the European Cup Winners' Cup, disposing of Roma and Feyenoord in the process. The final held in Lisbon was a huge anticlimax. Monaco were favourites to defeat German rivals Werder Bremen and become the first French side to lift a European trophy, but their preparations were thrown into chaos by events on the eve of their big day. They had already reached the final of their domestic cup. The semi-final to decide their opponents was played at Bastia on the island of Corsica, between Bastia and Marseille. A stand collapsed during the game killing eighteen people and injuring hundreds. 'It was a nightmare,' Wenger recalls. 'We didn't have our minds on the game. We were up until three in the morning at our hotel the night before our game because some of our players were directly involved, with family and friends.' Even if tragedy hadn't intervened, Wenger had a strong sense of fore-boding about the final. Realising that in looking too far ahead and resting the whole team for the preceding league game he had failed to abide by the old cliché: take one game at a time. The players had too much time on their hands, time to get nervous and too wound up for the most important game in the club's history. It was no surprise that Monaco meekly surrendered to Werder Bremen 2–0. Nowadays the next fixture is always the most important one on the manager's calendar – with the exception of a League Cup tie!

Monaco's success both domestically and internationally was the result of Arsène Wenger's team-building technique, in the same way that he later would transform Arsenal. Experienced players such as keeper Jean Luc-Ettori and midfielder Marcel Dib, were joined by the attacking skills of George Weah and Rui Barros, with exceptional youngsters such as Emmanuel Petit, Lilian Thuram and Yuri Djorkaeff emerging. 'We developed slowly, like at Arsenal, a team who could cope with the different demands of European competition, and became stronger and stronger every year. Of course at Monaco we were in a situation that meant we always had to sell players. We bought Hoddle and Hateley but they weren't expensive. We couldn't spend big money. We got George Weah for nothing and sold him for £4.5 million – big, big money at the time. We replaced him with Klinsmann for comparatively little – £1.8 million. We played 4–3–3 in Europe with Rui Barros as a second striker making runs behind Weah – he was small but very quick. We were always dangerous, playing a high-pressing game, very mobile, very fast. We played the same game at home. We were quite impressive.'

Barros on the one hand, and Weah and Petit on the other, illustrate the two main methods that Wenger uses to secure his players. Weah was an unsophisticated raw talent, inexperienced in the ways of the world. A teenager from Liberia (later reportedly referred to as 'the big librarian' by Ron Atkinson) found through Wenger's network of contacts and gradually developed by his coach, who sowed the seeds that precipitated a talented and versatile attacker and a sporting ambassador for his impoverished homeland. Off the field, Weah's commitment was unusual for a footballer and, even more worthy, he often dug into his own pockets to make sure his countrymen could perform on a level playing field with their football opponents. Such players feel beholden to Wenger for his role in their development as both players and men.

Emmanuel Petit was taken to Monaco as a teenager and moulded by Wenger, firstly as a central defender and then, later at Highbury, as a World Cup winning midfielder. Petit emphasises the attributes of his former boss as a mentor, 'Arsène is a very good teacher who knows how to get the best out of the man before getting the best out of the player. He often succeeds in detecting problems before they arise. That leads to a climate of confidence between him and his players. The player feels indebted to him.'

Rui Barros was an experienced talent that Wenger could see would bring an added dimension to his team. 'I saw him first in a televised match. I liked him and when he moved to Juventus, I went to see him play. I thought I want this player and for me it is always a feeling. I try to imagine a player in my team, to see what extra he will bring to my team. Will he bring a quality we don't have, a quality we need? It's like a puzzle and he's another piece to help you solve it.' Wenger's dilemma at Monaco was that at the end of every season some of the pieces of his jigsaw could be forcibly removed, making his accomplishments all the more remarkable.

Before the Bosman ruling in 1995 that gave footballers in the European Community the right to change their employers when their contract expired without the payment of a transfer fee, there was already freedom of movement of sorts in France. Unfortunately this meant that at a club like Monaco, no sooner had you unearthed a jewel than it was plucked from your grasp by a bigger, richer outfit and there was a new puzzle for the coach to complete. It's no wonder that coaches in France, with the atypical exceptions of Wenger's contemporaries, Guy Roux at Auxerre and Jean-Claude Saudeau at Nantes – whose longevity exceeded even Wenger's seven-year term at Monaco – fought a constant uphill battle. Today's title challengers becoming, as a result of debilitated resources, tomorrow's relegation candidates with the poor coach paying the inevitable price (*limogé* – fired, is an all too common term in the vocabulary of the French football business). It was not only his coaching record but the skill with which Arsène Wenger speedily learned how to play the transfer market at a profit that kept him in his job. And he was not above resorting to the tricks of the trade when needs must.

Jürgen Klinsmann was already – like Glenn Hoddle before him – in negotiations with Paris St Germain when he was prised away from the clutches of one of Monaco's main rivals. A lovely *monagasque* seafront restaurant provided the setting in which

Internazionale's seasoned German international was seduced – in his native tongue – by Arsène Wenger's technical know-how and by the fact that the role the coach had in mind for him appealed to his sensibilities.

As Jürgen recalled: 'Apart from expecting me to score goals, Arsène wanted to use my experience in a leadership role, to guide the up-and-coming stars like George Weah.' The deal was done over lunch. But no sooner had Jürgen arrived, than George departed. 'You told me you would play me alongside George Weah,' Klinsmann confronted his new employer. Wenger apologised, feeling as frustrated as the new signing, but explained that the president had just been offered more money for Weah (who had been bought for a pittance and was now on his way to Paris St Germain for £4.5 million) than Monaco could turn down. However the rapport between superstar and coach was so immediate as to make the change in circumstances forgivable.

Arsène Wenger's exceptional record of consistent success at Monaco remains unequalled to this day. By contrast his greatest rival Marseille had no less than eight changes of coach during their five successive title wins between 1989 and 1993. Although it could be argued that in their case the main man was President Tapie who was pulling the strings all the while.

After the Marseille scandal broke, Monaco, by default, found themselves once again competing for the European Cup. The competition had been relaunched in 1992 as the Champions League. A group stage, introduced the previous year, was maintained to justify the change and placate the big clubs agitating for more guaranteed fixtures than the old-style knockout formula could provide. Despite being the holders, having beaten Milan 1–0 in May 1993, Marseille had been stripped of their domestic title and were withdrawn from the 1993–94 contest by the French Football Federation. Paris St Germain had finished as runners-up in the French league, and as domestic Cup winners had qualified for the Cup Winners' Cup. PSG were detested by Marseille fans and the club would have been vilified if they had entered the premier competition by dint of Marseille's expulsion, so they remained in the Cup Winners' Cup and third-placed Monaco became France's Champions League representatives. It was ironic that Arsène Wenger's club should benefit from Marseille's punishment, having been thwarted due to their rival's shenanigans over previous seasons.

Monaco progressed through the first two knockout rounds beating AEK Athens and Steaua Bucharest. The eight teams remaining were split into two groups and Monaco finished second in their group behind Barcelona, eliminating Spartak Moscow and Galatasaray. Wenger's team beat the Turks 3–0 at home and 2–0 in Istanbul, which must have been particularly satisfying given their elimination by the same side in their previous European Cup campaign. The semi-finals were not aggregate two-legged affairs as they are now, but one-off matches. Monaco, finishing second in their group, had to visit the home of the other group's first placed side – Milan. The home advantage told, as the Italians won 3–0, progressing to the final where they hammered Barcelona 4–0.

But the scoreline flattered Milan. According to Wenger, 'We should have won this game. Possession was 70:30 to us,' he claimed, but you don't have a strong case when the result is 3–0. 'I was pleased to get to the semi-final, but I wanted to win. For Monaco, the achievement was great, but I always play to win.' That Monaco troubled Milan was evidenced by the fact of Alessandro Costacurta's dismissal for a foul on Jürgen Klinsmann. Television revealed that Klinsmann probably dived, but he subsequently explained that he had warned the defender that if he didn't desist the continuous fouling that was not being picked up by the referee he would get him a red card. (The manager claimed he was unaware of the incident at the time. It was a pose that critics of his desire to give his players the benefit of the doubt, even when there was none, would come to regard as an unfortunate trait.) However, Milan made the most of their opportunities and scored at key moments to ensure their passage to the final.

Possibly due to their Champions League campaign, Monaco's domestic form slumped in 1993–94 and the team finished outside the top three for the first time in Wenger's tenure. Despite this, Wenger was in demand elsewhere. 'I had an offer from Bayern Munich, but Monaco didn't want to let me go because I had one year left on my contract. They offered me two more years, and I said no, I will honour my contract and then I will go. Of course that created friction.' In fact Wenger may not have been too perturbed by Monaco's refusal to sanction his departure. Bayern had contacted him when they were enjoying a warm weather training break on the Côte d'Azur and Jürgen Klinsmann had picked up the vibes from his fellow countrymen. Taken aback when Jürgen asked him what was going on, Wenger admitted the approach and said, 'I'm kind of thinking about it.' Klinsmann was surprised at his downbeat reaction. 'Come on Arsène,' he said, 'this is Bayern Munich. What is there to think about?'

The 1994–95 season began badly for the team and in September, Wenger was dismissed. This was harsh and ironic after having been refused the chance to leave in the summer to take up the post in Munich, and then having his contract terminated before it had run its course. Since this experience, Wenger has felt the final year of any manager's contract to be practically worthless in terms of security, although he, as a man of honour, feels that the loyalty that a contract implies should work both ways.

Although Bayern may no longer have been an option, he had other offers of employment. One was from the Greek side Olympiakos, and another came from the Japanese club Grampus Eight, based in the city of Nagoya. 'I had ten years in the French First Division without stopping. I always had it in my mind to have an international career. I was forty-four and thought, let's go for something completely different – a culture shock, a completely different way of working. On reflection it was an audacious choice. I was on my own and I didn't speak the language. People said I was committing commercial suicide, but it was terrific for me. I was able to put some distance in my life away from all the European pressure.' (His relationship with Annie Hollville, his long-term partner – so much so that she now calls herself Annie Wenger – and mother of his daughter Léa, now five and a half, was in its infancy. She had children from a previous marriage and could only visit him in Japan during the school holidays.) 'It was difficult but also very positive, making a break from what had gone before, reflecting on my life, what I had done and what I wanted to do in the future. And to interact with a different society which operates in a different way which seduced me and I am still in love with today.'

He arrived in Nagoya in January 1995. 'What I did first of all,' he maintains, 'was to inject confidence into the players by saying repeatedly that they are competent enough to win. They were used to being defeated and lacked confidence in themselves.' After a slow start, Wenger's way began to take effect and his club finished as runners-up in the league and for the first time in their history, won the Emperor's Cup, in effect, the Japanese FA Cup. He still talks fondly of his time there, leading one to believe that he would happily return.

While Wenger was in Japan, the manager's office at Arsenal's Highbury Stadium might as well have had a revolving door fitted. George Graham, Stewart Houston and Bruce Rioch were all in the hotseat during a period of four months from February 1995. 'When they [the board] approached me,' recalls Wenger, 'I said I would take the job, even though I knew there would be resistance. After all, there was no history of success or foreign coaches when I arrived. And at this stage, Arsenal was still regarded as a very conservative sort of club, very conscious of its history and traditions.'

Wenger was a long-time student of English football. 'The first game I saw in England was between Liverpool and Manchester United and it was a big discovery. I could feel that football had been created here. There was a different quality of passion and the way the supporters lived the match was distinct from anywhere else in Europe. I thought that if one day I was given the chance to work in England, I would do it.' As Monaco often played before home crowds of under 5,000, no wonder he was taken aback by English football, particularly the Premiership. While managing in France, he would often use the league's winter break to come to England and watch matches at White Hart Lane, there being a close association between Tottenham and Monaco thanks to the transfer of Glenn Hoddle, and resulting friendly matches between the two clubs.

With Highbury in close proximity, Wenger's trips facilitated regular visits there too. On one of these, in 1988, he got lost and stumbled into the directors' wives' lounge (no women were allowed in the boardroom at that time). He was taken by Barbara Dein to meet her husband, and the two men struck up an immediate rapport. Dein, as is his wont with those who share his enthusiasm for his two loves – football and theatre – generously took Wenger to dinner with some friends, as he was on his own in a foreign town. After dinner, a game of charades ensued. Dein explained, in French, what was required of his guest in order to participate. Wenger's command of English then was not what it is today, nevertheless, he readily picked up on what he had to do, acting out *A Midsummer Night's Dream*, and making an immediate impression on David Dein. Some years later the roles were reversed, as Dein recalls: 'In Arsène's first year I had to negotiate the contracts of Patrick Vieira, Remi Garde, Nicolas Anelka, Manu Petit and Gilles Grimandi. The French boys were coming in thick and fast and it was putting my basic command of the language to the test. So after about a year, I asked Arsène, "What's the biggest improvement you've seen at the club?" Expecting him to say something about the style of play or the passion of the fans, he shot back instead, "Your French!"'

It was evident that here was a man not exactly in the mould of your average sheepskin-coat-wearing British football manager of the eighties, the antithesis of the kind of man of whom it might be said: 'He who only football knows, knows nothing of life.' Dein's initial good vibes were reinforced when he saw Wenger at work, with his players, the Monaco directors and the media. He realised that 'here was one for the future' and their friendship grew. Dein had a yacht moored at Antibes along the coast from Monaco, and would often take in a game and dinner with the coach afterwards, and it became obvious that his friend was an exceptional man who would eventually reach the top of his trade. Given the opportunity, Dein determined that Arsenal would be the beneficiaries – an arrangement that would satisfy both parties.

Wenger agreed to come, moved by his love of the English game – 'played with fluency and passion' – and the control he would be granted at Arsenal, despite the club being tainted by the George Graham saga that saw transfer funds misspent. 'At Arsenal, I have freedom in my work. That is most important and the most difficult to give up once you have it.' Always seeking to widen his horizons, there was also the challenge of changing the conservative, not to say, outmoded, outlook of his new employers and by so doing explode the myth that a foreign manager could never win the Premiership. The official announcement that Arsène Wenger would actually be the full-time successor to Bruce Rioch was not made until September 1996, a few weeks after it was an open secret that he would be arriving, and a few months after the deal was done in a Japanese hotel bedroom. Arsenal players, Arsenal fans and the football world were in for a culture shock.

Chapter Two

Arsène Who?

They were an incongruous sight – three middle-aged Englishmen struggling through the Tokyo rush hour to try and find the right shinkansen (bullet train). As Peter Hill-Wood recollected, 'How the hell we got there I don't know but we found our way somehow.' Along with his vice-chairman David Dein and fellow director and largest shareholder Danny Fiszman, the trio had come to try and persuade Arsène Wenger to manage their club.

Both parties had been down the same track before. Early in 1995, during the turmoil of the last month of George Graham's reign, at David Dein's request, Peter Hill-Wood had entertained Arsène Wenger at his favourite restaurant – Zianis – a stone's throw from his Chelsea home. With Josef Venglos hardly blazing a trail at Aston Villa, Hill-Wood cast his mind back and reflected, 'I think at that moment we were nervous of hiring a foreign manager. We hadn't the nerve to do it and I might not have been wrong. I don't think it hurt him going to Japan.' Indeed there was strong support for Hill-Wood's view from an indisputable source. Jürgen Klinsmann felt that, 'There was a different Arsène Wenger after Japan. He came back, and for the first time truly believed "I'm ready for a big club now" '. And as it happened, Arsenal were now ready for him.

'It was a big decision,' recalls Hill-Wood, 'to reverse the one we'd taken two years previously.' However, it was quick and painless. An hour's discussion in Arsène Wenger's hotel room and it was handshakes all round. 'We felt we'd got the right man,' affirmed Hill-Wood. But not right away as Arsène Wenger did not seek to break his contract with Grampus Eight. He had a year to run, but said he would endeavour to find his replacement to

13

expedite his release. After Carlos Queiroz (who became Alex Ferguson's assistant at Manchester United before landing the top job at Real Madrid) got his feet under the table, Arsène finally left Japan for London in October 1996.

Although managing to keep their prize acquisition under wraps for a few weeks, it became, as Hill-Wood commented at the club's AGM in September, 'One of the worst kept secrets of the year.' Pressed to reveal the identity of the new manager, the chairman refused, claiming that having given an undertaking he couldn't formally announce the name of the incumbent. 'An undertaking to who?' asked one of the shareholders. 'An undertaking to Mr Wenger and ...' cue dissolution of meeting into riotous laughter drowning out the rest of Hill-Wood's sentence.

Arsène Wenger first appeared before the English public on the Jumbotron screens at Highbury in the build-up to Arsenal's Monday evening Premiership match against Sheffield Wednesday on 16 September 1996. The manager in waiting was in Japan but had videotaped a message so that the fans could see and hear for themselves the man who would be guiding their team after his business with Grampus Eight on the other side of the globe had been concluded. Though the inability to hear his words of wisdom – the sound system and the crowd noise do not combine to make easy listening at Highbury – might not have conveyed a perfect first impression.

'Wenger looked like a 1970s throwback French professor ... mmm, nice choice Mr Dein,' was one fan's reaction. Most Arsenal supporters had never heard of Wenger before he was revealed as the successor to the recently departed Bruce Rioch. There was a feeling of anticlimax after the media had trumpeted former Barcelona coach and Dutch hero Johan Cruyff as the favourite to take over, but it soon became clear that Wenger would be the man, as new French signings Patrick Vieira and Remi Garde spoke of looking forward to working with him, oblivious to the fact that he was still some time away from starting his new job.

Wenger understood that the fans would have preferred a famous name, such as Cruyff. In reaction to the leaked news of his appointment, he had some words of consolation for them. 'Don't allow yourselves to be manipulated by a minority just because a few people are shouting the loudest. Names die, fame can be short term. It is the quality of your work which can survive the longest. The Arsenal fans are intelligent. They know to judge someone on his work and ideas, not just his reputation.' As it turned out, Wenger was correct in his wishful thinking.

With only a couple of days between the announcement of Rioch's departure and the revelation an unknown would be taking over, fans did not have very long to establish a groundswell in favour of a particular candidate for the job and largely reacted to what they gleaned from the media. However, once it was obvious who the new man was, they were prepared to give him time to show what he could do and judge him on his accomplishments in his new role.

This did not mean that the supporters, despite never really taking to Bruce Rioch, approved of his treatment. The fact that he was dismissed only days before the side's opening Premiership match of the season was indicative that the board's impatience with what they perceived as Rioch's intransigence had finally evaporated. It had been hoped that he might remain until Wenger could leave Japan, but the situation became farcical with Rioch, not allowed to sign any reinforcements, realising that he had no support from above and was only marking time.

'We were a club in crisis,' says David Dein of that period. And no wonder. Whoever heard of a club embarking on their pre-season training and friendlies under a coach that the directors fully intended dismissing regardless of results. With the player registrations of the two new French signings about to enter the public arena, Bruce Rioch had to be ushered through the exit door before it was known exactly when his replacement would arrive. Rioch's last act of any note was to qualify for the UEFA Cup on the last day of the 1995–96 season with a somewhat fortuitous home victory against Bolton Wanderers. Wenger's video appearance at Highbury four months on preceded the first match Arsenal would play under Pat Rice, Arsenal's second caretaker manager in as many months. Rice's predecessor, Stewart Houston, had quit the club (with few tears shed by the fans) frustrated at not being given a chance to wield the managerial whip for the long term, and having the opportunity to do just that across town at Queen's Park Rangers, where, ironically, he would employ Bruce Rioch as his number two, in a role reversal to their positions at Highbury.

Rioch's season at the club had certainly seen him leave it in better shape than it was on his arrival. Not only were Dennis Bergkamp and David Platt now on the playing staff, but Arsenal had embraced a more attractive playing style, which the paying public had not experienced in the last three seasons of George Graham's time. Despite this improvement on the field of play, one of the priorities was a happy ship at Highbury, and off it an increasing dissatisfaction with the manager was emanating from all quarters. Peter Hill-Wood put the players' point of view. 'They are very astute. I think they can pick up the vibes quite easily. They respected George and probably were quite frightened of him but I don't think they did respect Bruce and therefore weren't frightened of him, however rough he may have been.' Although Messrs Bergkamp and Platt had been captured (widely believed to be the result of David Dein's efforts rather than the manager's), as the director responsible for team affairs, Dein became more and more frustrated by Rioch's indecision. (Arsenal only have a handful of directors and apart from the chairman and managing director, all supervise a key area of the club's activities. In addition to Dein, Daniel Fiszman and the then managing director Ken Friar oversee the stadium project and Richard Carr works with Liam Brady and the academy.) The manager vacillated over potential purchases and indeed never even got round to signing his own contract, which the club honoured anyway when he was dismissed. The chairman succinctly summed up: 'Frankly I don't think he was up to the job.' Neither apparently was Stewart Houston.

Houston's failure to earn permanent promotion could also be put down to a lack of respect from the players. Their nickname for him was 'The Coneman', a derogatory reference to his status reflecting his function in placing out the road cones employed for various training exercises. Players used to years of being barked at by a succession of disciplinarians would soon welcome a very different approach. Goodbye sergeant major and the coneman, hello professor.

The tabloid press were not as open-minded as the club and its followers about the new man at the Highbury helm. Theirs was a different agenda and they were not about to give Arsène Wenger an easy ride. Media insularity and a touch of xenophobia came to the fore, with back page headlines such as 'Arsène Who?' That Wenger did not conform to the criteria of what a football manager should sound or look like did not help his cause. His meagre playing career meant there were bound to be questions about his coaching credibility when it came to gaining the respect of the 'hardened English pro', accustomed to being abused by a succession of fiery Scottish managers, or former England internationals with their 'caps on the table' approach as justification for the 'boss' or 'gaffer' moniker which they insisted upon.

Fortunately, the supporters and the board ignored all attempts to destabilise the club and were willing their man to succeed. The furore ultimately said more about the insular reactionary English football industry than it did about a man who was strong enough to keep faith with his own principles; which had proved successful in France and Japan and would soon do exactly the same in the Premiership.

However, before he had time to be judged on his team's football, Arsène Wenger experienced a baptism of fire, as the media picked up on a whispering campaign spreading scurrilous false rumours about his private life, culminating in a news report that he was about to be dismissed by the club because of the allegations. Peter Hill-Wood later revealed the baseness of this view. 'I didn't think for a moment there was a shred of truth. It certainly didn't rattle us. It just annoyed everybody that people could spread that sort of rumour.'

It was just the kind of thing the media was looking for to back up their initial hostile reaction to Wenger's appointment. On a Thursday lunchtime in November, the press descended on Highbury Stadium like a pack of vultures awaiting confirmation of the manager's dismissal. It was to be a watershed in their attitude to Wenger. Against the advice of colleagues, he faced them on the steps to the Marble Hall and challenged them to state exactly what the rumours were. The assembled hacks failed to find the courage of their convictions and meekly backed down as it became apparent that they were there on a wild-goose chase stirred up by their own prejudices. Wenger told them: 'Nobody who knows me will tell you anything bad about me. I do not have to explain anything, but I am sad because Arsenal should be respected and so should I. It is a strong club and I am a strong person.' His bold front had bought him some time, the media monkey was off his back – for now.

The modus operandi of the football professional was much the same at Highbury in the 1990s before the arrival of Wenger as it was at most other top clubs in England. Training designed to get the peak physical performance out of athletes was impaired, because clubs turned a blind eye to the all-pervasive drinking culture which was perceived as 'good for bonding' and 'building team spirit'. With hindsight the attitude defies logic, although old school devotees would point to the remarkable success English sides had enjoyed in European competition, especially in the decade before they were banned from competing as a result of the Heysel disaster in 1985. The Norwegian goalkeeper Erik Thorsvedt who played in Sweden, Germany and in England for Tottenham succinctly summed up the reason why: 'They (the English professionals) eat the wrong food, drink too much, don't train properly but have a tremendous will to win.'

Such an attitude continued to prove fruitful up to a point, after English clubs were readmitted to the UEFA fold. In 1991, Manchester United won the European Cup Winners' Cup, and three years later, Arsenal repeated the feat. However by the time of Arsène Wenger's arrival in 1996, neither the Champions League nor the UEFA Cup (competitions with a greater number of quality sides than the Cup Winners') had seen the winners' podiums seriously threatened by the legions of Albion as the leading Continental sides emulated Milan, who adroitly harnessed English spirit to Latin technique to create their all-conquering pressing game, subjugating the cult of the individual to the benefit of the team ethic.

Moreover, a key aspect of football changed after Italia '90, which unquestionably put the English sides at a disadvantage. FIFA, dismayed at the number of negative matches in their showpiece tournament – not least the final itself – decreed that changes had to be made to create a better spectacle. New regulations were introduced to try and eliminate time-wasting. So, goalkeepers were no longer allowed to pick up the ball from a back-pass. They were only permitted a limited number of steps if the ball was in their hand before releasing it (later changed to the current six seconds rule.) In the major competitions, a number of footballs had to be available around the playing area so that play could resume more quickly without needing to retrieve the ball after a clearance into the back of the stands. In short, the game was speeded up with the ball in play – and out of the keeper's hands – for a greater amount of time.

The superior physical condition of Italian sides in particular may have made little difference when the likes of Juventus were playing at the slow tempo they preferred, but with the pace of the game quickened, the discipline and dedication off the field now made a difference. The regime required greater physical aptitude by players, but they were conditioned for it by the exercise and dietary programme, to say nothing of their well-stocked medicine cabinets, at the top clubs' first-class training complexes. When Arsenal bucked the odds in 1994 and beat Parma to win their first European trophy for twenty-four years it was a 'backs to the wall' effort. It may not have been entertaining, but it was effective. Nine out of ten times, as the superior side, Parma should have won, but on this night Arsenal's endeavour paid off. However, as a strategy for consistent Continental success, it fell some way short of the dominant teams in the bigger Champions League – none of them English.

With the recently formed Premier League and the growing wealth of their members, it was not immediately apparent that domestic football required a revolution to mount a viable challenge in Europe. However, with the amount of money swilling around in the sport, it was a palpable nonsense that the key individuals upon whom the sport depended – the professional players – should not be fully prepared for their duties. A 100-metre sprinter with any intention of beating his opponents is not going to pour half a dozen pints of beer into his highly tuned body thirty-six hours before he takes up his position on the starting blocks; but that was exactly what Premiership footballers were doing. It was time for a long overdue revolution. The arrival of an unassuming man from Japan in the autumn of 1996 was about to turn English football on its head.

Chapter Three

Changes, Changes

'What does this Frenchman know about football? He wears glasses and looks more like a schoolteacher. He's not going to be as good as George. Does he even speak English properly?' When Tony Adams reiterated his initial thoughts about Arsène Wenger in his autobiography *Addicted*, the Arsenal captain was in all probability reflecting the views of the majority of the 1996–97 first-team squad. And this before his new boss had even taken a training session.

Arsène Wenger first witnessed his new charges in action in Germany, as the team were eliminated from the UEFA Cup by Borussia Mönchengladbach. The prospective manager intended to take no active part in the tie, but just observe. However, he did suggest in the dressing room at half-time a change in formation from 3–5–2 to 4–4–2 which acting manager Pat Rice adopted, but to no avail. Whether a suggestion or an instruction, it was somewhat foolhardy given that the team had not used that system for over a season. 'It didn't work,' said Wenger, 'but the qualification had already been lost at home.' (Arsenal lost both legs 3–2.) Wenger flew back to Japan immediately after the match to complete his arrangements before returning to England permanently a couple of weeks later.

The first thing the new man wanted to do was introduce an afternoon training session in addition to the morning one. It was not an idea that was well received. Arsène Wenger decided to retain Pat Rice, whom he later described as 'embodying the culture of the club', as his assistant, and use him as a go-between to liaise between himself and the players. By doing so he broke with the tradition of most English managers who immediately sack the incumbent assistant in order to bring their own man in. It illustrated Wenger's self-confidence that he felt no need to do this. He had, though, a lot of other changes in mind and knowing the necessity of having the players on his side, he heeded the feedback and withdrew the proposal in exchange for being able to make some fundamental alterations to the daily *métier*. He explained, 'The English train less than the French. For them, as long as they have given their all in a match, training is just an accessory. I am trying to change that attitude, to make them realise that training is crucial.'

The players' diet was revamped. He was convinced that an increased level of carbohydrates (already used in endurance sports such as marathon running and long-distance cycling) would make a significant contribution to the players' ability to cope with their tasks in the last quarter of a match when many goals are conceded due to fatigue-induced errors. Fluid intake was also monitored, and alcohol frowned upon.

With regard to gaining the full cooperation of his squad, converting his captain to his way of thinking was a prerequisite. So it was a pivotal move that Tony Adams had decided – in the weeks between the revelation that Arsène Wenger was to take over and his eventual arrival – his days as a practising alcoholic were well and truly over.

The summer of 1996 had seen Adams indulge in a seven-week bout of alcohol abuse triggered by England's semi-final defeat in the European Championships. It culminated in his decision to seek help and go public on his problems, as team-mate Paul Merson had done two years before. 'He wanted to change,' said Wenger, 'so I used him as an example. I thought that the other players should help him change and that the best way to ensure that happened was to ban alcohol completely so they had to behave like he behaved.'

Adams chose a fresh perspective to look at his life outside of the game as the innovatory methods of the new manager encouraged a reappraisal of his life within it. Indeed it would be no exaggeration to say that if he hadn't embraced Wenger's way then his whole future would not have changed for the better. Initially, so focused was he on his battle against his demons that he ceased to be the vocal presence of old and now carried out the captain's role leading by example. As he grew into his new persona – leaving behind the laddish Essex bloke whose natural habitat was the lounge bar – he gradually became more outspoken. After spending a few weeks rehabilitating at the beginning of 1998 in the south of France with Wenger's long-time fitness guru Tiburce Darrou, the captain returned ready to stand up and be counted in all aspects of his job. Happy at last with his fitness after months of just making do, he said, 'I just can't wait to show everyone that I am one hundred per cent. The problem for everyone now is that I am going to be on their backs.' His recuperation provided a terrific bonus for Arsène Wenger. The skipper had even added a subtle touch to his motivational skills. One of the first effects of his new course of action was a quiet word with Dennis Bergkamp just before the FA Cup Fourth Round tie at Middlesbrough in 1998. After praising his colleague for his abilities, he added, 'Isn't it about time you won something with Arsenal?' Four months later the Premiership and FA Cup double would be paraded on a bus journey from Avenell Road to Islington Town Hall, after Bergkamp had played some of the best football of his outstanding career.

The transformation of Adams the man was evidenced by events after England were eliminated from the 1998 World Cup Finals by Argentina. He consoled David Beckham when his manager, believing him to be culpable for the defeat, ostracised him. And his sympathy extended beyond his team-mates. Adams had invited a couple of friends – sixth-form girl students who were neighbours – to the match, and it was he who did the consoling afterwards. The girls were in tears, but Adams told them, 'It's only a game.'

Only a game! Oh, how the Arsenal captain had changed. Before facing his addiction, football was a kind of therapy from the excesses of his social life. Now, it was his work – pleasurable nonetheless – but he had developed cultural pursuits to gainfully employ his off-duty hours. The girls introduced him to literature and music; he started taking piano lessons and going to the theatre. Adams continued to expand his extra-curricular activities by writing a best-selling autobiography, noteworthy for the candour with which he tackled and subdued the evil eye. By 2002, he knew that if he was to continue on his voyage of discovery, he would – at least initially – have to leave football behind. Occasional thoughtful pieces for the *Observer* and enrolment for a sports science degree at Brunel University showed that if he was ever to return to the game in a managerial capacity, he would not be adopting the George Graham or Alex Ferguson method; he had become a disciple of the sympathetic, scientific approach favoured by his last mentor.

The special relationship between the two was evidenced by a meeting Wenger called once Adams had made the decision to retire. 'There have been some really special people over the years I have loved to bits,' recalls Adams. 'Arsène is one of them. I thanked him too for the last six years and we hugged. It was very moving and I was holding back the tears. I said, "I hope our paths cross again because you really are a lovely man".'

If evidence were needed of how Arsène Wenger refashioned the face of football, the decision of a former England captain to favour Wenger's way, to manage himself, is a significant pointer. A look at the training and dietary regimes at an average Premiership club in 2003 would be an even more persuasive argument. Yet back in 1996, compromise was the key to long-overdue change now so patently apparent.

In agreeing to compromise on certain issues, Wenger showed that he was as willing to be open-minded, as he asked his squad to be. After years of playing a flat back four under George Graham, Bruce Rioch had adopted a 3–5–2 formation using Lee Dixon and Nigel Winterburn as wing-backs. It encouraged the players' passing ability, not only by placing less emphasis on long ball tactics but because of the presence of newly-arrived gifted technicians in the form of David Platt and especially Dennis Bergkamp. Having started the season with the same system in spite of Rioch's departure, the players were not happy about reverting to 4–4–2. As 'it ain't broke', Tony Adams suggested leaving any fixing until the following season, and the manager relented.

In a sense, the team that Wenger inherited did too well for him to make the sweeping alterations that he envisaged were necessary. With the first choice defenders all the wrong side of thirty, it was widely anticipated that new blood would be arriving to replace them. In fact, the manager's methods actually extended their careers, allowing him to concentrate on other matters. With his scientific approach to the sport, he believes that defenders can enjoy more extended careers than those in other positions stating, 'There are appropriate ages for different positions. Beyond thirty it is difficult to play attack, beyond thirty-two you collect fewer balls in midfield, and in central defence you can play longer. As a goalkeeper you can be up to forty.'

From the position in August when it looked as if the team was bound for a season of transition at best the fact they were able to mount a credible title challenge was wholly unexpected. The possession football remained and improved, and Arsenal would have finished runners-up to Manchester United and qualified for the Champions League but for a controversial draw with Blackburn Rovers at Highbury near the end of the season. With full-time approaching, Arsenal kicked the ball into touch so that an injured player could receive treatment. Sporting convention decreed that Blackburn returned possession, and although the ball was given to Nigel Winterburn near the corner flag, before he could get it under control, Chris Sutton bore down on him and forced a corner. The sense of injustice spilled over into anger when the corner resulted in a Blackburn equaliser, which denied the home side two crucial points. Years on, the mishap still rankles with Wenger, 'You don't forget incidents like that because it cost us a place in the [Champions] league.'

Perhaps Arsenal were premature in claiming the moral high ground so far as unsporting behaviour was concerned. In an FA Cup tie against Sheffield United less than two years later, they themselves scored from a similar situation when new signing Kanu, unaware of the accepted protocol, challenged for a ball that had been thrown back to the opposition after they had deliberately conceded a throw-in. He won the ball and passed to Marc Overmars who scored the winning goal, to the astonishment of the opposition defence who expected possession to be returned to them. At the final whistle David Dein was out of his seat like a greyhound out of the traps. He told Arsène Wenger in his view the tie should be replayed and the manager immediately concurred. Ten days later, the game was restaged as if it had been abandoned (with the outcome the same 2–1 scoreline). Wenger's principles of fair play found a natural habitat in England. When performing the Ron Atkinson role (though without introducing the watching French public to exotic new football terms) during the 1998 World Cup match between France and Denmark, he made a point of emphasising that Manu Petit's conceding a throw-in so that an injured opponent could receive attention was in keeping with the sense of sportsmanship that was encouraged in England.

Of his early days at Highbury, with typical understatement Wenger later claimed, 'I was lucky at the beginning. To be accepted you have to win. If you tell players who were successful before that you must do it this way they may enjoy it, but if they lose they will say: "We enjoy it but we don't win," so maybe they will have a reluctance to do it. If they win of course, things are easier.' Wenger likened it to a singing teacher who had extended the range of his pupils' ability and given them the chance to express themselves. Surprised at their discovering hidden depths, they liked the sound of their own voices. Maestro.

Here was a man who offered something over and above the usual managerial clichés. He came across in the media, although not speaking in his own language, as erudite and engaging, more so than many British bosses speaking in their native tongue. He exuded confidence, authority and a certain charm. Arsenal ceased to be a club in turmoil. Innovatory and progressive, they exemplified style and promise.

A poor disciplinary record though was an odd bedfellow for the added élan, but the yellow and red card count could not be denied. It was the price to pay for the pressing style Wenger had imbued into the team. To demonstrate ability in possession, the ball has first to be won and Arsenal were under instruction to do so quickly. Tackles were more numerous and more hurried than hitherto – resulting in more reckless and mistimed challenges. It is hard to think of Wenger as a cynic sending his players out to deliberately foul opponents, although this was hinted at in some quarters. The reality was that he instilled such confidence and will to win in his players that they believed they could win tussles that they had no right to compete for. When they were unsuccessful it looked bad, and cards were the inevitable consequence. In mitigation, with their host of foreign players, there were bound to be communication problems, to which the officials tended to turn a deaf ear.

It was instructive that Patrick Vieira was a key early signing, as here was a player who succeeded in gaining possession when the odds were stacked against him. The supporters took him to their hearts on his debut, coincidentally the same night Wenger appeared on the Jumbotron to address the Highbury crowd for the first time. The words of intent came from Japan via the videoscreen, but the evidence of what was said was there in the flesh for all to see. Arsenal were 1–0 down to Sheffield Wednesday when Vieira made his entrance from the substitutes' bench. The game finished in a 4–1 victory to the home side, driven on by the determination and enthusiasm of the newcomer. The immediate impact of Vieira was as strong a sign as you would wish that Wenger knew his onions.

Under Bruce Rioch, Arsenal had finished fifth. With few but vital changes in personnel, viz Bergkamp and Platt, they had improved despite adhering to a formation that the new manager did not really believe in. The move to 4–4–2 was inevitable though, and came after he had allowed the wing-back experiment to take Arsenal to third place at the end of the season. With all the major continental clubs having switched to 4–4–2 in the light of Milan's success in the early 1990s, it confused Wenger that English sides should be experimenting with Continental systems which were no longer fashionable. He said, 'It is really strange, because in all Europe people are going to the old English system of 4–4–2 and England is going the other way. But with three at the back you have to come a little deeper and I like offensive football and winning the ball early. It is much more difficult to pressurise up the field with three at the back.' This was particularly so in Arsenal's case because the primary instincts of the wing backs concerned – Dixon and Winterburn – were defensive.

They were once again serious contenders for the league title. Indeed, but for a couple of key losses late on, they could even have been crowned champions. Yet Arsène Wenger had not enjoyed the luxury of taking the players for the pre-season period, when the groundwork could be laid down to ensure, for example, that his charges would not falter at a crucial stage, namely, February and March, when the home losses to Manchester United, Wimbledon and Liverpool had cost them so dear. They would have the time to adopt to Wenger's 4–4–2 and quickly reassure themselves that systems are only there to provide a comforting protective shell, within which as Thierry Henry succinctly states, 'We are free to express ourselves.'

The summer of 1997 not only saw the slate wiped clean, but the Gunners in better shape than they had been for years, eager and ready to follow *Le Technicien Alsacien* to the promised land.

Chapter Four

Wenger's Way

It is a twenty minute drive – to the accompaniment of Classic FM – from Arsène Wenger's Totteridge home in North London to Arsenal's London Colney training complex near St Albans (assuming the M25 isn't playing up). The man behind the wheel has been down this road literally and figuratively so often in the last six years that he will work out on the way which approach or type of session is required in light of the current situation. Whatever he decides, certain fundamentals will be adhered to.

Wenger's way is to ensure that his players are in the optimum physical condition. Right from the start, more lengthy warm-ups and warm-downs were introduced, usually led by Boro Primorac or Pat Rice, involving stretching exercises, designed to prevent injuries such as pulled and strained muscles. The players were told that their wives and girlfriends would also experience the benefits, although they were reticent to confirm subsequently the accuracy of the prognosis. Despite agreeing to forego his planned afternoon session, Wenger believed that training went on for too long. This may have led some players to believe that life was going to get easier, but nothing was further from the truth. Former Arsenal forward Alan Smith, forced to retire the year before Wenger's arrival, was still in touch with his ex-colleagues and relayed that, 'Even when the sessions had been cut down, the players were exhausted ... Wenger's coaching is very intense, with little respite between exercises.'

'Because,' according to Wenger, 'that's down to the targets you set for your work and the type of football you want to play.' Refined by experience but also open to innovation, 'I try and improve every year,' he says, 'and I believe every manager can only survive or become better if he tries to think about what's involved, what you have done before and the targets you set for your players. I don't believe that there is a single method but there are certain rules.'

In between the warm-up and warm-down, for the key session it will be his master's voice calling the tune, although it won't often be heard above the shrill sound of his whistle, 'To regulate the intensity of the training,' he says, 'to achieve exactly what I want to achieve, considering the intensity and the physiological target.' Experience has taught him the value of short sharp sessions and according to Bob Wilson, loyal Arsenal servant both as goalkeeper and coach, 'If he says it's going to be eight minutes thirty seconds then that is exactly what it will be,' sometimes to the disgruntlement of the players when time is called in their training games. (Bill Shankly would turn in his grave at this scientific approach, as at Anfield the legendary era of Liverpool dominance was built on five-a-sides in training that were played with as much commitment and will to win as the real thing, and were never halted until Shankly's team was ahead.) The bottom line for Wenger is to work out precisely 'how you can get the exercise as close to the type of game you want to play'.

Aided and abetted by a veritable army of a supporting cast: 'A doctor, an osteopath, a dietician – we have all kinds of people,' says Wenger, augmented from time to time with literally flying visits from France by specialists such as his friend Doctor Phillipe Boixel. The mental and physical side of every player is catered for on an individual basis.

Training itself is strictly limited time-wise because, contrary to the 'practice per se makes perfect' principle, extra-time, in Wenger's view, can be counterproductive. As Thierry Henry emphasises, 'Arsène doesn't appreciate it if I do it [too many free kicks] after training because I will risk a thigh strain.' In this regard, he could be described as a control freak with the best of intentions. Robert Pires emphasises the point: 'Before Arsène, Arsenal had its own character. He (Wenger) arrived with a lot of experience: experience from France, experience from Japan. That created a mixture which he transposed on to the English culture, the English players, and that gave Arsenal recognition in England and Europe. People love Arsenal's way of playing, especially in France. Today

Arsenal can say thanks to Arsène. He is the big chief of this business.'

The Monaco training ground at La Turbie in the hills above Nice was conducive to a relaxed environment even it was rather too compact for Wenger's liking. Determined that if he couldn't guarantee the weather or the bougainvillea, the Arsenal players would be more than compensated by the extent and quality of the training facilities he would persuade the board was necessary. He must have been horrified on his arrival to find that not only did Arsenal not have their own training ground, but they were restricted in the use of what were less than adequate facilities by the leasing arrangements with the owners, University College London. The arrangement was such that the students had first claim to the grounds on some afternoons.

In August 1999, Arsenal fan and then Minister of Sport, Kate Hoey, opened a state-of-the-art training centre for first-team reserves and youth usage. There are eleven pitches in total, complemented by a gym, medical centre and offices. At Mr Wenger's insistence, a hydrotherapy unit has been created which has a key role in both *décrassage* (the day after match relaxation routines) and in aiding recovery and recuperation from injury and fatigue. The complex is a stone's throw from their old training ground but as different as day to night and ushered in a new era.

Designed to facilitate the tasks of the players and coaches, Arsène, according to David Dein, 'was involved right down to the last teacup'. Not that there would be a need for many of these as the cafeteria and tea ladies were replaced by a first-class restaurant, and chefs who had the menu compiled for them by the coach. Wenger had his charges eating white meat, such as chicken or fish, served with mashed potatoes and boiled vegetables, particularly greens like broccoli. Rice and pasta dishes also became regular items on the menu. The traditional favourite of steak was banished.

It is not unusual for the manager to have an early afternoon lunch with half a dozen of his closest colleagues before he retires to his office. A workaholic – 'I don't switch off' – videotapes of games, reserve and youth matches mean a twelve-hour day, occasionally augmented by a twenty-four-hour one when an overnight scouting trip is crammed into his agenda. So much so that David Dein, protective of his friend, will put pressure on anyone who tries to eat into his free time, not that there is much of that. He is fortunate that, according to Dein, 'the chemistry between us is very good' and because of affection and respect – not just from Dein but the rest of the board, as well as the players – what Arsène wants Arsène gets.

This trust between the board and manager was unquestionably a major factor in his decision to prolong his stay at the club and, in late 2001, Wenger signed a contract extension keeping him at Arsenal until at least the summer of 2005. When he moved into his certainly desirable detached house in salubrious Totteridge, though not a patch on the multi-million pound residences of his neighbours, as part of the deal all the existing fixtures and fittings were included so that he could have a comfortable homebase from day one and not be distracted from his primary duties.

Over the years his partner Annie has gradually imposed her own tasteful preference for a stylish but unostentatious blue décor which Arsène has happily gone along with, his only prerequisite 'luxury' being a state-of-the-art satellite system and accompanying extra-large screen. With Annie, their daughter Léa (who bemoans papa's long working hours which is why she is often in his arms when they are together) and a new addition to the family – Lilly, a Yorkshire terrier – home life is pressure free. When in response to Alex Ferguson's claim that every player wanted to play for Manchester United, Wenger's riposte that 'everyone thinks they have the prettiest wife', was as true as it was gently dismissive. An elegant, friendly lady, Annie played basketball at the top level in her native France, so she sympathises with the pressures Arsène is under. So if his job makes going out difficult, friends and family often come to stay.

Despite the demanding pressures on his time, he will occasionally find it impossible to say no, usually when the request is of a personal nature. In 2002 he took the 'double' trophies to a local junior school and in the view of the staff was exceptionally considerate and kind to the clamourous pupils. The same open-handed approach was also apparent when on one occasion, surrounded by young fans as he left work, one excitedly told him, 'Mr Wenger, Mr Wenger, I can play for Arsenal!' And the considerate response came back, "Yes, I'm sure you can, but the question is, how well?' A pity then that he didn't ask Igors Stepanovs the same thing.

Occasionally, David Dein will drag him to the theatre but if you are going to get him out of the house on a non-footballing matter subterfuge has to be used. Arsène and Annie are so removed from the trappings of fame that neither had a clue about the existence of the *BBC Sports Review of the Year* television programme nor its significance. Television *chez Wenger* usually means live matches or highlights. The fact that the annual sports showcase event might attract eight million Sunday evening viewers does not mean it would even register in one particular football obsessed Totteridge household. So when Dein (tipped off by the BBC that his friend was going to be awarded the 'Coach of the Year' award for the second of his 'double' seasons) was requested to get the couple to the ceremony he had to tell them that they were going to a swish party. Having to wait around, and unaware of what was planned, Arsène got increasingly agitated. He viewed it as a wasted hour, when he could have been at home watching *Jour de Foot* on Canal Plus – a round-up of the weekend action across Europe and regarded as essential viewing.

Nevertheless contrary to popular myth, which he himself contributes to when he says, 'my hobby is watching football', he has a fertile enquiring mind and a nice line in sardonic humour. Asked by the author to give him a scoop, he declined saying, 'I have many scoops but I will keep them for my own book.' Then he relented, leaned forward and in conspiratorial tones whispered, 'I've had an offer from Grimsby Town and I'm thinking about it seriously.' Despite the long hours put in for Arsenal's benefit he makes time to have two or three books on the go simultaneously, chiefly biographies and politics; and he has eclectic musical tastes. When at Mulhouse and Strasbourg he would often make the tedious journey to Milan not to go shopping but to go to La Scala. Less highbrow but no less edifying, a current favourite is Norah Jones.

Annie, on the other hand, is enamoured with Elton John and as bad luck would have it, when Arsenal played Watford in the FA Cup, it was one of those rare occasions when she could not be by her partner's side in the boardroom for the post-match mingling of directors and their guests. Watford vice-chairman Elton showed

Arsène due deference and told him, 'I know a woman who adores you – my mother.' Arsène responded: 'And I know one who adores you – my wife.' Even the invitation to a celebrity bash starring Sir Elton couldn't persuade the Wengers to go on the razzle. It was left to David Dein to explain their absence to the man himself, who promised that if they couldn't come to him, one day he would go to them.

Arsène Wenger likes to make active use of his time, even if he is not the best of timekeepers (despite his love of the stopwatch) when it comes to the press. Michael Hart, the experienced London *Evening Standard* reporter can testify to this, having spent so long waiting around for managers just to get a quote or two that he has become immune to it. Pre-match conferences at London Colney called for noon rarely see the manager appear before one. And although Arsène may not be punctual as Hart states, 'at least he turns up. I've never known him not to'. Unwilling to give one-to-one interviews except occasionally to *France Football* or *L'Equipe*, he nevertheless is unfailingly polite and will answer any question put to him candidly and often with a touch of sardonic humour. However, he keeps his distance and never refers to a journalist by name. So no favouritism at play here for any individual – whether from the tabloids or the broadsheets. In fact, although he regards it as a bit of a chore he will continue talking, often because he enjoys the verbal jousting, until a member of Arsenal's press team calls time, usually leaving the journalists frustrated, with many questions unasked.

His patience must have been severely tested when, like thousands of others, he was caught in a freak snowstorm that gridlocked South East England. After a tortuous car journey which took him within a couple of miles of home, it was a case of so near and yet so far as he came to the aid of a couple of stranded ladies. Retracing his steps to take them to Barnet, he ended up completely lost. It was only through the aid of David Dein navigating him through the back streets by phone (he himself was marooned at a Heathrow hotel) that he eventually made it home at around midnight. A trip that would normally have taken him thirty minutes, due to his Good Samaritan act ended up taking six hours.

Persuaded to remain at the BBC Sports Review junket by Dein, the penny dropped as to the real reason he was in attendance and although he expressed his pleasure at receiving the award and was his usual generous and magnanimous self in his acceptance speech, that was it ... a pleasant little interlude. Surprised by friends who saw them on television, Annie never even saw the programme till some months later when an acquaintance gave her a video recording of the show. Arsène still hasn't seen it. Boro Primorac's wife babysat Léa on the evening in question and didn't even switch on the television. None of the trophies or awards Wenger has won for his coaching achievements are on show at home. Heaven forbid he should reflect on past glories or rest on his laurels. Every season must see progress.

And this is what he tells the players. Used to George Graham's ranting and raving, the experienced campaigners were surprised by his pragmatic downbeat approach. The build-up to matchdays is low key, the ultimate training session being paramount, and concentrating on raising his own team's performance level rather than worrying about the opposition. Whether home or away in the Premiership or for a midweek European game he attempts to ensure that pre-match training at London Colney is sacrosanct. After training, for key games, rather than dispersing to their homes the squad will be kept together at a hotel in Chelsea Harbour, south-west London. When distance dictates, morning training on the day before will be followed by an afternoon flight or coach journey leaving matchday for gentle loosening exercises and walks before the afternoon or evening encounter.

At 2.30 before the clash with Chelsea on New Year's Day 2002, the man who should have no time to spare, spotted an acquaintance on the landing outside the boardroom at Highbury, went over and wished him seasonal greetings and then spent the next ten minutes debating the merits of Continental goalkeepers and whether in reality Arsenal's 4–4–2 is more akin to the 4–2–4 of Brazil in 1970. Points in the dressing room are made before the adrenalin starts to flow, or after it subsides. Words at half-time are left until the last few minutes in the belief that they will be absorbed better. According to Bob Wilson, his goalkeeping coach, 'Arsène believes you can only rollock a team, have a real go at them a maximum of three or four times a season. More often and the impact would be lost.' There have been only two occasions when he actually lost his temper in the dressing room, and understandably so, given the abject displays at Coventry in 1999, and especially when 5–1 down to Manchester United at half time in 2001. Lee Dixon confirms that an angry Arsène Wenger was a rarity: 'There were times when Tony Adams and I felt things should have been said after games, but he did not believe in saying things in the heat of the moment. Even on a Monday after a poor Saturday, when we were waiting for him to say something, nothing would be said. That silence often said more. Using the art of auto suggestion, something he learnt in Japan, he left you to figure it out.'

For a coach who values so highly the beauty of the football his team plays, it is interesting that he foregoes the opportunity to watch the first half of matches from the directors' box, where he would enjoy a far better perspective on the patterns weaved by his charges. But he explains that he remains in the technical area for the complete ninety minutes because, 'Physically, I can't take the separation from the team. I started my coaching career like that and always did it like that.' His view at pitch level is one of the reasons he does not see every incident, although the idea of his selective myopia has become a running joke in the press. He claims, 'It's true, I can't see everything from the dugout. Because I have this reputation now, I used it once or twice not to come out against my players, as a trick. It's true you are in a bad position to see everything, but now even when I am honest, people don't believe me.'

According to Robert Pires: 'Everyone who is influenced by Wenger's hand succeeds. Certainly his work helps many, that's what he's brought in terms of improvement to we players. It's not necessary to say anything, just look at the pitch.' The Wenger affect is omnipresent, according to Thierry Henry: 'He gives a player responsibility. Contrary to what certain people think, he is not hard, not the type who shouts, "do this, do that". He lets you express yourself. He knows when to speak to you and when to leave you be. He takes players at face value, he doesn't try to reshape them. He respects their individuality, improving them according to their own attributes. He puts the emphasis on our strong points, not our weak ones. When I try a manoeuvre that is too complicated he knows that's part of my make up so he doesn't rebuke me.' Robert Pires again: 'Arsène has asked me to play more quickly and be more confrontational. We work at it in training and try to apply it on the pitch. He stresses my strong points and if people notice it (the changes) it is because Wenger's work has paid dividends.'

The tag of best striker in the world is bandied about on a regular basis. When Arsenal hosted Fiorentina in the Champions League in 1999, goalscorer Gabriel Batistuta would have been mentioned. His decisive strike that night was witnessed by Thierry Henry from the substitutes' bench, but now it is the Arsenal striker's name that pops up in the company of Raul, Christian Vieri, Ruud van Nistelrooy, Ronaldo and Andriy Shevchenko. In Henry's fourth season as a Gunner, the number 14 only takes a place on the sidelines when his manager chooses to rest him, such is his import-ance to the team. And vice versa. Asked on the occasion of his one-hundredth Arsenal goal about his contractual arrangement Henry replied, 'Here the contract is with my heart. If I ever came to leave it will be because Arsenal will have fired me.'

The player had been given his league debut as a seventeen-year-old in August 1994 in the final weeks of Wenger's Monaco tenure after graduating from the national school at Clairefontaine. Playing as a winger, his career progressed under Jean Tigana, who took over the coaching reins in 1995. Henry first came to the attention of an English audience when Tigana's side faced Man-chester United in the Champions League quarter-finals in 1998. David Trezeguet and Thierry Henry lined-up for a Monaco team who were expected to succumb to Alex Ferguson's more experi-enced campaigners, but both shone over the two legs of the tie, which saw the French side go through on the away goals rule. The two players must have impressed semi-final opponents Juv-entus, as despite losing, both were subsequently signed by the Italian side. Henry was first to make the move, in January 1999. He brought with him the cachet of being a member of the French World Cup-winning squad, appearing in every game except the final itself, scoring three goals in the process.

The move did not really work out. His French international colleague Marcel Desailly, who himself spent five seasons in Italy with Milan, felt, 'He needed a bit of time to be able to play at the level that he is at now. The Italians didn't really have time to look after him and to explain things to him.' And it dismayed Henry that he was expected to defend rather than attack. 'I was the fifth midfielder on the left side, making the run between defence and attack.' After three goals in sixteen *Serie A* appearances and about to be loaned out to Udinese, the summer of 1999 saw Arsène Wenger spend £8.5 million (the media estimate inflated the figure by a couple of million) of the money he had received from Real Madrid for Nicolas Anelka, to once again get Henry under his wing. Desailly credits Wenger's perspicacity for the improvement out of all recognition at Highbury. 'When he came to Arsenal, Arsène Wenger spoke to him and put him in his correct position and gave him a lot of confidence. Soccer players definitely need confidence, it is fifty per cent of the player.'

So, Thierry Henry the wideman became Thierry Henry the marksman. On joining Arsenal, he was shocked to discover what his new manager had in store for him. He recalls, 'I remember my first press conference, when I arrived. Arsène said that he'd play me as a central striker, and I heard quite a few laughs in the audience.' In fact, his memory is playing tricks with him, as certainly no journalist would have thought it was an absurd notion. After all if they had done their homework, they would have discovered that he scored seven goals in nine appearances in Monaco's run to the Champions League semi-final the year before. Henry adds, 'I myself was a bit sceptical, I looked at him in surprise. It seemed a bit too much to me. Then, once again, he'd been right. He knew, and I didn't know. I showed him afterwards that he wasn't wrong.'

Initially, Henry struggled to make the starting eleven, but after the Champions League exit at the hands of Batistuta's Fiorentina, he superseded Kanu as Bergkamp's partner. The new man rewarded Wenger's faith with twenty-six goals in his first season at the club, six more than his league total at Monaco during his five seasons there. Finally it looked like Arsenal had found someone who could compete for the Golden Boot – the new Ian Wright.

'Arsène insisted I could play that role, and finally I came round to that view.' So did Roger Lemerre the France coach, but he dallied before doing so. After his World Cup success Henry was surprisingly banished to the *espoirs* (under-21s) and at the beginning of 2000, although in a rich vein of form for Arsenal, when he was rejected for the senior side against Poland, he began to despair of ever regaining a squad place, not to mention the prospect of a *titulaire* (starter). As he remembers, 'Arsène is not a clairvoyant, he told me to remain positive and upbeat and I would be part of the team that wins Euro 2000. He gave me confidence and that helped me a great deal.' And so it came to pass, just as Arsène said it would. After a paucity of quality strikers, France were now spoilt for choice for Euro 2000, being able to call upon Henry, Nicolas Anelka, David Trezeguet and Sylvain Wiltord. They won the tournament, with Henry re-establishing his importance to the team scoring three goals in five appearances. He has not looked back.

The self-belief that Arsène Wenger imbued in Henry was only part of the learning curve that transformed the player into one of the most feared strikers in world football. The physical development came on the training pitch courtesy of his team-mates, who had to prepare the new boy for the challenges he would face in the Premiership. Henry explains: 'I have had to work on my physical strength since coming to England. During training, Martin Keown would always keep hitting me – sometimes all the way to the dressing rooms. There were some fantastic battles between us during training. I used to get knocked aside at the start but this has helped me. That was because they wanted to instil the English way of playing into me. It was their way of being cruel to be kind.'

Even under George Graham, one of the tasks with youngsters on the periphery of first-team action was to get them bulked up both in the dining room and the gym. Graham wanted his players to be physical powerhouses and that is an aspect of the preparation that did not alter with Arsène Wenger's arrival. However, after trying creatine because he believed 'it could help with recovery', he subsequently 'banned it completely because some players put on weight and I read some studies that said it was the equivalent of ten steaks. I hate it. I don't like weight. I think footballers need coordination more than muscle.'

Technically, Wenger worked on teaching his willing pupil the specific skills of his new role, playing with his back to goal and 'everything concerning keeping possession'. Henry's goals tally continued to grow as he became a pivotal figure at the club. Twenty-two in season 2000–01, were followed by a Golden Boot tally of thirty-two goals in the Premiership-winning campaign of 2002. His repeat tally the following season, coupled with an astonishing twenty league assists persuaded both his fellow players and the football journalists to elect him their player of the year. If he remains at Arsenal for the foreseeable future, it is difficult to see Ian Wright's club record of 185 goals surviving. Certainly his Premiership strike rate as a starter of a goal every 1.59 games is comparable to Wright's 1.5 and of course he has many more assists to his name than Wright, who was essentially a penalty-box poacher.

Nevertheless, his appetite for the big stage has been questioned by some, who feel that he fails to do himself justice when it really matters. Yet this criticism seems at odds with a player who has been a prominent member of an international side who swept all before them in 1998 and 2000. It also goes against the statistics that show Henry has scored twenty-six goals in forty-nine Champions League matches for Monaco and Arsenal – by definition goals scored against the best defences in the world. His ratio at this level is comparable to the competition's record holder Raul, and his peers Filipo Inzaghi, Ruud van Nistelrooy and Alessandro del Piero. Moreover, like the Juventus captain he would certainly be near the top of any 'assist' chart as well.

The lightning pace of Henry is the most effective weapon in his armoury. To see the forward leave a defender for dead in the first five yards of a run is a breathtaking feat to behold. (It has inspired Renault to use him as the personification of their 'va va voom' theme in a successful advertising campaign, although the irony of his marrying a girl called Nicole may be lost on him.) Defences have to be wary of pushing too far up the field when he is lined up against them. Given the space to run on to a ball between a back-line and goalkeeper, his sheer speed from a standing start means he will invariably earn himself a one-on-one scoring opportunity. This fear factor often works in Arsenal's favour by creating gaps between the opposition midfield and defence, especially when more cautious sides will attempt to throw a tight barrier around their own goal. The Gunners can then use their possession jostling for an opening, trying to break through until inevitably the dam is burst open. The talent that Arsène Wenger spotted in Henry that others had missed is now blindingly obvious. He says he is probably the most talented footballer he has ever worked with, yet expects him to continue to improve and suggests the answer lies in Henry's genes. Perhaps the truth is somewhat more prosaic. If Henry casts his mind back to his Parisian upbringing, he'll remember the fifteen-a-side games played in a small court-yard with his brothers and their friends who were half a dozen years older. A small, slight seven-year-old had to be quick and skilful to flourish. Then there was his father, who was a hard taskmaster because he always hoped his son would become a top class footballer. Praise was scarce. 'I always tried my hardest and it was never enough. When I scored he criticised me for not making the goal. On the other hand he was never pleased if I had laid on goals without scoring myself.'

Similarly with Jean Tigana at Monaco, as he recalls: 'I didn't always understand his decisions. He took me off after a good performance and would criticise me if we had been unsuccessful.' Though with the benefit of hindsight he now appreciates that, as in his childhood, lack of approbation was an impetus to improve. Now, of course, he does both with equal facility. 'Normally,' according to Dennis Bergkamp, 'to say a player is the finished article you would say he is good at all the necessary skills, but Thierry is exceptional at them.'

One quirk that perhaps needs addressing is Henry's tendency to head towards the left wing as if he is being magnetically drawn towards the corner flag. When his striking partner is Dennis Bergkamp, the end result is often no attacking presence in the penalty area; once Henry has beaten his man on the flank, there is no one to pass to. Although Henry says the absence of Robert Pires led to him calling on his Monaco experience and contributing more in the construction of the attacking play. 'When he (Pires) is there it is not worth the trouble of going there (on the flank) because I know what he is going to do.' To be categorised as just a *chasseur des buts* (goalscorer) fills him with dread. 'When certain strikers don't score their team effectively plays with ten men. I don't want to be this type of limited attacker. That's why it is just as important to make goals as to score them myself.'

Yet Henry's pace sometimes meant he became a one-man attack, if only because his team-mates couldn't always keep up with his bursts from deep. As he said of his remarkable length of the field dribble and resultant goal against Tottenham in November 2001 (voted Goal of the Season by ITV's *The Premiership* programme), 'I didn't see anybody so I had to do something myself. It worked.' That situation was atypical. Usually the tactics are geared to exploit his attributes to the full. As he himself puts it, 'At Arsenal the play is conceived for the attacker to finish the action. I feel that Dennis Bergkamp does everything to put me in a position to score. The same goes for Robert Pires, Sylvain Wiltord and the others. They know me, they know the runs I make, how I like the ball to come to me. I am there to finish the preparatory work. That's my job. I must do it and fulfil the efforts of my team-mates by scoring.'

Arsène Wenger can't help himself spontaneously enthusing about the latest Henry exploit. Looking to the future he has forecast: 'Thierry could become the Michael Jordan of football.' Hopefully a reference to the basketball player's supreme skill and powerful personality rather than the salary his team is forced to pay to retain his services. Yet the relationship between the two runs to another deeper level. Managers and coaches have a pre-dilection for certain players because they embody both in manner and deed precisely what is deemed the pivotal fulcrum of the team's *raison d'être* on the field of play. So Bill Nicholson's ethos was represented by Danny Blanchflower; George Graham by Tony Adams; Alex Ferguson by Roy Keane; and it is to Arsène Wenger's credit that the heartbeat of his team exemplifies the freewheeling, *joie de vivre* attacking style – both as a goalmaker and goalscorer – that he rejoices in, rather than a defensive colossus or a combative midfielder, despite the magnitude of Patrick Vieira's role.

For Arsène, defending is a means to an end. 'I am a fan of good defending. I want my team to defend well to express what they have to say when they have the ball. The target is to defend because you want to say something. When I listen to you, I defend; when I speak, I attack. And the first target is to listen well to you. And that's defending.' The emphasis though is firmly placed at the other end of the pitch. 'The art is to have a balanced team that is always dangerous offensively and can defend well. I would say my evolution was to become more offensive. I was more defensively oriented when I was younger and as I get more experienced I try to get closer to the game I dream to play.' He believes some teams are so great – the Real Madrid of Di Stefano, Puskas and Gento; Arrigo Saachi's Milan – that they belong to all of us. 'Sometimes it can just be a fight for ninety minutes, both teams give absolutely everything and you can enjoy it, but there must be something more as well. It's like when you have been to the theatre. There is a magical moment during the second act and when you go home you remember that. It can happen with a football team as well.

'The imprint you make in the spirit of people is more important than the result. It's somewhere where people can identify with the way you play. It remains in the spirit and they are grateful for what you give them. They really enjoy a moment of happiness that is so much more than when you win just 1–0. You cannot keep people happy for years if it's boring every time and they just come out at the end with a 1–0 victory.'

Chapter Five

We Have Got To Get It Together

He stood alone in the corner of the Wembley pitch, celebrating in front of the opposition fans. Having just applied the *coup de grâce* by scoring the second, clinching goal in the 1998 FA Cup final, to the outsider it seemed puzzling that Nicolas Anelka was not mobbed by joyous team-mates. Eventually Ray Parlour, Arsenal's most energetic and best player on that stiflingly hot May afternoon, trotted over to offer a congratulatory pat on the back. Perhaps it was the unseasonal weather and Anelka's cohorts were simply too shattered to run half the length of the playing surface. Then again Nicolas Anelka was such a loner that perhaps the team spirit that underpinned the Gunners' success simply didn't extend to him. Undoubtedly, though, without that spirit and sense of purpose there would have been no platform for Anelka to score his goals.

It was unlikely that the striker would have flourished so soon at Highbury were it not for two key events in that double season. Ian Wright picked up an injury that ruled him out for most of the second half of the season, opening the door to a precocious teenage talent acquired from Paris St Germain for £500,000. Important though the capture of Anelka turned out to be – not least because he was subsequently sold to Real Madrid for £23 million, financing the purchases of Thierry Henry and Davor Suker and leaving a healthy profit for the bottom line – another more prosaic occurrence proved to have the most far-reaching of consequences. It would be no exaggeration to say that it was the turning point of Arsène Wenger's short Arsenal career to date. In the midst of a losing streak a routine December team meeting saw an *entente cordiale* struck between the English central defenders Tony Adams,

45

Martin Keown and Steve Bould; and the French central midfield Patrick Vieira and Emmanuel Petit. To prevent the scoring opportunities that were all too readily opening up for Arsenal's opponents it was agreed that more cover was needed in front of the back-line. The central defenders were perturbed about the lack of protection afforded them, and demanded a bulwark to prevent the opposition being able to reach them so easily. Under George Graham there was an understanding that the team's defence began in central midfield. Several different partnerships had proved adept at accomplishing this task, the most successful being that of Paul Davis and Michael Thomas, which played a key role in securing two league titles. If one player ventured forward, usually Thomas, the other would hold back to ensure the defence wasn't unduly exposed.

By the time of Arsenal's defeat to Blackburn in the final home game before Christmas in 1997, twenty-one goals had been conceded in eighteen games – more than any of the four sides above them in the table. The influx of Continental players including Marc Overmars and Emmanuel Petit, had undoubtedly added to the attacking armoury but the sum of the parts had not yet been forged to form an effective whole. Arsène Wenger had laid a continental quilt over the bedrock of George Graham's famous back five, but the cover was threadbare in places. It was agreed that the midfield should be the fulcrum of a seamless unit from the point of the attack to the last line of the defence. The Graham holding tactic was to be rigorously applied, Vieira and Petit would take it in turns to support the attack, with the other covering in the event of a breakdown. The team meeting proved to be a watershed in Anglo-French relations and Arsenal's next eighteen league outings saw the addition of only seven in the 'goals against' column.

A concomitant spirit – which called to mind the initial double side of 1970–71 – accompanied the change in fortunes. After the Blackburn defeat Arsenal embarked on a run that saw them lose only once – a League Cup semi-final second-leg – in all domestic competitions and blow away all opposition in the process before Tony Adams lifted the Premiership trophy in early May.

If there was one game that exemplified the new found resolve of Wenger's Arsenal it was the FA Cup quarter-final replay at

46

Upton Park against West Ham. The opposition had become familiar foes and this was the fourth meeting between the two in just over two months. Having dramatically defeated Manchester United at Old Trafford in the Premiership only three days earlier, Arsenal could have done without another midweek match, but their inability to capitalise on their home advantage ensured a semi-final place had to be earned the hard way. As if the odds were not already against them, a deserved red card for Dennis Bergkamp meant that, with extra-time, the visitors would end up playing almost ninety minutes with only ten men. Adams and Keown in central defence saw Vieira and Petit work like Trojans in front of them, while stand-in keeper Alex Manninger put on a sterling show behind them when called upon. Up front, Anelka was the lone striker in all senses of the word, but still managed to give the ten men a vital lead just before the interval. West Ham equaliser by Highbury old boy, John Hartson, with only six minutes of normal time remaining, might have demoralised lesser teams, but Arsenal held firm and managed to see out the thirty minutes of extra-time in a backs-to-the-wall effort that George Graham would have been proud of. Manninger's heroics continued in the shoot-out to send his team-mates to a semi-final against Wolves that produced yet another 1–0 win.

Resilient was a word that was often used by Graham to describe his team's best exploits, and this replay came in the middle of four league clashes that all ended 1–0 to Arsenal to demonstrate that although Graham was long gone his legacy lingered on, notwithstanding changes in the cast. Vieira and Petit were Arsène Wenger's men, midfielders who had no equals with their ability to dictate the pattern of play under any circumstances. The old guard and the new wave had combined to secure a result that not even the most optimistic of Arsenal fans would have dared predict with Bergkamp's dismissal after thirty-four minutes.

Of the fourteen players that represented this resolute unit, more than half had been brought to Highbury by Wenger. The Upton Park triumph was undoubtedly the moment when the December agreement bore its most vivid fruit. 'If spirit won prizes, Arsenal would win the lot,' said a proud manager somewhat prophetically as his side went on to triumph in both League and Cup. They simply would not be beaten.

It was a first Premiership medal for Martin Keown. Unlike Adams, Bould, Dixon and Winterburn, he had not been at the club when they won the league in 1989 and 1991. He progressed through the ranks at Highbury to become a familiar face in the first team in the mid-1980s, often alternating with fellow defender Tony Adams in partnering David O'Leary at centre-back. Following a pay dispute, George Graham sold him to Aston Villa, subsequently admitting his mistake by having to pay £2 million in 1993 to get him back from Everton. Even then, Steve Bould was still the manager's preferred choice as Tony Adams' central defensive partner, and Keown was often deployed as a midfield man-marker to subdue a key creative opponent. Graham used him this way in Europe to great effect as Arsenal reached two successive Cup Winners' Cup finals. His versatility also allowed him to cover at full-back on either flank in an emergency.

Bruce Rioch's switch to three at the back allowed Adams, Bould and Keown to all play in the back-line, and once Arsène Wenger took over and 4–4–2 was restored the younger Keown invariably got the nod over Bould when both were fit. Since 1996, the only time when he was not an automatic selection was for a handful of games in 2001–02 when both Adams and Sol Campbell were available. He is a shining example of how the ways of Wenger can prolong a player's career. He was a ready convert as unusually, although one of the 'old school' of English professionals, invariably he chose to return home after training, instead of partaking in the pub sessions that were the norm at the time. Keown remembers, 'When everybody is having a drink and being matey, to stand up and say, "No, I'm not doing it" is very difficult. I looked around and didn't see it as a good example for others to be sitting in a pub all day. I hadn't come to London for that. I'd come to be a professional footballer and to learn as much as I could. Anything I thought wouldn't help that, I binned.' It is a reflection of his strength of character that, at a young and impressionable age, he elected to go his own way. Arsène Wenger would doubtless approve. 'If I didn't want to follow the group, I wouldn't,' Keown explains. 'That took a fair bit of mental strength on my part, but that was the way I was brought up. My mum and dad told me, "You've got a fantastic opportunity in life", and I wasn't going to piss that up against the wall.' Always somewhat of an outsider, he continues to live in Oxford, as he has done for most of his Arsenal career, and as an example of his prudent ways he has become like Soames Forsythe, a man of property. Approaching his thirty-seventh birthday and still a cornerstone of the defence he admits, 'You have to be lucky with injuries to play for that length of time. You also have to retain your desire. Given that, Arsène will keep you going.' When he was out of contract in the summer of 2002, he agreed to a wage cut to remain at Arsenal, but significantly five other Premiership clubs offered him a better deal to join them. It was a tribute to Arsène Wenger's life enhancing properties that he should still be in such demand and to his loyalty and sense of values that he stayed put.

Few would doubt the desire of a player whose man-marking skills are the reason that he is sometimes referred to as 'the rash', as he is all over opponents. Keown is unambiguous about his approach, affirming, 'I set out to impose myself on the game. If I upset people that is unfortunate.' Certainly, he is a very 'in your face' defender, and as a back-handed compliment, he is frequently named as the man opposition forwards least like facing. He has had many notorious run-ins with the likes of Mark Viduka, Jimmy Floyd Hasselbaink and Ruud van Nistelrooy, often resulting in disciplinary problems for both himself and his opponent, reflecting the ferocity of the personal duel. As a 'wind-up merchant' – a legitimate tactic in any contact sport – he may be one of the finest exponents of the art. How else can the antics of Roma's Francesco Totti in the 2003 Champions League tie at Highbury be explained? An experienced international forward thoroughly versed in competing with cynical markers, the *giallorossi*'s captain, after the referee had already told the players to cool it a matter of seconds before, took a swing at his marker and duly received the inevitable red card when Keown theatrically went to ground. (So far as the Italians were concerned, there should have been no cause for complaint as it was a long overdue case of the biter being bit.) It was almost as if Totti simply didn't fancy ninety minutes in the company of Keown and decided to self-destruct, despite his side's desperate need for points from the visit.

The contest between the two could have been portrayed as beauty versus the beast, with the Italian's pin-up boy status contrasted to the Arsenal defender whose looks may not challenge

David Beckham's when the cola companies are casting for a face to front their next campaign, but the fact that opposition supporters take the mickey out of Martin with their 'he's got a monkey's head' chants is a back-handed compliment and in reality they would be delighted to have him playing for their team rather than against it.

More of a bridesmaid than a bride for much of his career he has lived in the shadow of his defensive colleagues. Lack of top of the bill status may not be significant at Highbury, but at international level, Keown has seen first Tony Adams and then Sol Campbell prevent him from adding to the forty-three England caps he has been awarded since being given his debut by Graham Taylor. A succession of international managers have made him a regular in their squads, but he has never been regarded as an automatic starter. He has travelled to two World Cup Finals without kicking a ball, and although being involved in the tournament was an experience he would not have missed, his frustration was apparent as he watched events unfold from the bench. His most rewarding moment came when he partnered Sol Campbell in the Euro 2000 finals, when England beat Germany 1–0. 'It was nice for my family finally to see me on the pitch,' he reflected, 'because, for the last two tournaments, they thought I was working for the media.'

Whereas some of the imported stars are accused of not giving one hundred per cent to the cause, Martin Keown's combativeness, so obviously apparent in his battles against opposing marksmen, has led Arsenal supporters to never question his commitment or desire. His presence in the starting line-up is a reassurance that a little bit of the old Arsenal, the renowned Arsenal, is alive and kicking in the days when attack, attack, attack is the priority.

The defensive grit, embodied by Martin Keown coupled with the invention and imagination of the attack enabled Arsène Wenger to build a championship-winning side in his first full season in England. Appetites had been sharpened not sated and expectations raised so that fans now anticipated the level of performance witnessed in the first months of 1998 to be reproduced as a matter of course. A few months later after an uninspiring home draw against Middlesbrough, Wenger admitted he might have made a rod for his own back. Commenting on the criticism of his team's performance he said, 'Maybe we have given them too much too soon. When you eat caviar it is hard to go back to sausages.' The man from Alsace had led his followers into the promised land. Now they expected it to be overflowing with milk and honey, having conveniently forgotten the false prophets – McGoldrick, Carter, Hillier et al. – of days of yore.

The only reinforcement of note in the summer of 1998 saw Argentine defender Nelson Vivas join from Swiss club Servette. Although back-up defenders Steve Bould, Gilles Grimandi and Matthew Upson were potential replacements at centre-back, Wenger had been fortunate that neither Lee Dixon nor Nigel Winterburn had suffered prolonged absences since his arrival. However, his next two purchases perhaps reflected where his instincts lay. Ian Wright had been sold to West Ham, so although Christopher Wreh had enjoyed a purple patch in attack after his March 1998 debut, it didn't appear as if he would be able to consistently maintain the goalscoring form needed at this level. When a player is discarded, according to Bob Wilson, it is because, 'Arsène's judgement is based on the best – not the second best or nearly the best – and if any player, in his mind, falls below that criterion then he is vulnerable to the chance that Arsène Wenger will find someone better.' Freddie Ljungberg arrived early in the 1998–99 season and was joined a little later on by Kanu from Internazionale.

Although they went close to retaining both their trophies, Arsenal only had the Charity Shield to show for their efforts. The defence remained consistently ungenerous, but they were another year older and time demanded – in the absence of likely prospects from the youth system – that this area of the squad was prioritised. So in the summer of 1999, it was time to ring some more changes. The sale of Anelka funded the spending spree that brought both Thierry Henry and Davor Suker to Highbury (prompting David Dein's quip, 'We are going from a sulker to a Suker.') Suker was brought in for a modest sum, having been mainly a substitute in his final season at Real Madrid. Wenger was thinking of the future with Henry, but hoping to get a good season out of Suker, after the purple patch he enjoyed at France '98 (scoring six goals to win the Golden Boot) suggested he wasn't over the hill. However he never approached that form again. His Arsenal career was characterised by a mix of memorable goals and horrendous misses, but ultimately too many of the latter. He proved an inexpensive gamble that didn't work out, and was even more ineffectual after subsequently moving across town to West Ham.

George Graham had a reputation for collecting centre-backs, but with the number of attackers that were coming to Arsenal perhaps Arsène Wenger was overdosing at the other end of the pitch. Granted Dynamo Kiev's Ukraine skipper Oleg Luzhny and the Brazilian Silvinho from Corinthians arrived with a view to phasing out Dixon and Winterburn – Vivas had proved ineffective in that department – although the big money signings always seemed to have an attacking bent to them. As if to confirm this, Robert Pires and Sylvain Wiltord joined in 2000, the latter being the club's record transfer signing. Wenger justifies spending more heavily on attackers by claiming, 'Strikers are more expensive. Only Manchester United buys a defender for £30 million.' As for Wiltord's cost seeming disproportionate to other buys, he remembers, 'We spent £11 million on him in a year when we got £29 million to spend from Barcelona. It is the highest transfer ever for us because of that income. If we had not done the transfers we had, he would never have come. It was an exceptional year, like you have with wine. And I had defenders.' For all that, Wenger later admitted that the goals conceded in the subsequent season's FA Cup Final defeat and the Champions League exit in Valencia were no accidents, but a result of age catching up with his back four. Even so, his belief that you can't win without a first-rate attack means he will always spend more money on forwards, even if he had Manchester United's resources. An example was his flirting with the thought of acquiring Harry Kewell from Leeds United in 2003, only to be denied by financial obstacles, despite knowing that there were gaping defensive holes to be filled in a side that had demonstrated the one thing it could be relied upon to do was score goals on a regular basis.

So although Pires and Wiltord were paid for by the sale of Overmars and Petit to Barcelona, neither of the new players could be seriously regarded as potential central midfield partners for Patrick Vieira. The manager's predilection for the purchase of attacking players was further evidenced by his willingness to take a gamble on a number of low cost forwards, possibly in the hope that he might uncover another bargain find to rank alongside Nicolas Anelka. In addition to Christopher Wreh, Luis Boa Morte, Fabien Caballero and Kaba Diawara and Tomas Danilevicius were all on Arsenal's books without making significant impact on the first-team selection policy. Collecting attackers – good, bad and indifferent – indicated that there was a lower criteria of quality needed for a forward to get his chance at Highbury, whereas defenders invariably needed to be experienced, with the exception of the then promising teenager, Matthew Upson. Arsène Wenger seemed less inclined to take such chances in giving places in his squad to defenders, because maybe he wasn't so sure of his touch in this area.

The 1997–98 double side had found the right balance between defence and attack. There were matches when the likes of Overmars, Bergkamp and Petit would combine to produce some devastating and beautiful football. But there were plenty of 1–0 days too. The ability to take maximum points under all circumstances is the mark of a great side. The 1998–99 Arsenal were the nearly men – unable to build upon a remarkable season. Arsène Wenger would have to reconstruct almost the entire side before glory would once again be grasped, before the balance between defence and attack was again what it needed to be.

Chapter Six

European Misadventures (Part One)

The Parken Stadium, Copenhagen, 17 May 2000. At the scene of one of their greatest triumphs six years earlier, Arsenal were moments away from one of their biggest disenchantments. As three peeps of the referee's whistle marked the end of the second period of extra-time, and thus left the destination of the UEFA Cup to a penalty shoot-out, Arsenal's chairman Peter Hill-Wood turned to his counterpart Faruk Suren from Galatasaray and offered him a congratulatory handshake. The bemused Turkish president responded that the contest wasn't over. 'Yes it is,' came the reply, 'we always lose on penalties.'

The incident was typical of Peter Hill-Wood. Dignified in defeat and magnanimous in victory he gives the lie to Brian Clough's hyperbolic description of club bosses: 'Hooligans? Well you've ninety-two club chairmen for a start.' But then he comes with an inimitable pedigree. Since his grandfather Sir Samuel Hill-Wood joined in 1919 there has been a Hill-Wood continuously on the board at Arsenal for eighty-four years. 'Quite a good record really,' comments the present incumbent, who became a director in 1962 in his mid-20s, and chairman twenty years later on the death of his father Denis.

As he was working his way up the ladder at Hambros bank, eventually running the investment department, Peter Hill-Wood recalls his Arsenal duties as 'a nice little hobby. Your employer didn't mind you taking the odd afternoon off. It's not quite the same nowadays.' Understatement punctuates the speech of a modest unassuming man whose sharp sense of humour helps him through the public functions he has to perform in his role of company chairman.

Only too pleased to take a back seat on such occasions, his fellow directors have every reason to be thankful for their chairman's ability to meet the needs of the moment. At the yearly piece of theatre, otherwise known as the September Annual General Meeting, Hill-Wood's chairmanship usually carries the day. 'How on earth,' asked one shareholder in amazement back in the early 1990s, 'did you get £620,000 for Martin Hayes?' 'We couldn't stop Celtic giving us their money,' came the reply – and the occasional slip of the tongue – the undertaking to 'Mr Wenger' – earn the chairman the respect and affection of everyone who comes into contact with him. One suspects among them are the players. Unobtrusively available when needed – to help Tony Adams and Ray Parlour ('he'd walk through a brick wall for you') pick up the pieces of their lives – there is no ego at play here. He rarely ventures into the dressing room. 'I don't necessarily think the players need to see directors going around with big smiles on their faces. Frankly it's not going to make any difference to the way they play.' Nor are there any false airs and graces despite the privileged upbringing – Eton and country house estate. One suspects his heroes are not today's superstars, much as he admires their silky skills, but yesterday's 'double' winners, vintage 1971, as evinced by his spontaneous affection when he recalls stalwarts like Peter Storey, dismissing his criminal past as misjudgement which should not and doesn't, as far as he is concerned, impact on the present. 'I like Peter,' he says simply, 'I've got a lot of time for him.'

Not so much time though for many of the new breed of entrepreneurial Premiership chairmen: 'You see them for lunch and dinner and that's about it.' Though Mr Suren, the Galatasaray president, made more of an impression. 'I remember him, he was rather a nice man actually,' Hill-Wood recalls. When asked, three years after the event, whether he did indeed congratulate his opposite number before the penalty shoot-out, he laughs and says, 'It sounds like me, I might well have said that.'

That moment of whimsy could not have occurred without Arsenal's failure in UEFA's top competition in the first place. As Premiership runners-up in 1999, they had earned an automatic berth in the newly expanded first group stage of the Champions League. Now consisting of eight teams of four groups, the third placed clubs, although eliminated from the main competition, enjoyed entry into the third round of the UEFA Cup by way of compensation. It was the second year in a row that Arsenal had failed to get past the initial group stage in Europe's Premier club tournament, and there was little doubt of the major reason for these successive shambles.

As defending Premiership champions in 1998–99, the club made the bizarre decision to stage their Champions League home matches on neutral territory. And what neutral territory! Wembley Stadium was a venue that could easily inspire, rather than intimidate opponents in the way that sometimes the under-dogs will play the game of their lives against top-flight opposition in the FA Cup. The chance to play there would be a once in a lifetime opportunity for many of the visiting players. Also, Wembley was in no way as threatening for an evening fixture as the intimate surroundings of Highbury, despite the guarantee of almost double the number of home supporters. Arsenal ensured their 'home' fixtures would be sell-outs by offering a three-ticket package at prices as low as £10 and £15 per match. Thousands of fans could not get into Highbury due to its limited capacity as Arsenal were as exclusive a London club as some of those in Pall Mall. But, now supporters would be able to see their heroes in the flesh, and what's more, could afford to bring the kids.

Arsenal's justification for the choice of Wembley was that High-bury was simply not up to staging Champions League matches with all the media facilities, extra advertising boards and sponsors' hospitality that were a UEFA prerequisite. Given that some European stadiums were smaller and far more antiquated, this did not appear to be a persuasive argument and when Highbury was suddenly able to stage Champions League matches after all in the autumn of 2000, albeit with a reduced capacity, Wembley was consigned to the past as a worthy but ultimately self-defeating experiment. Arguably, the only long-term benefits being the veri-fication of an extended fan base, reassurance that there were at least an extra 30,000 fans that were eager to watch their team given the chance and the club had put down a marker, should circumstances ever make Wembley a more desirable alternative to their existing home. The national stadium may have delivered the club more revenue than Highbury would have, but if it was indeed primarily a piece of speculative market research or political schmoozing, the ultimate price would be a heavy one.

Having won the double, great things were expected of Arsenal; moreover, the draw looked exceptionally kind to them. They would face Dynamo Kiev, Lens and Panathinaikos. Other groups appeared far more difficult – certainly the names of the competing teams – Real Madrid, Bayern Munich, Juventus, Internazionale – were more glamorous. If Arsenal's opponents seemed unexciting, at least their lack of European pedigree gave the English champions a realistic chance of topping the group or at the very least garnering enough points to qualify as one of the two second-placed sides. Six groups of four teams each competed for eight quarter-final places, the winners joined by the two best runners-up.

Arsenal's four points from their three away fixtures was a respectable enough haul, but their pitiful home displays effectively put paid to their aspirations. A win against Panathinaikos was a good enough start, but the points subsequently dropped to Dynamo Kiev set up their match against Lens as a must win encounter for both sides to give the winner a chance of progressing to the last eight. Simple enough in theory, but with Dennis Bergkamp and Emmanuel Petit injured, the absence of Patrick Vieira due to suspension meant that the central midfield partnership was Remi Garde and Stephen Hughes, whilst Christopher Wreh partnered Nicolas Anelka in attack, hardly the personnel to set the opposition quaking in their boots. Thus there was no great surprise when Lens ran out the victors. If the defeat established anything, it was that Arsenal lacked the necessary strength in depth, the squad simply wasn't strong enough to compensate the unavailability of the key personnel.

The expansion of the competition in September 1999 to allow entry from a greater number of clubs from Europe's top football nations meant that the first group stage now comprised thirty-two teams of which sixteen would proceed into a second group phase. Arsenal were drawn against Fiorentina, Barcelona and the least known, unfashionable Swedes AIK Solna. So, in effect, it really came down to perming two from three to go through to the last sixteen. As a result there were now six extra games for the sides that progressed from their initial group, with all the attendant financial benefits, amounting to at least an additional £7 million to representatives of the larger television markets like Arsenal.

Arsenal again began well with four points from the first two fixtures, although they could so easily have secured the maximum as in the goalless opener in Florence, Kanu had a penalty saved with ten minutes remaining. Such profligacy was to become an unfortunate characteristic of Arsenal's Champions League performances. Even when they were on song, they lacked the ruthlessness to see off their rivals. Entertaining AIK Solna, a similar story threatened to unfold as the home team dominated but found themselves 1–1 as the match entered second-half injury time. Fortunately they took the two chances they carved out in the dying seconds to secure the three points they deserved.

Arsenal's trip to Barcelona was the game that looked least likely to produce any return, although it was certainly a test as to how they might fare if they reached the latter stages of the competition. Before the game, Wenger expressed his admiration for his side's opponents. 'I like their front six: Luis Enrique, Guardiola, Rivaldo, Figo, Kluivert and Cocu are all good. Because of the size of the pitch and quality of their technique and passing Barcelona can destroy any defence. If they run after the ball they can slowly kill you. It's like drowning, you cannot do anything against it.'

His worst fears seemed about to be realised, as Arsenal looked out of their depth, and were fortunate to reach the interval only one goal in arrears. Partly thanks to a Tony Adams rallying cry during the break – his motivation stimulated by the gate-crashing of Arsenal's pre-match training session by some of the Barcelona players, who mocked the proceedings (picking up the tone from their outspoken Dutch manager Louis van Gaal) there was no question that Arsenal gave a far better account of themselves in the second half despite being reduced to ten men after Gilles Grimandi was dismissed for a petulant foul. The visitors' revenge came through a scrambled Kanu equaliser with ten minutes remaining and they left the Nou Camp delighted with a point. Three matches, two of them in Italy and Spain, and still unbeaten. For all that, Arsenal were in exactly the same position as the previous year with five points at the halfway stage in the group.

Three weeks later the trial of strength resumed with Barcelona's visit to Wembley. Tactically, however, Wenger's side never really got to grips with their opponents' very fluid pyramid formation – notionally 4–3–2–1, but in reality far more flexible, with a constant interchange of personnel. An important disparity between the sides was the holding role of Guardiola – a seamless link between defence and attack. Patrick Vieira could have duplicated this task for the home side, but a two-goal deficit after sixteen minutes meant that caution and, sadly, discipline had be sacrificed. The absence of someone carrying out this vital function unquestionably contributed to Barca's two second-half goals in a final 4–2 scoreline. Further, Arsenal's midfield was also weakened by Emmanuel Petit's absence through injury. In the nine Champions League matches played up to this one, due to suspension or injury Vieira and Petit had partnered each other a meagre three times. But despite the defeat at least their fate was still in their own hands. With AIK Solna now out of the running, the runners-up spot, and resultant qualification for the second group stage was between the English and Italians.

Having more than matched Fiorentina on their own patch, Arsenal were entitled to feel confident about the visit of Gabriel Batistuta and company to London eight days after their epic encounter with the Spanish champions. At the conclusion of hostilities, if level on points the qualifier would be determined by the head-to-head results as opposed to overall goal difference. It meant that a win for either side would guarantee them second place and progress to the next phase, irrespective of the outcome of the final set of games. Fiorentina were suffering domestically, with coach Giovanni Trapattoni lambasted for failing to build on the success that had seen them challenge for the *Scudetto* the season before. He had even offered his resignation the previous weekend after a surprising loss against unfashionable Piacenza. On the other hand, Arsenal were buoyed up by a vibrant 3–2 win against Chelsea at Stamford Bridge due to an astonishing hat-trick by Kanu. And history was on their side – in six previous ties they had yet to concede defeat to an Italian club.

A first minute assault by Batistuta on Lee Dixon's ankles should have warranted a red card, but the referee allowed the striker to remain on the pitch with just a caution, a scandalous decision that was to directly affect the outcome. Fiorentina displayed a niggly, cynical manner that was clearly intended to rattle their opponents.

Notwithstanding, it was the same old story namely, the home side's inability to impose sustained pressure. They created enough decent chances to have emerged victorious, but as usual were predictably wasteful. Batistuta had one opening all night – fifteen minutes from time – and capitalised with a shot from a narrow angle that rocketed above David Seaman into the far corner of the net. It was a salutary comment on the quality of Arsenal's finishing as there was no further score. Arsenal were out of the Champions League at the first hurdle – again. So much for history.

It was a black night. Those who knew Arsène Wenger well said that the defeat, and its implications wounded him. His side had done the hard work in achieving away draws, but once again Wembley was their nemesis. Given that they had dropped five points out of nine the season before, it seemed as if the painful lesson of conceding *genuine* home advantage had not been learned. Why did they play a further season away from Highbury? Wenger's answer was, 'Because I thought we were stronger – strong enough to do it. But we had injuries during the period we played at Wembley, and put out some teams that were not strong enough to compete in the Champions League. In fairness it was a mistake. I didn't want to blame Wembley and use it as a an excuse; I know how it is in England if you say something like that.' By returning to the stadium for a successive campaign, he reasoned, 'I'll show them it isn't Wembley – but it is a mistake not to play your home games at home.' The point had already been underlined when after complimenting Arsenal on 'their great powers of recovery' at the Nou Camp, Barcelona's Brazilian virtuoso Rivaldo looked forward to the Wembley return without the slightest sense of apprehension. 'We are happy to be going there,' he said, 'because Wembley is large and spacious, like the Nou Camp. It will suit our style. It would have been much more difficult for us at Arsenal's stadium.'

Playing at bigger stadia to cater for the extra demand of special games is not unknown abroad, but what is unusual is for major clubs like Arsenal to feel that their existing home ground is obviously outmoded for the big occasion. There was no doubt that the club had outgrown its home, and due to the opposition of residents living behind the West Stand in Highbury Hill, expanding Highbury would, at best, raise the capacity to something around the

45,000 mark, from its current 38,500 capacity. Manchester United were adding another tier of seats at Old Trafford, and were effectively pulling away from all other sides in the world in terms of potential matchday revenue. Possibly Arsenal needed to confirm that there was a potential demand to watch the team should they decide to up sticks from their existing ground and use a bigger stadium for all of their home matches, and the Champions League provided that opportunity. The only team of any note to use another stadium on a regular basis with any degree of success was Ajax of Amsterdam, who moved to the Olympic Stadium in preference to their antiquated De Meer stadium when important foreign guests came to town and even for major domestic clashes against rivals like Feyenoord. Thus the players felt it was more of a home from home rather than neutral territory on temporary loan, (now though, all their home games are played in the Amsterdam ArenA, the new stadium they moved into in the mid-1990s, despite their lack of economic muscle compared to Arsenal).

Perhaps, the lack of depth in Arsène Wenger's squad might not have been so obviously exposed had they played on more familiar territory. Footballers, supreme creatures of habit and superstition, tend to perform better in home matches because familiarity breeds contentment; they settle into a comfortable routine. Travelling to play for Arsenal at Wembley Stadium was something associated with participating in the FA Cup Final, the League Cup Final and the Charity Shield, the climax of a successful series of engagements, with all the paraphernalia associated with a special one-off event played out in the unique setting of the national stadium. The 1999–2000 UEFA Cup that Arsenal entered as a result of their third place finish behind Barcelona and Fiorentina witnessed the return of European nights to Highbury. Back where they belonged genuine home advantage undoubtedly contributed to victories over Nantes, Deportivo La Coruna, Werder Bremen and Lens as Arsenal reached the ultimately disappointing denouement against Galatasaray. The run certainly added to their European experience, largely because the sides they faced were good enough – despite the obvious secondary status of the event – for nothing to be taken for granted, and they weren't having to take them on without the benefit of the full advantages of the home leg.

The elimination at the first Champions League hurdle was a huge blow to the ambition, pride, and revenue that the club would have enjoyed from another six matches in the next group stage. With a line-up of French World Cup-winning stars, world-class Dutch attackers and vastly experienced English defenders that together had no lack of exposure on the international stage, Arsenal were unquestionably worthy of a place amongst the best sixteen teams in Europe – on paper at least. But on the Wembley pitch, they had failed to even earn their spurs.

Chapter Seven

European Misadventures (Part Two)

Football has a way of throwing up the past and a heartbreaking example was provided by Arsenal's Champions League exit in the quarter-finals of the 2001–02 competition. Only needing a draw to progress to a semi-final against Leeds United whom they were confident they had the measure of, Arsène Wenger's side had kept Valencia, their Spanish opponents at bay for seventy-five minutes. Then, up popped an old adversary from the manager's time in Monaco. From a throw-in on the left side, Jocelyn Angloma – a former Marseille player – hit a quick cross into the box and John Carew rose fractionally ahead of Tony Adams to glance a header across the goal and into the far corner. As Arsenal made their exit on the away goals rule, Gunners fans with long memories doubtless recalled being foiled by the same club over twenty years before in the Cup Winners' Cup Final, losing the trophy on a penalty shoot-out.

Having won the first leg 2–1 at Highbury (Henry missing a gilt-edged chance to take the score to 3–1 and effectively kill the tie), Arsenal were now left with two strategical options for the return leg: play for a draw or stay true to their convictions and adopt a more attacking stance to try and cancel out Valencia's away goal advantage. Perhaps Arsenal were inhibited by Valencia's reputation as being a difficult side to break down, and felt their best chance was to rely on their own defensive unit to take them through. David Seaman had Lee Dixon, Martin Keown, Tony Adams and the emerging Ashley Cole in front of him; four of the famous five who had played in Europe for George Graham at a time when they could normally be relied upon to keep a clean sheet if it really mattered. But *Anno Domini* waits for no one. In

1994, Tony Adams would probably have been a microsecond quicker to react to the cross from Angloma, and done enough to prevent Carew's winning header. Now, over four years after Wenger's arrival at Arsenal, the legendary defence was inevitably winding down. The attack needed to assume more responsibility, but the team's reluctance to move forward to support Thierry Henry – despite the presence of Robert Pires and Sylvain Wiltord in the starting line-up, subsequently joined by Freddie Ljungberg for the second half – and attempt to relieve the pressure by maintaining decent possession smacked of undue wariness. Now Arsenal were forced to push forward frantically in search of an equaliser, but having got their noses in front, Valencia as their defensive prowess implied, were not about to relinquish their advantage. The final whistle blew and Arsenal were out.

Wenger's out of character cautionary tactics – a throwback to the George Graham era without the necessary practice to perfect them – would of course have been justified if they had succeeded, but the margin between triumph and tragedy is often wafer thin, as the manager's post-match reflections illustrated. 'We've paid a high price for one second's lack of concentration because until then we looked comfortable,' he reflected. 'Hopefully we'll be back next season, but we might not get a chance like this again.' That the Spanish side went on to dismiss Leeds United 3–0 and then only lose the final on a penalty shoot-out to Bayern Munich was scant consolation to Arsenal. Although it did demonstrate how close they had been to becoming realistic candidates to contest the European Cup final for the first time in their history.

Once before at a crucial juncture in a Champions League campaign Arsène Wenger departed from his tried and trusted tactics with a similar unfortunate result. As Monaco manager in 1994, in the group match at home against Barcelona he surprised his captain Jürgen Klinsmann by adopting a more defensive approach, moving from four to five at the back. Klinsmann pointed out that although they were a technically gifted team, they were not as mentally tough as their Latin opponents. With the group runners-up – the Barcelona fixture would determine the top spot – having to travel for a one-off encounter, in all probability against Milan, the only chance for Monaco, in Klinsmann's view, was to try and defeat Barcelona and thereby secure home advantage in the semi-final. Wenger though, according to Klinsmann, appeared obsessed with the need to counter the threat of the Brazilian striker Romario. But in the event, Barcelona's coach Johan Cruyff, restricted by the prevailing UEFA regulation to choose three foreigners from amongst his plethora of stars, opted for Bulgarian international Hristo Stoichkov, Danish star Michael Laudrup and Dutch defender Ronald Koeman, omitting Romario as he had done before. At the eleventh hour, Klinsmann tried to persuade his coach to resort to his attacking instincts. 'Let's go for it,' he urged, 'it's not too late to change the line-up.' But a forward might say that, mightn't he? Wenger understood Klinsmann's frustration, and, as he remembers, 'he was always pushing to attack.' In the event defensive reinforcements did not win the day, so the formation was changed to give the star striker more support, but to no avail as Klinsmann had an undistinguished match and Barcelona won by a solitary goal.

There was another uncalled for coincidence. The episode so disenchanted Jürgen Klinsmann that he succumbed to Tottenham's overtures. However, unlike Patrick Vieira – who made no secret of his unhappiness at the Valencia debacle – Klinsmann had gained his share of cosmopolitan club honours to accompany his World Cup winners medal so there was nothing to hold him in the Principality. Vieira on the other hand, was persuaded to stay and fight another day, after a summer of press speculation that he was unlikely to remain at Highbury.

That Arsenal managed to reach the quarter-finals, by finishing in the top two of both their first and second stage groups, showed how crucial it had been to use Highbury rather than Wembley. In 2000–01, they could afford the luxury of allowing their away performances to dip but still advance due to their strength at home. Whether that season's record on the road (four defeats in seven matches compared with only one in six in the two seasons before), was affected by a change in the selection policy regarding Dennis Bergkamp may provide the answer. In the two 'Wembley' seasons, Bergkamp travelled to France, Italy and Spain and the Gunners were not beaten. His trips made by sea and land because of his well-documented flying phobia, meant that special travel arrangements had to be made for him whenever the squad took to the air. He did not feature once in the seven away trips of the

2000–01 campaign, in spite of venues such as Rome, Lyon, Munich and Valencia involving similar journeys to those undertaken before in aid of the Champions League cause. It seemed as if Arsène Wenger had taken a contrary view to use other players, often Kanu, instead, wilfully depriving himself of someone he has described as 'super talented'.

In a volte face, it appeared that Wenger had decided that a team that stays together, plays together. Previously, he admitted that maybe he sometimes wrongly persevered with Bergkamp, reasonably justifying his actions by revealing, 'There have been some games when I thought Dennis didn't do a lot, yet when I watched the tapes I noticed that in the two or three moves from which we could have scored, it was always him who was involved. So I thought I couldn't leave him out because we would lack the final ball.' For somebody who always looks as if it is an indignity when he is substituted, it came as an ironic blow to be told, after retiring from international football to concentrate his energies for his club that he would not be selected as regularly as he had been. Injury exacerbated his hurt and it took some time to come to terms with his drop in status, only feeling recently that he has returned to the high standard he sets himself.

Of his goals – over one hundred for Arsenal – Arsène Wenger once said, 'Dennis only scores best-sellers'; meaning that more often than not they are from distance, or require the unexpected, as the player is rarely in position to score simple, mundane tap-ins. The great goalscorer and main man at Ajax had transmogrified into a scorer of great goals and 'shadow' striker at Arsenal. He tends to drift around the field in the space between the halfway line and the opposition penalty area, picking up the ball and either playing it simple or, when the moment comes, attempting a killer pass to set up a scoring opportunity for a colleague or scoring that special goal all by himself. As Bergkamp explains, 'I don't want to appear arrogant but this attractive way of playing comes naturally. I don't think of it as anything special it's just the way I imagine football should be played and the way I do it.' He dismisses the plaudits bestowed upon him by commenting, 'It is only natural that the fans go for players with style rather than those who just work.' Marco van der Wiel experienced the same Ajax schoolkids system that developed Bergkamp, although he failed to make the grade and became a supporter of the club. He says of the former Ajax striker, 'His touch is magnificent. If Bergkamp gives you a ball, you score easily.'

Van der Wiel was one of a huge throng of Ajax fans that travelled to London when Arsenal entertained the Dutch side in a 2003 Champions League tie. 'We are here to see Ajax,' he explained, 'but we also came to see Bergkamp. We love him because he earns our respect. He has got better with age.' Arsenal's goal that night included a typical contribution from Bergkamp, as he set up Sylvain Wiltord with a probing pass from just inside the Ajax half. In the blink of an eye he saw the possibilities and released the ball into his colleague's path. There was no time for the visiting defence to respond and Wiltord applied the final touch. The glory was the scorer's, but the goal, in truth, was all about the set-up and the vision it conveyed. As van der Wiel said before the match, 'Bergkamp plays for the team. He's a decent character, selfless.' Confirmation that this generous view of a former favourite was shared by other Ajax fans was the reception afforded Bergkamp when the Gunners fulfilled the reverse fixture the following week in the Amsterdam ArenA. Returning stars such as Clarence Seedorf, Edgar Davids and Frank de Boer, are often jeered on such occasions; but the Dutch appreciate artists rather than artisans, and Dennis Bergkamp is a special artist. A direct descendant of a line that reaches back to Johan Cruyff via Marco van Basten, he exemplifies Dutch football at its best.

A reclusive individual who shuns the spotlight, he had a miserable spell in Italy, after transferring to Internazionale from Ajax in 1993. Disturbed by the amount of attention he was subjected to, he says, 'You are made to feel like you are public property. The fans want to see you as a god or something. They want to touch you and that seems to be a big thrill for them. You have grown men wanting to touch you, it's unbelievable.' When told that Arsenal fans had taken to wearing replica shirts with 'God' and number 10 on them, he commented, 'Luckily in England there is a bit of irony behind it. In Italy they really believe it.' The decision to play him as an out and out striker was certainly responsible for his poor return of only eleven goals in fifty-two games – a far inferior ratio than the one in three he would go on to attain at Highbury (although the quality of defenders he had to face in

England must have been a relief to him). It seemed perverse that Internazionale paid £12 million for a player they didn't want to use in his best position. After all he scored more than a goal every other match for Ajax, often twenty-five or more in a season, but Bergkamp modestly tries to put his native success into perspective. 'Coming from Ajax you win everything; you dominate matches and are given four or five chances every game to score. So when I moved to Italy it was like moving to a different world.' Despite his difficulties in acclimatising he contributed enough in his first season at Internazionale to play a full part in lifting the UEFA Cup, repeating the feat of his former club two years before.

He was the first international star to arrive on these shores with his best years still ahead of him and despite the carping from the tabloids that the Premiership would soon lay bare the exorbitant extravagance of his £7.5 million fee, at a stroke his reputation made Arsenal into a top European club, although it took a virtuoso performance against Southampton a few appearances into his Arsenal career before the doubters were silenced. On a personal level, the omens were good. There is a story that when he made his Highbury debut in 1995 against Internazionale in a friendly arranged as part of his transfer deal, he was teased afterwards by former team-mate Nicola Berti (continuing the barbs he had been accustomed to receiving in the Inter dressing room). Bergkamp walked off, but Berti wasn't letting up. Following him, he ran into Tony Adams who sent his new team-mate's tormentor away with a flea in his ear. Bergkamp felt that he was amongst friends and belonged, and after a transitional season he was reassured that 'a new Arsenal was in the process of being created'.

Named after Denis Law and a fan of English football from the time his parents took him as a treat to White Hart Lane to watch Glenn Hoddle, Bergkamp seamlessly adjusted to his new surroundings. Most of his time in England has been spent in a salubrious secluded upmarket estate in Hadley Wood on the London/Hertfordshire borders. Here he resides in domestic tranquillity with his wife Henrita and his three children far away from the prying eyes of the tabloids who have nothing to get their teeth into. No social animal he, the only flash aberration from his chosen low-key lifestyle is a blue Ferrari with a 'DNB 10' number plate (signifying Dennis Nicholaas, but not Maria, his third – and to insular English ears unfortunate – forename). Then, traffic permitting, he can be back home from training in time for a late lunch.

His new found contentment was expressed on the field not only by his intimate understanding with the likes of Ian Wright, Marc Overmars, Thierry Henry and Freddie Ljungberg – all of whom acknowledge their goal tallies benefited from playing alongside Bergkamp – it also resulted in some of the finest goals ever scored by a player wearing an Arsenal shirt. The hat-trick at Filbert Street in Arsène Wenger's first double season was topped off with a virtuoso goal akin to that he would go on to score for his country in the 1998 World Cup quarter-final. Drifting into the area, he collected the ball from deep, deftly controlled it to beat his Leicester marker Matt Elliot, and created the space for a shot across the keeper into the top far corner of the goal. An astonishing display of skill which caused author and Arsenal fan Nick Hornby to wonder, 'Does Dennis Bergkamp have three feet? Probably not . . . it only looked that way.'

Another 'best-seller' was selected as goal of the season, as was his earlier effort against Leicester. In his second double-winning season in England, Arsenal triumphed 2–0 in the league at Newcastle. Bergkamp's exploit saw him receive the ball with his back to goal while being tightly marked by centre-back Nikos Dabizas. With a flick of his boot he sent the ball to one side of the defender whilst turning and running past him on the other. So quick was his speed of thought that he had time to move across the Newcastle man so that he was in position to pass the ball into the net with his instep. For gems like these the circumstances have to be just right. He recalls, 'The angle of Robert Pires' pass was perfect. Ten centimetres further and I wouldn't have been able to do it the same way.' Regarding the goal that knocked Argentina out of the 1998 World Cup, Bergkamp admits: 'You often say to yourself "I could have done better" but with this goal, I would never have been able to do it better.'

Of course, moments like this do not happen every time the man takes to the field of play, but the sheer audacity of his skill is so deeply etched in the memory that on the increasingly frequent occasions when he is substituted at Highbury, the home crowd invariably afford him a standing ovation, regardless of his performance on that particular day. He is the kind of player fans will doubtless talk about long after he has left the club. However, the line between prodigy and notoriety is a thin one and the number ten has been known to veer the wrong side of it more often than he should. Unhappy with some of the not so legitimate tactics used by defenders, he has sought retribution when he thinks it is called for, sometimes even getting his retaliation in first. Something snaps and his self-control goes belying his nickname of 'The Iceman'. It is an odd phenomenon that a man so calm and unassuming outside of a match situation can demonstrate such a mean streak on the field of play. Presented with the evidence of studs in the chest or elbows in the face David Dein refuses to face facts. Persistence eventually provokes the response, 'genius can be flawed'. The conundrum for his coach being which side of Bergkamp's mean, moody or magnificent personality will be brought forth: the spitefulness, the anonymity or the supreme skill.

With the passage of time the goals are definitely drying up – seven in forty-one appearances in 2002–03 – but the player himself does not feel unduly concerned for his place as long as there are others to capitalise on his contribution. 'The way I like to look at it is to combine the assists and the goals. I'd be more disappointed if I'd had a lot of chances and missed them. I'm trying to play with a balance between making goals for other people and trying to score a few myself.' Sylvain Wiltord, Freddie Ljungberg and Robert Pires all score more goals from wide midfield positions than Bergkamp these days, yet the number ten has again become a first-choice starter when fit, indicating that Arsène Wenger is well aware of the vital role he can carry out. Which makes the decision to not use him in Champions League away games since 1999, with the exception of two trips to Holland, all the more surprising. Whether the side would have improved on their record of one win and a draw in ten away games before his return at PSV Eindhoven in September 2002, and a 4–0 victory, has to remain hypothetical.

His presence undeniably lifts his colleagues, as the coach acknowledged, 'He can often find the way to score the goals we need. It's not always an easy decision to leave players out of a team; but with the amount of matches we are playing it is sometimes needed. However, we want everybody to be together, which creates a good team spirit and it is psychologically important for the team to have Dennis Bergkamp with us.' So why the enforced absence? Arguably it was in fact one heck of a self-imposed handicap, the equivalent perhaps of Real Madrid foregoing Zinedine Zidane or Juventus without Alessandro Del Piero.

So it was just as well that September 2000 saw Highbury back in use for Champions League football after the Wembley experiment. Nine points from their three first stage group matches meant that they headed Lazio, Sparta Prague and Shakhtar Donetsk. The second stage was harder work, although a win against Spartak Moscow and draws with Bayern Munich and Lyon were just enough to see them through because of a rare away win in France. However alarm bells rang with the abject performance in their final group game in Bayern's Olympic Stadium. In the simultaneous group fixture, if Lyon defeated the already eliminated Spartak Moscow, Arsenal would have to win in Germany to stay alive, which made their insipid display all the more inexcusable. Losing 1–0, a scoreline which seriously flattered them, they hardly deserved to progress, but fate was kind to them as Lyon's inability to defeat Spartak gave them the same number of points as Arsenal. Despite their inferior goal difference, their aggregate goals, 2–1, in the head-to-head encounters with the French team meant they squeaked into the quarter-finals by the narrowest of margins.

It was a case of no lessons seemingly learnt and *déjà vu* for the following season's campaign. Five away defeats out of six saw at least three dismal performances on a par with that given against Bayern. A curious feature of the solitary point earned at Bayer Leverkusen, was that Dennis Bergkamp actually made the 500-mile trip, only to sit on the substitutes' bench! To this day his journey remains an unsolved mystery. Perhaps the mere sight of the shadow striker warming up on the touchline sufficiently inspired his team-mates to rise to the occasion. The irony of the failures on foreign soil in 2001–02 was that domestically, the team couldn't lose; going through their away fixtures unbeaten (excluding the deliberately weakened side fielded at Blackburn to ensure they would not have to endure a protracted League Cup campaign), culminating in Arsène Wenger's second Premiership and FA Cup 'double'. No one could satisfactorily explain why the

Gunners froze once they crossed the English channel, although the number of defeats they were clocking up may well have contributed to the players feeling inhibited before a ball was kicked.

Once again, Highbury served them well. Maximum points from the visits of Schalke, Panathinaikos and Real Mallorca took them through to the last sixteen and the second group stage. There, a 3–1 win over Juventus and a 4–1 trouncing of subsequent finalists Bayer Leverkusen justifiably raised hopes that this was going to be their year. Ultimately though, the travelling disease became contagious and the first European defeat suffered at Highbury under Arsène Wenger forced them to make their premature adieus to the competition.

A home victory against Deportivo La Coruna would ensure Arsenal a place in the quarter-final draw for the second year running. In the reverse fixture almost three months previously, Deportivo did not really have to get out of second gear to overcome a poor Arsenal side on the night, so their true worth was unknown. However, it soon became apparent just how good they really were. The Gunners may have routed their Spanish opponents 5–1 two years earlier in the UEFA Cup, but that result exaggerated the disparity between the two. On 12 March 2002, the scoreboard proclaimed: Arsenal 0 Deportivo La Coruna 2. That result confirmed that the gap had been more than bridged.

Notwithstanding the loss, the vagaries of UEFA regulations meant that Arsenal could still qualify by equalling or bettering Bayer Leverkusen's result in the final round: the Gunners away to Juventus, the German side away to Deportivo with the proviso that in the event of both emerging victorious, computation of comparative results would eliminate Arsenal. The anomaly, as Arsène Wenger acknowledged, was 'that we are in a situation that we can lose and go through or win it and go out. It makes it a little bit strange and it would be very difficult to explain even to a mathematician.'

Deportivo coach Javie Irureta made encouraging noises about his team's task, even though their qualification was guaranteed; 'We will be trying to get at least a point against Leverkusen, we always play to win.' This claim proved to have a hollow ring to it as Deportivo rested some key players and played like a team who were indifferent to the outcome. Given that a defeat would relegate them to second place, and they would thus have to face a potentially more difficult quarter-final against a winner of one of the other groups, it seemed a short-sighted selection.

Leverkusen established a 2–0 lead and the news filtered through to Turin. With the Italians already eliminated, hardly any of their fans had bothered to turn up, and the atmosphere inside the Stadio delle Alpi can rarely have been as soulless. Despite Arsenal's respectable away support of around 1,000, the chants had a ghostly ring as they echoed around a near empty bowl. It was a difficult environment for players who had to raise their game, perhaps aggravated by having to face a second string Juventus line-up. It was not Arsenal's night. Thierry Henry missed a penalty just as he done against Deportivo the week before, and as if to confirm the fates were against them, with the outcome seemingly academic, the *bianconeri* scored the decisive goal with fifteen minutes remaining. The grapevine reported that Deportivo had pulled a goal back but the Gunners still couldn't find the necessary motivation despite an individual win bonus of £12,000 or £4,000 for a draw on the table. Perhaps players earn so much that they are indifferent to financial rewards of this nature. Still, there was no excuse for such a vapid performance, an insult that those who had taken the time, trouble and expense to support them would not forget. The evening was another blot on the European copy-book which has yet to be fully erased. There was no further score, and to nail down the coffin of Arsène Wenger's European ambitions, Leverkusen ran out 3–1 winners.

All the same Arsène Wenger was upbeat after the game, refusing to accept that his team was just not good enough. 'This will not stop us. Do I still believe we can become the best in the world? Yes, I do,' he declared. 'We will come back and win this competition next season. Arsenal are 130 years old and have never won it. Some other big clubs, like Inter Milan, have not won it for many years and Real Madrid had a long wait as well. We are in a good way and we have a team who are good enough to win it. We are not far away. We had the most difficult group and were close to going through. It was not only Arsenal who went out.'

He did not believe that there was any obvious reason for his side's difficulty on their travels, stating, 'Our away record could be a psychological problem but I don't think it is. We got a draw in Germany and were unlucky in this game. It's not a mental block for us. I believe we actually lost this group at home in losing to Deportivo. If we had at least drawn against them then they would have had to get a result tonight.' True enough, but the fact that Arsenal's progress to the quarter-final had gone down to the wire in two successive campaigns established that they were some way off being serious contenders for the Champions League crown – regardless of their manager's conviction.

That night in Turin provided a mirror image of their experience at the same stage the previous season. Away to another European giant in Bayern Munich they were unable to raise their game, and were reliant on other results to go their way. In 2001 they got lucky, with Lyon failing to win in Moscow. On this occasion, fortune showed its fickle face to them. However what made their dismal showing in Turin all the worse was that their opponents had nothing whatsoever to play for apart from their win bonus, and gave their stars the day off. Ultimately, if either of two results had been more positive, as they should have been, Arsenal would have advanced. Had they held on to a 1–0 lead away to Leverkusen they would have shown Klaus Topmöller's side the door after the 4–1 win at Highbury. Even after dropping two points in Germany, if their home form had been maintained with a win against Deportivo, they would still have made the last eight. As it was they were left to rue their missed opportunities and stand by as Liverpool and Manchester United made the quarter-finals. It was no consolation that Deportivo paid the price for foolishly sacrificing top spot in the group by drawing Manchester United and suffering the consequences.

Arsenal's chief Premiership protagonists finished seven points clear of the third-placed side in their own second stage group. Going into the last round of matches, United had, as usual, an unassailable lead. That Arsène Wenger's outfit on the other hand found themselves as perennial hostages to fortune in order to move to the knockout stage was sure-fire proof that although they undisputably had the measure of the English game, they were still on a steep learning curve abroad. For in Europe, it was still United who were indubitably England's top dogs.

Rather than curse the fates for their lack of progress in Europe,

Arsenal should take a leaf out of United's book. Making the quarter-final stages without fail since 1997, they were twice eliminated on the away goal rule. Even so, being in the last eight as a matter of course signified that they were operating on a higher plane to Arsenal. Home-grown stars like Beckham, Giggs, Scholes, Butt and Gary Neville; together with Keane, Solskjaer and Irwin had all racked up more than fifty Champions League appearances over the years. And there was no substitute for the savvy, the *savoir faire* which paid increasing dividends as time moved on. Arsenal, by contrast, not only lacked the European know-how but as an evolutionary side kept changing their line-up; only Kanu in the current squad had notched up more than forty games in the competition and a third of those were for Ajax. Sooner or later teams with the expertise seem to get the breaks that they have earned. When Manchester United won the Champions League in 1999, they made the most of their good fortune. In a very one-sided final against Bayern Munich their perseverance brought them two injury-time goals against the run of play to run out 2–1 victors. Such luck can also work in scenarios such as penalty shoot-outs – indeed Bayern Munich won the trophy themselves two years after the loss to United in precisely this manner. The fact that over four seasons of participation in Europe's premier club competition, Arsenal had only played in one tie in which a penalty shoot-out was even conceivable told its own story.

Carpe diem – seize the day – seemed an alien belief to the Gunners. In the most important club competition in the world, they had reached the last eight on only one occasion. They could blame the Wembley experiment for the early failures as subsequent European nights at Highbury exposed the move as an unnecessary folly of the club's own making. But their away performances in the 2000–01 and 2001–02 campaigns simply didn't merit a place in the knockout stages, despite the paradox of being undefeated away on English soil in their march towards the 'double' in the latter season. Obviously, Europe was quite a different obstacle, full of snags for the unwary. And for Arsène Wenger, good enough to make great strides against Continental allcomers in his time at Monaco, but with greater resources and better players, his comparative failure at Arsenal gnawed at him. In the cold light of day, Arsenal had gone backwards, and not only in terms of achievement. In the year between the defeats at the hands of Valencia and Juventus, the resolve shown at the stadiums of their English opponents was noticeably absent as soon as they crossed the channel. Was Arsène Wenger's claim after the abysmal capitulation to Juventus' second string that, 'We will come back and win this competition next season' the words of a man who saw something no one else could see or was he simply whistling in the wind to keep up his spirits? Either way, he had no opportunity to enjoy his domestic triumph. As his partner Annie says, *'Arsène ne savoure rien le moment,'* – never takes time out to enjoy his success. There is always another challenge and in his own mind he was determined to win the Champions League next time around.

Chapter Eight

Turning Over

The Porsche and the Mercedes parked alongside the normal vehicles on the gravel drive of a *recherché* Totteridge residence one early July day in 2001 indicated to the outside world that the Deins' had guests. One of those visitors, Arsène Wenger had been hard at work even though it was the close season, strengthening his squad with the signings of Tottenham's out of contract centre-back Sol Campbell on a free transfer, versatile Dutch international Giovanni van Bronckhorst from Glasgow Rangers, striker Francis Jeffers from Everton, and Ipswich's England goalkeeper Richard Wright. Whether these new arrivals satisfied the other guest *chez Dein* Patrick Vieira – who had accused the club of a lack of ambition based upon the goings, particularly of Emmanuel Petit and Marc Overmars – was debatable. That Vieira himself was still an Arsenal player with the squad about to report for pre-season training was a surprise to many, who after a summer of persistent tabloid stories about a move to Italy or Spain anticipated an irreplaceable loss.

Ambivalent about Nicolas Anelka's contribution and reluctant to hold on to players, however influential, when their hearts and minds were elsewhere as was the case with Overmars and Petit, the manager could nevertheless show the board a net profit on their sales of over £40 million that made their departures not only acceptable but palatable. Patrick Vieira however was a different matter; the *piece maitresse* of the team both as player and talisman. Dismayed by their meek exit from the Champions League and the failure to even hold on to Manchester United's coat-tails (Arsenal finished ten points behind the coasting title holders), Vieira wondered whether Highbury was the place to add to his trophy cabinet.

Both David Dein and Arsène Wenger laboured long and hard to convince Vieira that the groundwork had been laid and was about to bear fruit – to go now would be premature. Moreover, on a personal level with Tony Adams increasingly susceptible to injury, it was pointed out that there was now the opportunity to add another layer to his range, leadership by example. Confident that with the vice-captain on board, the club would be in a position to take on and overhaul Manchester United, the manager and vice-chairman eventually succeeded in persuading Vieira to share their conviction. Today the Premiership, tomorrow the Champions League. After this milestone meeting, hands were shaken on the realistic quest for domestic glory, and if the European dice fell their way, then that would be a bonus. But first things first. The domestic foe must be vanquished.

It was a bitter-sweet irony that Vieira was regarded as such a pivotal figure in the strategy to overhaul United, as it was his error that led to a momentous moment in the power struggle between the two clubs some two years previously; an FA Cup semi-final replay that ultimately tilted the balance of power back to the North-West. Defending their league and cup double of 1997–98, the subsequent season saw the holders neck and neck with Alex Ferguson's side in both competitions. Having seen Arsenal over-take him, Ferguson responded by splashing a record £25 million on defender Jaap Stam, and forwards Dwight Yorke and Jesper Blomqvist. The United manager had to wait six years for his first league title. As his counterpart at Highbury accomplished the feat in his first full season he was determined that it would be an aberration. There would be no repeat performance. The fiery manager reputedly called 'the hairdryer' because of his occasional tendency to express his explosive temper right in the faces of people who failed to live up to his expectations certainly took any loss suffered by Manchester United as a personal affront, and his record of bouncing back by regaining the title at the first possible opportunity was testimony to his ability and his ambition.

Arsène Wenger might have felt that the 1998 World Cup did him few favours, as both his French and Dutch internationals were involved until the tournament's final weekend. Certainly, fatigue was to play its part in the concession of the club's trophies at the culmination of the 1998–99 season. The semi-final replay took place three days after the initial 0–0 draw after extra-time at Villa Park. Usually, the police require ten days' notice for a replay to be staged, although with United still involved in the Champions League, this proviso was conveniently bypassed.

Although United scored first through David Beckham, after Dennis Bergkamp equalised in the sixty-ninth minute, Arsenal dominated proceedings, in no small part due to the dismissal of Roy Keane for a second bookable offence. The Old Trafford side were on the rack as their opponents created chance after chance, but could not apply the killer blow. Nevertheless with extra-time looming, the outcome suddenly appeared a foregone conclusion as Phil Neville conceded a penalty. Dennis Bergkamp stepped up to take the kick that would eliminate United and put his side through to Wembley to face Newcastle in the final for the second year running. Although well struck, Peter Schmeichel guessed right and parried the ball away from goal. The goalkeeper had thwarted Bergkamp seven years before when Holland were eliminated by Schmeichel's Denmark in the Euro '92 semi-final as a result of a penalty shoot-out. Although not personally responsible for missing one then, nor indeed when Holland exited both Euro '96 and the France '98 World Cup in the same manner, perhaps the concept of sudden death from the penalty spot was weighing on the number ten's mind as he strode up to strike the spot-kick. Having already failed twice that season, the trauma of Schmeichel's save and its ultimate effect meant that Bergkamp hasn't taken a penalty since.

All the same, Arsenal had an extra thirty minutes against ten-man United to avoid a penalty shoot-out. However, as so often on the big occasion, Wenger's Arsenal have been unable to apply the killer touch – seemingly lacking the ability to put depleted troops to the sword. Conversely, when they themselves have found their numbers reduced, their fortitude often makes them appear the better side, frequently overturning the odds. Although a team featuring the outstanding attacking talents of Bergkamp, Overmars and Anelka had few problems prising open the most determined of defences, far too often the profligacy of their finishing undermined their efforts, and so it was to prove their undoing on this night of all nights.

The decisive moment came in the second period of extra-time

when Patrick Vieira played a sloppy ball across the midfield. It was intercepted by Ryan Giggs who proceeded to outrun the Arsenal defence and launch an angled drive above David Seaman's head. That the *coup de grâce* was a phenomenal individualistic goal made it all the more painful for Gunners fans who would have to endure, in the years to follow, endless television replays of that heartbreaking moment. The Arsenal defence had enjoyed an outstanding Premiership season, and would end the campaign with a miserly seventeen goals conceded, but against Giggs they were simply outdone by pace and skill. The tie ended 2–1 and Arsenal were forced to witness Alex Ferguson's jig of joy as they trooped off to gather themselves for the one trophy they could still retain. Psychologically, a hammer blow had been struck. Now United had momentum, and did not lose another match for the remainder of the campaign, which meant that going into the final round of fixtures their destiny was in their own hands.

Although Arsène Wenger's side responded well to their FA Cup exit by winning four consecutive league matches, including a derby at White Hart Lane, a trip to Elland Road was a game too far. They could curse ill fortune there too, as late in the match full-back Nigel Winterburn picked up an injury, and his substitute Nelson Vivas was at fault for Leeds' winner, scored by Jimmy Floyd Hasselbaink. The defender purchased to bolster the backline failed to come up to the mark when needed.

With Arsenal losing, a point for United away to Blackburn twenty-four hours later meant they simply needed to beat Tottenham at Old Trafford to regain the title, which they duly did. The FA Cup Final was a formality with Newcastle effectively beaten in the first half. Not content with wiping out the pain of the previous season by emulating Arsenal's double, United went one huge step further. The victory over Arsenal in the FA Cup undoubtedly convinced them they could weather any storm. Apart from overcoming a 2–0 deficit in Turin to beat Juventus 3–2 on the night and 4–3 on aggregate in the Champions League semi-final, at 1–0 down going into injury time against Bayern Munich in the final despite having been comprehensively outplayed, Ferguson's side refused to accept they were down and out. Two goals from corners broke German hearts and completed United's trio of trophies, an unparalleled feat for an English club.

Looking back at the semi-final, Arsène Wenger is still frustrated by what might have been. 'It was a turning point in the season. It gave Man United that extra belief, that extra bit of luck as well because they were hanging on the ropes. When you have a penalty against you in the last seconds to decide whether you go into the Cup Final and you recover from that, it gives you the belief it is your season.' The FA Cup may have been the least of United's three trophies, but the manner of Arsenal's defeat was a traumatic blow consigning the 1998–99 side to the status of nearly men. It was no consolation to learn that Alex Ferguson's words in the Nou Camp dressing room before his side took the field against Bayern were, 'You shouldn't have any problems beating this lot. They're nowhere near as good as Arsenal.'

The stupendous task now for Arsenal was to demonstrate that the double had not been a flash in the pan, particularly as they had conformed to the precedent of failing to win anything following their *annus mirabilis*, although there was at least some small consolation to be had from the fact that their points total was the same as in 1998. In this sense the team had not gone backwards, United had merely overtaken them, and only by a single point. However, there wasn't even a pyrrhic victory to be gleaned from the two campaigns that followed. They regressed, they went backwards in terms of points won.

At the end of November 1999, the portents looked promising as Arsenal found themselves at the top of the table despite having incurred four defeats, including one at home to United. There was bitter controversy over the FA's decision to allow Alex Ferguson's side to forego their defence of the FA Cup in order to participate in FIFA's World Club Championship tournament in Brazil. However their absence should have seen Arsenal leap ahead but they simply failed to take their chances. In the five games leading up to their visit to Old Trafford in late January, they accumulated only eight points from the fifteen available. A creditable 1–1 draw in Manchester put them on parity with United – both sides with forty-four points – but the home side had three games in hand to accompany their Brazilian suntans. The holders went on to retain their title without looking back, but if they had done so at the season's end, they would have seen Arsenal a distant second, a colossal eighteen points in the rear.

It was nothing less than a chastisement for a club that had been nip and tuck with United over the last two seasons. In mitigation, Arsenal had been forced to adapt to life without first Nicolas Anelka, and then Petit and Overmars as the board found it impossible to turn down the huge amount of money offered by their Spanish buyers. United's financial clout, on the other hand meant that not only were they never forced to sell any players they wished to retain, but could add to the pot whenever a player took Alex Ferguson's fancy, which appeared increasingly so as he sought an insurance policy to cement his hegemony. Maybe the gap was a lot bigger than had been thought. Arsenal were certainly good enough to stand toe to toe with United in the head-to-head conflicts between the two, but the reputation of Ferguson's side intimidated opponents and gained them valuable breathing space on off days, something Arsenal had not yet earned.

The 2000–01 campaign saw Arsenal finish as runners-up again. They recovered from a mid-season hiatus with a run of eighteen league games that saw only two losses to ensure another second-place finish. Symbolic of United's supremacy over their nearest rivals was a 6–1 hammering at Old Trafford. None of the 'old guard' who were still on the staff: Seaman, Adams, Keown and Dixon, were available for selection, and the back-ups that Arsène Wenger had brought to the club were simply not up to the required standard. Lee Dixon's injury forced Wenger to tinker with the defence that had been effective even without the first-choice centre-backs, so with Oleg Luzhny moved out to right back, the combination of Gilles Grimandi and Igors Stepanovs was given its debut. Ashley Cole was removed at half-time (United were 5–1 ahead) to spare further trauma in a defence that played like its constituents were hardly on nodding terms. Stepanovs and Luzhny might have resembled a pair of gargoyles (according to Arsenal fanzine *The Gooner*) in the FA Cup win over Chelsea the weekend before, but maybe because they at least spoke the same language, they were able to develop an understanding and helped their side to a 3–1 win. If Wenger had opted to play Grimandi in place of Dixon, perhaps the visit to Old Trafford would have seen a more respectable display. It was as if David Bowie had taken over as team manager for the day and wished to re-enact on the football field the famous session for 'Boys Keep Swinging', when he forced his musicians to play instruments they were unfamiliar with. In Bowie's case, the bum notes did not lead to a poor performance and he recorded a hit. If only the same could be said of Arsène Wenger's experiment.

One redeeming factor in this season, although too late to make up lost ground, was that the manager's training methods were bearing fruit, enabling his players to peak from February until the season's end. This may go some way to explain why he has only failed to reach a cup final once in his six full seasons at the club; and it should not be forgotten in 1999 Arsenal were only a penalty kick away from Wembley. So although fans felt that they were living in the constant shadow of an Old Trafford dynasty, the reality was that Arsenal were over-achieving, by consistently out-performing the likes of Liverpool and Newcastle who enjoyed far greater financial resources. Not that this was any consolation going into the 2001–02 season with the prospect of United winning a record fourth consecutive title.

The agreed objective of manager, vice-captain and vice-chairman may have been to prise the Premiership from United's grasp. But with an outlay of around £50 million on three players: Juan Sebastian Veron, Ruud van Nistelrooy and Roy Carroll, to strengthen his hand in what was scheduled as his final season before retirement Alex Ferguson had ensured, on paper, Arsenal's task was as hard as ever. However, the side that had endured the Villa Park trauma had by and large been replaced. To Thierry Henry, Robert Pires, Sylvain Wiltord, Sol Campbell, Lauren and Ashley Cole, that unfortunate page of the club's history had been turned over, and the group of players Wenger had assembled were about to write their own chapter, but not before, Campbell excepted, they had suffered their own nightmare. The FA Cup Final, played in Wales for the first time due to the closure of Wembley, saw bad luck, wasted chances and two late Michael Owen goals deny Arsenal their deserved winners' medals. Maybe the pain felt lying on the Cardiff turf produced the resolve that enough was enough.

Although Arsenal got off to a flying start with a 4–0 victory away to Middlesbrough, a subsequent home defeat to Leeds United three days later abruptly halted any premature sense of euphoria. The team bounced back by taking three points at home to Leicester, again by a 4–0 scoreline. The result was tempered by Patrick Vieira's dismissal for two yellow card offences – the second after getting needlessly involved with the Foxes' agent provocateur Denis Wise, who shared his opponent's fate in leaving the field prematurely. With Vieira having suffered two red cards within days at the beginning of the previous season and made noises about quitting English football, the Highbury public feared the worst, but a few weeks after his summit meeting in Totteridge, the player was just concerned with getting the one-game ban out of the way and returning to assist the cause. It was just as well, as in the subsequent fixture – a draw with Chelsea at Stamford Bridge – Tony Adams was substituted with an ankle injury. After one further appearance a fortnight later confirmed the severity of the damage, he could not return to Premiership action until the end of March. Effectively Arsenal had a new leader who now had more to play for.

By the time of United's visit to Highbury in late November, Arsenal's disappointing home record of five points from the fifteen available put them a point behind United in fifth place. Only their outstanding away form, undefeated in seven games with four wins, allowed them to keep pace with the leaders. The fixture against United was the acid test of the accord agreed over four months before and it was fortunate for the Gunners that the Old Trafford side had foregone their habitual flying start and not already pulled clear. If Arsenal were to make up the deficit of 2000–01, then they had to put their chief rivals to the sword themselves when the occasion arose. Unfortunately, against the run of play, they went behind. But the second period saw the goals reflect the dominance of the home side as they rallied to score three and demonstrate the kind of drive and determination so noticeably absent in their concurrent European ventures. Freddie Ljungberg nabbed the equaliser before sheer pressure brought its due reward as United keeper Fabian Barthez made two howlers that allowed his compatriot Thierry Henry to notch a brace of goals.

The 3–1 win at an electrified Highbury Stadium made it a red-letter day. Graciously Ferguson acclaimed the victors exclaiming, 'We were well beaten, outplayed. Arsenal played magnificently. That's the best they've ever played against us in my time at United.

They were never off the bite all night and the football was terrific.' Arsène Wenger must have been a relieved man to see his team play with the conviction that was too often absent in the preceding weeks: 'We had that added determination to turn things around and came out like lions in the second half.' It was an interesting simile, given the dwindling number of English players on his books, but highlighted a virtue that was a prerequisite for success in the Premiership.

The win over United was the first in a series of events which boosted the feel-good factor at Highbury at the time of some major uncertainties, chiefly over the future of the stadium project and Arsène Wenger's failure to sign an extension to his contract, now only half a season from expiring. Yet within a few days, the future looked a lot brighter as the manager decided to extend his stay until at least the summer of 2005. His predilection may have been partly influenced by the decision of Islington Council to give the go-ahead to the club's plans for a new 60,000 capacity stadium at Ashburton Grove, a stone's throw from the existing 38,500 Avenell Road Stadium. Arsenal could now envisage a long-term future that would enable them to compete financially with other clubs who possessed significantly bigger and better facilities.

This was a crucial decision all round. As chairman Peter Hill-Wood recalled, 'We didn't make any secret of the fact that Arsène was important to the development of the new stadium, that he should be seen by everybody as being under contract at the time we opened the new one.' Well into the last year of his existing deal, the manager in Hill-Wood's words 'quite rightly took a bit of time to think about it'. In fact he wavered. There was a solid offer from Barcelona. According to Hill-Wood money wasn't the issue. 'Barcelona would have probably paid him more than we do. We pay him enough. I don't think he spends any.' What persuaded the manager to stay was the realisation that there was still a major role for him to play at Arsenal. Having convinced Patrick Vieira that together they were on their way to wresting domestic dominance from Manchester United, it would ill behove the admiral to jump ship. Moreover as Peter Hill-Wood puts it, 'I think he's got a very nice job with us. The board don't interfere with him. Normally we say yes when he asks for something. Also we are quite a stable group. If we lost a number of matches in a row we wouldn't say "my God, let's get rid of the manager".'

With the key personnel secured and the Champions League placed on the back burner for a couple of months, domestic concerns assumed priority. A stirring 3–2 victory against Aston Villa at Highbury came on the eve of the news of the manager's new contract and the green light for the stadium go-ahead. From two down at half-time, the comeback was evidence that the old fire had been rekindled.

Arsenal's last domestic defeat of the season against Newcastle came ten days before Christmas. The feelings of injustice about the result, largely influenced by some highly questionable refereeing by Graham Poll, compounded by the sending off of Ray Parlour – seemed to galvanise Arsenal in their subsequent fixtures, not least the next one at Anfield where they again found themselves on the wrong end of more controversial refereeing decisions, one of which saw Paul Durkin dismiss Giovanni van Bronckhorst after thirty-six minutes for alleged diving. The away side rode the punches, and the in-form Freddie Ljungberg won a penalty, converted by Henry, before scoring the winner himself in a 2–1 victory – the Gunners' first at Anfield since 1992. Referring to the second consecutive red card suffered by his side, Wenger joked, 'Maybe we should try playing with ten men in training as every game we seem to be in that situation.' He could however afford to smile, as he had witnessed an outstanding display, the denouement of an astonishing few weeks of proceedings both on and off the field that had put this watershed season right back on course. There were no more questions about the desire of the players. The Arsenal spirit was alive and kicking.

Five wins and three draws from their next eight league games kept them at the top of the table and they were still chasing trophies on two other fronts as well. However, talk of a possible treble to emulate United's achievement in 1999 was extinguished as the end of March witnessed their Champions League exit in Turin. In the FA Cup, a quarter-final draw at St James' Park set up a replay with Newcastle which proved to be Robert Pires' final appearance of the season as he suffered a cruciate knee injury which also ruled him out of the France squad for the World Cup finals. Arsenal's consolation, after winning the replay 3–0 was a semi-final against Middlesbrough. Newcastle manager Bobby Robson unwittingly referred to one of the differences between the domestic Arsenal and the European Arsenal when he talked after the game: 'Dennis Bergkamp is a genius, we couldn't control him, and we didn't have such a player.' Neither did Arsène Wenger for too many of his continental sorties.

Bergkamp's rich vein of form and the return from injury of Freddie Ljungberg helped to compensate for the loss of Pires for the critical climactic weeks of the season. Two points dropped at home to Southampton on the first weekend of February were the last ones conceded as the Gunners showed the grim determination not to be Manchester United's fall guys once again, as they put together a phenomenal run of eleven straight victories. That took them to within a point of securing the title with two games remaining before the FA Cup Final on 4 May against Chelsea, after Arsenal had eased past Middlesbrough, Manchester United's conquerors in an earlier round, 1–0. In a change to tradition, the FA, with the World Cup finals in mind, had scheduled their annual showpiece to precede the ultimate Premiership weekend. The timing meant that the FA Cup could supply the first half of the domestic double.

A tight game with few clear-cut chances witnessed a commanding display from Arsenal's centre-back pairing of Tony Adams and Sol Campbell. The trophy was won with two late goals from Ray Parlour, partnering Vieira in central midfield, and Freddie Ljungberg. It was Adams' final competitive match, and symbolically, when the trophy was lifted, he raised it in tandem with Vieira, for so much of the season the skipper as Adams recuperated from the injury picked up against Chelsea in September. The baton was handed over for good when confirmation came in the close season that Adams would not sign for another year.

It was both appropriate and unsurprising that Ljungberg scored the decisive goal, having enjoyed a run of five successive league games in which his name was on the scoresheet, converting key goals in the race for the title. If a player was earmarked to enjoy a purple patch, it could not have been better timed. The Internet site Arseweb summed up the feeling of the fans towards their

Swedish hero: 'That red patch in his hair, it's not dye you know. It's just the Arsenal red streak that runs through his body, seeping out through the top of the midfield dynamo's head.'

To many who were underwhelmed by the sometimes overly casual approach perpetrated on occasion by certain of his highly skilled colleagues, Ljungberg exemplified the true spirit of the club. The season was a pivotal one for a player who had not always received a regular starting spot since his move from Halmstaad in 1998. (Wenger admits he bought the player having seen him only on television because he was a £3 million bargain and, 'I was scared someone else would take him.') Although Ljungberg could play wide on either flank or as a forward, his versatility initially appeared to count against him as the make-up of the squad meant that he would often be competing for a place on the right side of midfield with the similarly enthusiastic Ray Parlour, as first Marc Overmars and later Robert Pires, when available, were invariably picked on the left. It was apparent that when a starting line-up incorporated both Parlour and Ljungberg there was an extra dose of vigour and tenacity sometimes conspicuous by its absence when neither of them was selected.

Lungberg was sanguine regarding the concept of squad rotation. 'I believe it is good for me because I am small and rely on my speed,' he explained. 'I do not have the body strength of other players and if I played ten games in a row I would lose my speed. When Arsène Wenger says I don't need to play in certain games that's good for me and it's good man-management, but fortunately I always seem to be picked for the important games. I always feel it's a privilege to play in the big games,' he says. 'So many people want to be in your shoes, so I just think you should just take the opportunity and enjoy it.'

It took a while though to win the affection of the fans. Visually, his playing style is not easy on the eye, reflecting his unkempt appearance on the pitch, with his shirt hanging out and socks rolled down towards his ankles, but importantly, the man scores the kind of messy goals that the likes of Henry, Bergkamp and Pires appear to disdain and anyway are rarely in position to claim for themselves. Tenacity and sheer dogged determination, rather than finesse may be his trademark, but fans will always support a trier, someone who gives his all – all the time.

There was another factor that endeared Ljungberg to supporters, namely, his appalling hairstyle, with a strip of his punk hair dyed flaming red. It may have looked like a skunk on a bad hair day, but by the season's end had given birth to a new chant that reflected the esteem in which he was held. To the tune of Andy Williams' 'Can't Take My Eyes Off Of You', the chorus adapted to a paean of praise, rang:

We love you Freddie
Because you've got red hair
We love you Freddie
Because you're everywhere,
We love you Freddie
Because you're Arsenal through and through

And sometime later after the initial shock of seeing their favourite with his hair cropped, when it emerged that a dramatic style change had not been the result of a Beckham-like whim but was a spontaneous reaction to an unexpected setback, he cemented his popularity. 'I was very angry so I told them to cut it all off. Normally I like to have hair on my head, but I just had it cut off.'

The special talent that Ljungberg offers his colleagues is his omnipresence. He can pop up anywhere, particularly in attack – and for this reason is a troublesome player for the opposition to pin down. As Wenger said after his number eight had scored against Juventus in a rare memorable Champions League triumph, 'Ljungberg was unbelievable. He worked so hard and gets on to the end of things.' The understanding he developed with Arsenal's other attackers, and especially Dennis Bergkamp, was a key factor in many of his goals in the 2001–02 season.

Ljungberg says of the singular rapport he has with the number ten: 'We think the same way about football. Dennis has a special vision that I don't think many players have. It's very quick, difficult for opponents.' Bergkamp concurs: 'I know how he likes to make those runs. At certain moments we both get the same feeling, we know exactly what we're going to do and that's difficult to defend against.' Ljungberg notched seventeen goals from thirty-nine appearances in all competitions by the end of the campaign; successful strikes without which Arsenal would quite probably have finished empty-handed for a fourth successive season. The combination of Bergkamp's sublime vision and Ljungberg's perceptive runs – the knack of arriving in the penalty box a split second before a marker – was a weapon that many sides found impossible to combat when both players were on song. Ljungberg's twelve league goals in 2001–02 doubled his totals of the two preceding seasons.

Hitherto Arsenal had suffered from the lack of a penalty-area poacher which was why Francis Jeffers had been bought from Everton. However Jeffers' move was blighted by injury and anyway he would have had the nigh on impossible task of displacing either Henry or Bergkamp to get his chance as a starter. Although the player was brought to the club to fulfil the 'fox in the box' role, as Thierry Henry termed it, revealing the same ease with his adopted language as his skill on the field, and with Ljungberg in the kind of form he demonstrated during the 2001–02 season, maybe the club had such an animal on their books all the while.

With the FA Cup in the bag it was an opportunity for the supporters to party hard and rejoice in the first trophy for four seasons, but the players had to put their own celebrations on hold for a few days as an imminent date with Manchester United beckoned the following Wednesday evening. Alex Ferguson's side were now the only remaining threat to the second double of the Wenger era. Beating their visitors would reduce the gap to two points, and give a glimmer of hope that the last day visit of Everton to Highbury might induce an attack of the collywobbles giving United the chance to pip their rivals on the finishing line. Statisticians might have viewed the game from another perspective as the toughest test to establishing two astonishing records for Arsenal; a score draw or better would mean, 1. an entire league season without an away loss – not achieved since the nineteenth century, then only eleven away fixtures were undertaken – and, 2. up to that point they had scored in every single league game.

As if the possible ignominy of watching their opponents wrench the title from their grasp on their own patch wasn't incentive enough, United had a point to prove to their own public after their Champions League involvement was terminated by Bayer Leverkusen the week before. Signs that the pressure was telling on Alex Ferguson were revealed in a press conference two days prior to Arsenal's visit, when he lost his rag and hurled a volley of abuse at reporters who had the temerity to query the value-for-money of £28 million record signing Juan Sebastian Veron. Although 2001–02 was scheduled to be Ferguson's final season in the manager's seat at Old Trafford, with his charges faltering midway through the campaign, he changed his mind and committed himself to a further three years, perhaps mindful that he didn't want to end his career empty-handed. However, anything but a win against Arsenal would ensure he did so that year. To boost United's chances, injuries left Thierry Henry in London and consigned Dennis Bergkamp to a place on the bench, entailing a second choice pairing of Sylvain Wiltord and Kanu up front, with Brazilian Edu drafted into midfield.

United's approach to the game was to try and shake the visitors out of their stride by unsettling them with some stiff early challenges. However, Wenger's side withstood the physical battle and gradually reduced the tempo of the play to one that suited them. It was perhaps ironic that it was the reigning champions who were trying to outmuscle their pretenders, given that it was their outstanding passing play that had delivered so many trophies in the past. United's manager had himself accused Wenger's Arsenal of approaching games in the manner his own team now used in an attempt to intimidate his opponents. This time though, the tactics weren't working as the champions elect went in at the interval perfectly content with the 0–0 scoreline.

The second half saw Arsenal with even greater possession as their hosts appeared to wilt, a tacit acknowledgement that they had given their best and had failed to break down the resistance they faced. The defence of Ashley Cole, Sol Campbell, Martin Keown and Lauren had a commanding ninety minutes and provided the platform for their team-mates to win the game in the fifty-sixth minute, when Ray Parlour was gifted the ball by Mikael Silvestre. He fed Wiltord, who in turn supplied that man Ljungberg. For a change, it was to be a match without the usual name on the scoresheet, as his shot was parried to the waiting Wiltord, who scored the only goal of the game, signalling the return of the Premiership trophy to join the FA Cup on display in the oak-panelled boardroom at Highbury.

Afterwards Arsène Wenger was ebullient. 'We wanted there to be a shift of power and to bring the Premier League trophy back home. Now we want to win it again next season. Since I arrived at Arsenal, we have won the title twice and United have won it three times. So they are 3–2 ahead and now we want to equalise next season. It's fantastic to win it here as they are the team we want to beat, who have dominated English football for the past three years. What Arsenal have achieved is tremendous and will go down in history.'

Patrick Vieira felt vindicated after the doubts about his loyalty that were voiced in the summer. 'I've proved Arsenal means a lot to me, I hope I've given the club back what it deserves. We showed how badly we wanted to win it here. From the start of the season we knew we could win the Premiership and had the players to do so.' The celebrations of the players on the pitch at the conclusion of the match indicated that the sweet smell of success did indeed mean as much to them as it did to their vociferous travelling support.

So, on their own pitch no less, the domestic foe had been vanquished and the new champions went on to finish ten points clear of a demoralised third-placed United, a role reversal of the year before. Now it would be Alex Ferguson's turn to play catch-up.

Chapter Nine

Young at Heart

'One of the greatest achievements of Sir Alex Ferguson was the fact that he created this strong youth policy. Manchester United had their own way in many aspects. I think it's a level playing field now, but when Beckham, Scholes, Giggs, all those kids came through, he was ahead of the game.' So says Liam Brady, the head of youth development at Arsenal. When he was appointed in the summer of 1996, David Dein commented, 'He has the most important job at the club.' Before the year was out, Arsène Wenger was in the hot seat and events since indicate that perhaps Arsenal's vice-chairman was way off beam in his assertion.

Dein, though, had good reason for believing that a rosy future for his club was inseparable from the cult of youth. At Old Trafford, the Premiership title had just been regained from Blackburn Rovers after the release of such stalwarts as Paul Ince, Andrei Kanchelskis and Mark Hughes in the preceding close-season to be succeeded by a number of youngsters Alex Ferguson had brought through the youth and reserve ranks. He was rewarded with a League and FA Cup double, duplicating the feat of their more experienced elders two years before, and revealing the baselessness of *Match of the Day* pundit Alan Hansen's early season prognostication: 'You'll win nothing with kids'. Although Ryan Giggs was an early bonus of the policy the manager had prioritised, now it was suddenly bearing the substantial fruit – Beckham, Butt, Scholes and the Neville brothers – that would form the basis of the side that would go on to thwart Arsenal and dominate English football for the next few seasons.

Liam Brady's task was to take a leaf out of the Old Trafford book, although the subsequent arrival of Arsène Wenger ensured that the club was now perusing a different script and in another language as well. The immediate future was shaped not by the produce of the academy, but the manager's activity in the transfer market. On one level, this predilection for experience was perverse as Arsène Wenger had been instrumental in the development of the academy. When the new training complex was designed, the youth set-up formed an integral part. As Brady points out: 'At London Colney we have four pitches for our under-17s and under-19s, three for the reserves and the first team have got four. The board have also made a very substantial investment into our other training ground in Walthamstow at Hale End. It's used by Arsenal schoolboys – our nine- to sixteen-year-olds train there. They have artificial surfaces which are floodlit, so they can work out there after school. It's first class.'

That the schoolboy wannabes enjoy better facilities than some Premiership senior squads – Chelsea's antiquated Harlington quarters come to mind – makes it all the more surprising that Arsenal do not appear to enjoy the end product of the set-up to any substantial degree. At least not so far. Granted the stakes at Highbury are higher that at most other clubs, based upon expectation levels, all the same there are circumstances when Brady believes a calculated risk could be taken in order to provide a youngster with some valuable experience. 'We at the Academy, feel that Arsène could have given some of the kids a chance and maybe put them on the bench and given them a run-out, especially in games where you're winning 3–0, but I also understand he has to get results and he's super-cautious.' Precisely. When hosting some of the lesser lights, when anything but an easy three points would prove a major upset, having one of the brighter prospects as one of the four outfield substitutes could hardly be described as throwing caution to the wind. Away to Manchester City in 2003, did the manager not feel a pang of regret when, with his side 4–0 up and coasting at half-time, there were no kids amongst the substitutes to give half a game to? 'Yes, maybe,' he says, 'but it is not as simple as that because you are already preparing for the next game and then you have a player who is searching for confidence and another who needs the competition.'

Maybe it is not a question of risk but loyalty. The manager's obligation is to the more senior players he has been instrumental in persuading to join him in the quest for glory. In the Champions League, a win brings the eighteen players involved in the fixture, including the non-playing substitutes, a £12,000 per man bonus. Appearances on the sidelines such as that made by under-19 goal-keeper Graham Stack in the December 2001 victory over Juventus (the absence of David Seaman and Richard Wright through injury led to Stuart Taylor wearing the gloves, with the fourth choice on the bench) are likely to be a rarity. Truly a case of major to minor when it was back to reality and his £6 youth team fee on the following weekend. The four figure performance payment for Premiership points may also be substantial enough to influence the manager's selection of bench warmers. If an established performer were to miss out on a financial windfall through a kid being picked in preference, it might well spread disharmony among the ranks, although the set-up at London Colney is specifically aimed at preventing a 'them and us' situation. The first-class facilities are used by young and old alike, and as Brady says, 'Arsène has youth players train with him regularly as part of first-team squad sessions. David Bentley [then a seventeen-year-old] went on a pre-season trip with the first team squad.'

So at least there is some attempt to integrate and filter through the more promising material. David Bentley made his first-team debut for Arsenal as a substitute in an otherwise routine FA Cup third-round victory at home to Oxford in January 2003. Playing on the right wing, he turned a placid affair into a memorable match the fans were still talking about for some time afterwards. Many regulars felt they had just seen the most electrifying debut since that of a certain will-o'-the-wisp Irish lad called William (Liam) Brady thirty years before. However, young Bentley did not see the first-team bench again for the remainder of the season, not even for the subsequent FA Cup tie against non-league Farnborough Town. And on the rare occasion that Arsenal summon up the gumption to take a gamble, Murphy's Law intervenes to spite them. Having conceded the Premiership title in May 2003, two further fixtures had to be fulfilled before an FA Cup final brought the season to a close. With the runners-up and, effectively, a Champions League place secured, at last the manager could blood some kids with a clear conscience, but of the obvious candidates, only right winger Jermaine Pennant and left back Ryan

Garry were available for consideration. Doubtless, were they not injured, Bentley, Sebastian Svard, Moritz Volz and Jeremie Aliadiere might conceivably have enjoyed a run out against either Southampton at Highbury or a few days later Sunderland at the Stadium of Light. Although Pennant and Garry made the most of a rare opportunity (a 6–1 thrashing of their future cup final opponents Southampton showed they didn't let the side down), the visit to Wearside saw them both back on the bench, only Pennant seeing any belated action as the manager decided that it was a better bet to field his likely cup final side in order to keep them sharp and match fit.

While the principle of *carpe diem* served David Bentley well on his debut, when Jermaine Pennant gets an all-too-rare crack at the first-team whip, perhaps he feels the need to do too much. In the eighth match of the 2002–03 Premiership campaign away to Leeds, Pennant made his second substitute appearance. With his side comfortably up 3–0 and only eleven minutes remaining, his failure to track the run of Lee Bowyer led to a consolation goal for the home side. Although the nineteen-year-old had time to make amends by creating a fourth goal for his side, it didn't prevent him being farmed out on loan to Watford. He would not see any further Premiership action until over seven months later, coincidentally also against Leeds, in the return fixture at Highbury in which Arsenal needed a win to maintain any chance of retaining their title. Coming on with the sides level at 2–2, maybe it was Pennant's need to impress after waiting so long for another chance, that led him unsuccessfully to try the 'clever stuff' when a simple pass to Dennis Bergkamp appeared the sensible option. The consequence was a reprise of the Elland Road scenario, as his indiscipline cost the team. He lost the ball and Leeds scored, this time with dire consequences as Arsenal's faint title hopes were finally extinguished.

It would be tempting to lay all the blame on the folly of youth but Arsène Wenger, supposedly one of the better bosses when the question of man-managing superstars is raised, has to be allotted a portion. Quite why Pennant should be marginalised when he was obviously a capable contender for a starting place, at first sight appears a mystery. But Liam Brady categorically states Pennant 'has only got himself to blame. He's not punctual enough, he was sent home from England just recently (for ignoring a Saturday night curfew between two under-21 international matches). He has to demonstrate that he can handle that side of it as well, because Arsène Wenger has a lot of options to choose from and behaviour like that can make a difference.'

It is Brady's responsibility to try and produce what the game likes to term 'model professionals', and he tries to stress the importance of self-discipline. 'I always tell the young kids that coaches want reliable players whom they know when they put them on the field are going to be able to do a job for them. And to get coaches to depend on you, you've got to be professional and reliable and turn up on time and be enthusiastic about your training.' That Brady feels that Pennant is at least part author of his own misfortune through his inappropriate approach to his well-paid career would seem to indicate that his time at Arsenal has reached a watershed, particularly as the academy director would be keener than most to see Pennant as a first-team fixture. The reality of what is at stake for both parties was highlighted when Pennant followed up his costly mistake against Leeds by scoring a hat-trick in his full league debut against Southampton three days later. Brady succinctly lays it on the line for Pennant: 'I don't think he's helped himself. He needs to become more professional and perhaps he will make the break-through.'

Is it possible that Pennant's misdemeanours typify the attitude of a certain type of English player? Self-discipline is an integral ingredient of the manager's scientific approach. What use the stopwatch and the carefully pre-planned sessions if a footballer cannot manage to arrive on time for training? Perhaps some of the wages based on promise rather than ability imbue players with a false sense of their own importance, but careers are only fashioned by application, a lesson the likes of Jermaine Pennant must heed if he is to fulfil his potential. As Brady says, 'It's down to the talented players to show the right attitude because they won't make it at Arsenal if they haven't got it. It is sad that some players are beyond shaping and advice and we lose a lot of talented lads because they just haven't got the head for football. They have to realise it's more than just kicking a ball or running around the football field – it's the whole package. You bump into them later on and they say "I wish I had listened to you", but they won't listen at the time.'

Could it be that the manager holds a caustic view of the traditional

English professional, shaped by his early experiences with certain members of his inherited squad? Neither John Hartson nor Ian Wright formed a part of Wenger's long-term plans. Both are wilful individuals who had frequent brushes with authority. Granted, Wright continued to score the goals that made him the club's all-time record scorer, but after a particularly indisciplined exhibition in a defeat against Blackburn, he was injured and Arsène Wenger promoted teenager Nicolas Anelka to the starting line-up in his stead. By the time Wright recovered, Anelka had become an established partner for Dennis Bergkamp and the older model didn't get a look in, and was offloaded to West Ham.

The English players who had no qualms with the requirements of the new regime were for the most part the defenders who had been moulded by George Graham. But then the football maxim of Tony Adams, Martin Keown, Lee Dixon, Nigel Winterburn and Steve Bould was discipline. The team ethic was paramount. There was no room for egos in the Arsenal back-line; individually they knew they were good, together they believed they could see off anyone. And these players quickly appreciated that the Wenger way was the most likely one to prolong their cherished careers.

Perhaps it is not surprising that the academy's one irrefutable success is a young Londoner who has made one of the defensive positions his own as the long-standing back-line was gradually wound down. Ashley Cole made his Premiership debut at Newcastle in May 2000 as most of the first team were rested ahead of the UEFA Cup Final against Galatasaray three days later. A year on and he was an automatic choice for both club and country. Liam Brady remembers, 'He was recruited from schools football as a forward, but you find that a lot of players who go on to make it have been forwards at some time or other because they're probably the best player in the school team so they push them up front. Ashley fell into that category.' Born and raised in Stepney, Arsenal's scouts spotted the youngster knocking in one hundred goals a season for his schoolboy team Puma FC, on Wanstead Flats. Cole recalls, 'I used to play against Ledley King (of Tottenham) and John Terry (of Chelsea) who played for a team called Senrab. I was a striker for Puma and we had some real battles against Senrab, some real scraps.'

Phenomenal goalscorer or not, the teenager was only ever going to play in one position as far as Brady was concerned. 'He was quick, he was shaped like a full-back and obviously is very left-footed, so for us it was his natural position. He was very tough and good in the tackle. As a left-back he quickly flew through the various teams in which he was playing – above his age at all times really.' His ascension was made all the more easy by the expertise on hand at Arsenal. Cole confirms, 'I had to learn how to play as a defender but was lucky I had good coaches like Don Howe and Don Givens. Pat Rice has also been very good to me; as a former full-back himself, he has taught me a lot.' He was still only nineteen when he scored his first senior goal in a 1–1 draw at Bradford in September 2000. Nigel Winterburn had moved across town to West Ham and so Cole only had the Brazilian international Silvinho ahead of him in the queue for a first-team berth. The established player however was enjoying a rich vein of form, and the youngster had to bide his time before he could return to the side, though it quickly became apparent that he was a more than adequate replacement for the injured Silvinho.

Cole had spent the latter stages of the previous campaign on loan at first division Crystal Palace, whose manager at the time was Steve Coppell. He remembers Cole fondly: 'Our youth team had played Arsenal a year before and I saw this little left-back with a real whip of a tackle, lightning quick and aggressive.' Coppell was only too delighted to arrange a loan, but then felt that maybe his critical faculties had been awry. 'Funnily enough, he is not the best of trainers and on his first day with us you could see the players and even a couple of the coaches thinking blimey, he is only a tiddler and he wasn't putting himself about. Then we played and the transformation was amazing. He is a terrific player and a delightful young man.'

Cole impressed his temporary employers so much that they offered £1 million for him; a not insubstantial amount for a teenager from a club struggling to make ends meet. There was no question of a sale though and indeed Brady denies his accession to the first team at Highbury was only a result of Silvinho's sick leave. Indeed he claims, 'It was by design. After he'd been over at Crystal Palace for a few months Arsène Wenger decided that he was ready for the first team. We all felt he was ready. He was still a bit rough around the edges and you'll always need a few games under your belt, but

I predicted within the club that he'd very quickly be the England left-back. It wasn't hard to do because England didn't have a left-back! I said he'd do it before he'd played twenty first-team games. And I think he did it before he'd played ten.' Cole made his full international debut when England visited Albania in March 2001 for a World Cup qualifier. He had under his belt nine Premiership starts for Arsenal, six in the Champions League, four in the FA Cup and one in the League Cup. Of course Brady felt vindicated, 'You don't hear a lot from him but he's got great character and determination, and the right temperament for being thrown in at the deep end. We're thrilled for the club as well, because we've been accused of favouring foreigners and this shows that if you are good enough and, just as important, want it as much as Ashley, you can come through.'

In August 2000, Arsène Wenger needed cover for Silvinho. Nelson Vivas was used occasionally, but he was fundamentally a right-sided player, and to take a cynical point of view it seemed Cole owed his chance to another's misfortune. That he turned out to be as good as he is facilitated Silvinho's transfer to Celta Vigo the following summer. When Arsenal subsequently paid tribute to a number of recently departed players on the Highbury Jumbotron, Silvinho, although a fans' favourite, had been forgotten. Allegations had been made about the authenticity of his Portuguese passport and it was as if a revisionist historian had been at work on the club's records. If Arsenal had to sweep one left-back under the carpet in an attempt to avoid the prying eyes of the authorities, it was as well that Liam Brady's academy had developed another to get them out of a hole.

Cole was fortunate to arrive in the first team when Tony Adams, Lee Dixon and Martin Keown were still very much an intrinsic part of the set-up, and indeed, he started alongside those three brothers-in-arms along with David Seaman, in the 2001 FA Cup final team. His sudden elevation to elite company did not make the ensuing defeat any easier to bear. 'Losing the final against Liverpool was awful,' he recalls. 'It was my first final and just to be there was great, but the game was so disappointing. To be honest, I was overawed by it – the crowd, the occasion.' He was being unduly hard on himself for he lived up to the standard expected of an Arsenal defender.

Possibly as a throwback to his early days, Cole's speed and control invariably enable him to overlap and support the forward players and as a result he finds himself frequently in shooting positions on the left side of the penalty area. Critics can point to the need to sharpen up his defensive aptitude but it would be wrong to suggest he is any less tenacious than his long-serving predecessor Nigel Winterburn. And that is why the fans forgive him for his sometimes naïve defending, when he brings to mind some of Phil Neville's more inept performances in an England shirt with his positioning and rash tackling. So whilst he continues to sparkle going forward, there's a lot of leeway to make up going back.

The first to acknowledge he had a lot to learn, being able to develop under the watchful eye of mature teachers could only improve the eager student. 'They've told me to just keep working at my game and helped me out on my positional sense which has made me a better player,' he says. Humility is a rare quality in today's pampered players, nevertheless, riding high a couple of months from the conclusion of the 2001–02 double season, Cole was still taking nothing for granted. 'Since everyone said I can't defend, I have been working on it a lot with the manager and the team,' he revealed. 'Your position is under threat all the time. I've only just come in so I don't see my selection in the team as cemented.'

Actually, not only was he one of the first names on Arsène Wenger's team-sheet, but there was little debate over his automatic selection for all of England's matches in the 2002 World Cup Finals. After an industrious display in the 1–0 defeat of Argentina, Cole felt he had finally proved his doubters wrong, stating, 'It was a chance to prove I could defend against a great team like Argentina. It was nice afterwards to hear people say I defended well. Playing well against players like Ortega and Aimar did give me more confidence.' His club manager subsequently paid his own tribute, declaring, 'Since the World Cup, Ashley has become a respected player in Europe. He has character, he's a winner, a fighter, he's very ambitious. He has Nigel Winterburn's steel and determination.'

Not that Cole himself is resting on any laurels, 'The perception of me has changed,' he says. 'People now are treating me like I have been in the team a long time when I haven't really. It does make it harder, being young in the team. I have more to prove. I have to keep playing well.'

Held up as a shining example of what can happen if youth is given its head, Cole unfortunately appears an atypical case. Although surely frustrated at the lack of academy end-product in terms of first-team players, Liam Brady is candid enough to admit that those who have come through the ranks but have not been able to establish themselves were simply, 'not good enough for us'. Stephen Hughes was one who looked set to buck the trend. A left-sided midfielder who made enough appearances in the 1997–98 double season to perhaps believe he had made the grade. Two seasons later and a solitary first-team start told its own story. In Brady's words, not good enough. Perhaps his attitude might have been his downfall too, as a loan spell at then First Division Fulham was cut short after the player expressed his disquiet at being named as a substitute. Subsequently sold to Everton, Hughes was a product of the youth system before Wenger had got to grips with it, but nevertheless he appears to be a victim of the manager's preference for Continental which has permeated right through to the academy. Rightly so, Brady admits reluctantly, 'In the first two years (I was here) I thought we could recruit solely in England and Ireland, but I'm afraid that's not the case any more, kids have got other things to do. The pool had dramatically shrunk and that's why we have many foreign kids in our academy, because we have to go further afield. In all the countries in Europe that have a good standard of living, perversely that has been to the detriment of young footballers. That's why Brazil nearly always win the World Cup.'

With this in mind, the net has been cast wider, and Arsenal have established links with St Etienne in France and Beveren in Belgium. 'We've got first option on any of the good young players at St Etienne. That's the relationship we have,' say Brady. 'With Belgium, it's mainly to do with talented African boys. They go to Belgium (who have a more flexible policy towards the *nouveau arrivé* than the UK), obtain a passport and could be good enough to come here, and we give them a bit of help with that.' Without established international status, players from outside the European Community find it hard to obtain the necessary work permit to join English clubs, although new test cases may give Bosman freedom of movement to any countries with only the most flimsy of EC connections. Thus Kolo Touré was able to join Arsenal directly from his African side whilst his nineteen-year-old younger brother Yaya is at Beveren until either he has an international record of his own or has served the necessary time to qualify for a Belgian passport. Wenger's appraisal of Yaya – 'he is still young but has true potential. I see him as a future great player for Arsenal' – points up his self-interest in the arrangement.

With Arsène Wenger's preference for pace, power and youth, it is puzzling that the academy has not borne more first-team fruit. Although analysis revealed that the team who faced Middlesbrough just before Christmas 2002 was the second youngest, in terms of average age, of all Premiership sides fielded that weekend – highlighting Wenger's policy of rejuvenation – it was an all international selection, with Ashley Cole the only product of Arsenal's youth system (although to stretch a point Martin Keown was another example of growing your own, albeit from a bygone era). So, notwithstanding his support for the academy – 'Arsène knows everything there is to know about our good young players,' according to Brady – it appears that the manager prefers the more finished article, such as Lauren, Ljungberg, Henry and Wiltord to which he can add the final polish to take them to his required level.

Football has seen consummate change since the days when the home-made Brady himself graced Highbury. Yet if asked to name an all-time eleven, many fans, despite stuffing their selections with Wenger's men, would invariably find a place for 'Chippy' Brady, a genuine Arsenal prodigy. The Irish midfielder, who made his debut for the Republic as an eighteen-year-old, had been the only genuine star in a workmanlike Arsenal team during the 1970s as the club marked time after the 1971 double. With his gifted left foot and extraordinary vision, he masterminded Arsenal's astonishing cup runs with four finals in three seasons at the end of the decade. The solitary win came in 1979, when Brady initiated the move that saw Alan Sunderland score the last minute winner in the 3–2 FA Cup victory over Manchester United. With Liverpool monopolising the league, a move abroad was Brady's best chance of winning a championship. The embargo on foreign stars had just been lifted in Italy and Brady's spell-binding displays in the 1980 Cup Winners' Cup semi-final persuaded Juventus coach Giovanni Trapattoni to splash out the sum of £600,000 on the sole *straniero* (foreigner) they were now permitted.

Brady became a hero in Turin too, despite spending only two seasons there. His impact was immediate, as Juve won the championship. Not only were his not inconsiderable creative powers at their peak, he scored thirteen *Serie A* goals over his two seasons, an extraordinary feat for a midfielder, and the eight netted in his first season made him the club's top scorer, illustrating how difficult goals were to come by, even for forwards in a *Scudetto* winning side.

As his second season drew to a close, he got wind that despite his undeniable success, the club had lined up the French maestro Michel Platini to replace him. In the final game against Catanzaro, in which Juventus needed to win to be certain of retaining their title, they were awarded a penalty but volunteers made themselves scarce. Although he knew he was being jettisoned and that one of his final acts for Arsenal was to fail from the spot in the shoot-out of the Cup Winners' Cup Final defeat to Valencia, Brady shouldered the responsibility and scored the only goal to enable Juve to take the *Scudetto* by a solitary point from Fiorentina. For that act of courage as much as his sublime skill he is fondly remembered by the *bianconeri* supporters to this day.

Brady stayed in Italy for five more *Serie A* seasons with Sampdoria, Internazionale and Ascoli, before returning to London to end his playing career at West Ham. Uncomfortable spells in the manager's seat at Celtic and Brighton preceded his current occupation.

Although spending sixteen years away from the club, Arsenal is ingrained in his soul. A man of high ideals, loyal and discreet to the point of paranoia, he will not acknowledge that he feels any frustration or that much of his work might be in vain. Within two years of his arrival, Arsenal were crowned FA Premier Youth League champions, and successive FA Youth Cup trophies followed in 2000 and 2001. Even so, hardly any of the boys have made the quantum leap required. It is almost as if the bar has deliberately been set too high for Brady's charges to clear it. 'The team that won the two youth cups – I think those players would have played at many Premiership clubs. But we've had a senior team that have won five major trophies and have been challengers all the other years. It's not going to be easy to get into a team like that.' Or indeed, despite Brady's view, other Premiership sides.

The bottom line, as Brady admits referring to recently released academy prospects such as Jason Crowe, Stephen Sidwell, Julian Gray and Rohan Ricketts, is that 'the people who have been let go from this football club weren't good enough, but they have been groomed to be good enough for the First Division and there's talk that Julian Gray of Crystal Palace might go to Spurs. Some of them may bounce back, but we haven't made any mistakes. We've got one of the best youth systems here in England, if not Europe and we've got a lot of talented young players and quite a number of them whom I believe will be Arsenal players in the future.'

Of course, effective youth policies are not developed overnight. So before Brady and his team of coaches are judged too harshly, there are at least a couple of years to wait, although the equivalents of Beckham, Scholes, Butt and the Neville brothers should already be making their mark. Worryingly though, there appears to be a trend to bypass the academy. Eighteen-year-old Phillipe Senderos has just been acquired for a fee of £500,000 from Swiss club Servette, and is likely to go straight into the senior squad, following in the footsteps of Kolo Touré and Stathis Tavlaridis who joined Arsenal as twenty- and twenty-one-year-olds respectively from clubs in the Ivory Coast and Greece.

So, just as the first-team stars splurge on shopping sprees in Rome or Paris, Arsène Wenger too goes abroad for his more important purchases. Moreover, many promising English youngsters, having served their apprenticeship at Highbury are then questionably shipped out. Recent examples are David Noble and Paolo Vernazza, now plying their trade at West Ham and Watford respectively. Noble's parting shot was that 'it was frustrating at Arsenal because there was no real opportunity for young talent'. Jermaine Pennant has claimed that Everton's Wayne Rooney, a full England international at seventeen, would not have got a look-in at Highbury, and the cold shoulder given to David Bentley after his debut only seems to confirm this, not to mention Pennant's own lack of first-team opportunities, in spite of regular selection for the England under-21 team. When twenty-year-old defender Ben Chorley signed for Wimbledon in February 2003, he claimed, 'I've played so many reserve games and it was never going to happen at Highbury. There were so many good players in front of me and others that I didn't rate like Igors Stepanovs, who I think played because he had played for his country and the club had to justify the money they'd paid for him. It got to the point that I was playing as well as I could and not getting anywhere, so I had to move.'

The paucity of academy product raises another issue as well. Is it possible to develop a tight-knit team spirit amongst a group of players of disparate origins from all corners of the globe? The much vaunted British bulldog never-say-die demeanour unquestionably played a cardinal role in bringing Arsenal the six trophies under George Graham, and underpins Alex Ferguson's prosperity at Old Trafford. In prioritising foreign recruitment even in the academy, and circumventing it to sign foreign starlets, has Arsène Wenger made a rod for his own back? Without British backbone, can he build a team that can challenge the greats in Europe? With the exceptions of Patrick Vieira and Freddie Ljungberg, Arsenal's most resolute players – the ones who will get stuck in and lift their colleagues when the tide is flowing against them – are arguably all English: Campbell, Keown, Cole and Parlour. Alongside Vieira, these players were conspicuous by their all-too-frequent absences (through injury or suspension) as the attempt to retain their league title was derailed towards the climax of the 2002–03 season.

Liam Brady acknowledges the vital contribution of the English contingent: 'They bring a great passion and loyalty to the club, and also an understanding of what the English game is all about. It takes foreign players time to adapt. Some never adapt. It was the same when I went to Italy. There were a few successful foreign players, but not that many. Ray Parlour is Arsenal through and through, Ashley Cole is Arsenal through and through. With foreign players, they can move about much more.' Although perhaps he reflects the manager's thinking when he admits, 'As far as areas like spirit are concerned, British players give you that bit more but can Ray Parlour do what Henry does? Can he heck!' In mitigation Wenger might point to Francis Jeffers as an example of an English player on whom he has spent serious money (£8 million) but the expense and his injuries notwithstanding, Jeffers has never been given an extended run in the starting eleven, uncharacteristic behaviour by a man who does not spend his employer's millions lightly.

It is not surprising that Arsène Wenger was seriously tempted by Barcelona's offer late in 2001 before eventually deciding to stay in England. For of the acknowledged European mega-clubs – Real Madrid, Barcelona, Juventus, Milan, Internazionale, Bayern Munich and Manchester United – only the Catalan giants have mirrored the strategy at Highbury in permitting a foreign manager to colonise the club with stars from his own country, thereby changing the face, perhaps even the culture of the club. So just as Louis van Gaal filled Barcelona with Dutch players (testing the allegiance of the supporters in the process), Arsène Wenger frequently buys French, to the extent that his compatriots often outnumber their English team-mates on the field of play. Although both van Gaal and Wenger have enjoyed the sweet smell of domestic success, given the talent at their disposal, they have fizzled out in Europe.

There is a common denominator to their non-fulfilment. Every Champions League finalist since 1996 – Juventus, Ajax, Borussia Dortmund, Real Madrid, Manchester United, Bayern Munich, Valencia, Bayer Leverkusen and Milan – featured a significant proportion of players born and bred in the same country as the clubs themselves. It is almost as if keeping faith with the national character, reflecting their own football traditions and only borrowing a touch of foreign stardust to top up the formula, is a prerequisite to success at the highest level. These clubs may also be venturing further afield than hitherto to increase their complement, but they still manage to put together a good enough nucleus, even if some of it is developed at another club in their country, bonded together by their own common culture to mount a sustained bid for the ultimate prize.

It is ironic that, from the manager's own backyard, there are countless examples of how a well-orchestrated youth policy cannot only bring a club halcyon days but ensure its very survival. The success stories of Auxerre and Nantes have been based upon a conveyor belt of teenage talent to regenerate their teams, as the *titulaires* (starters) are picked off by the wealthier clubs. World Cup winners Didier Deschamps and Marcel Desailly both began their careers at Nantes while the current Auxerre team – Djibril Cissé, Philippe Mexes, Olivier Kapo, Jean-Alain Boumsong et al – are merely the latest rich crop coach Guy Roux has presided over. The systems to produce a steady supply of new blood were put in place much earlier in France than their neighbours because, even before the Bosman ruling, France had freedom of contract. This led to a lot of fluidity with clubs often paying the penalty for their success as the cream of their crop took the opportunity to leave the rest and move up in the world.

However, the viability of small town clubs such as Lens, Auxerre and Guingamp, based in a catchment area numerically inferior to practically every English professional outfit, proves that they can survive and flourish with a prescient youth policy. Auxerre coach Guy Roux succinctly states his case that shames Arsenal if not most Premiership clubs. 'Auxerre won *la coupe Gambardella* (under-18 cup) six times over the last twenty years. When you have a good youth team and afterwards the coach has the opportunity when they are a year older to integrate them into the first team for a number of games you can produce on average four good professionals, one of whom will become an international. That's the general rule at Auxerre.'

Arsène Wenger, doubtless cogniscant of happenings across the channel, might argue that such a commitment would risk a fallow season, and a year without Champions League involvement could not be tolerated, but the club stands condemned by the painful knowledge that Ashley Cole is the only player to have come through the youth system and gain an undisputed first-team berth during the manager's six years at the club. Something is not right, at least the academy should be regenerating the squad on the margins if not at its heart, but the harsh facts cannot be denied: rather an import with a bit of experience than the home- grown product. Arsène Wenger is surrounded by hand-picked staff willing to 'bust a gut' for him as evidenced by Brady's seven-day working week and goalkeeping coach Bob Wilson's willingness to postpone his retirement at the manager's request. He will always take the time to listen to his specialist advisers, then he will go off and do his own thing.

Doubtless one of the reasons why Arsène Wenger is not working elsewhere is because of the amount of control he has at Highbury. Wenger's stamp is discernible not only on the playing side. The fact that he was so involved in the design of both the new training complex and is regarded as instrumental in the plans for the stadium at Ashburton Grove means that, decades after his departure, his legacy both in terms of his record and the infrastructure will remain. The ambivalence he wrestles with is the insatiable demand for immediate returns that preclude any thought of indulging Liam Brady.

Arsenal's academy director can only continue to set his own course of action. 'I strive for the day when it will publicly be acknowledged that Arsenal have done well in the area of youth development under Liam Brady. I'm not surprised that hasn't happened yet, but we will strive to make it happen. The challenge for us is to produce better players so that there'll be no argument. We have to produce players of Ashley Cole's standard, of Nicolas Anelka's standard, of Henry's standard, of Ray Parlour's standard. The best way to work on him (Wenger) is to push talent that he can't really ignore.' And with no pun intended Brady says, 'I'll keep chipping away at Mr Wenger.' Though in spite of the restrictions on the purse strings effected by the Ashburton Grove project, there has been no sea-change in the manager's view.

Speaking at the conclusion of the 2002–03 season, Arsène Wenger defended his conservative outlook. 'We have Svard, Volz, Aliadiere, Garry and Bentley. Some of those players will come through. But what you have to understand is that we have world-class players here. Over the last few years we have lifted the level of the academies and we have one of the best in England now. But the players who come through into our first team must be an exceptional talent. The work in the academies is to scout and find the players who have these qualities. For example, we got Kolo who has done remarkably well this season and Pennant is already there as well.'

Proud to say the standard has improved 'one hundred per cent' since his arrival, the manager is aware of the dilemma he faces. 'We have good young players in the academy and we have good players in the first team. It is a risk to put them in and it is a risk to let them go. They can make great impact but are they better at the moment to select in preference to players that are in the first team? That's the question you have to answer.' Alex Ferguson tends to answer it in the affirmative. Maybe if Arsène Wenger had found a higher calibre of personnel when he first came, he wouldn't have been forced into so many changes so quickly. Over his years there have been nearly one hundred player movements in and out of the squad and for the most part the changes have worked wonderfully well. But in so doing he may have created an insurmountable obstacle for most of the emerging talent from the academy.

So Brady is left to ruminate, his proudest moment being, he hopes, a harbinger for the future. 'To see Ashley Cole and Stuart Taylor pick up their championship medals in 2002 was very satisfying. That's two out of twenty-four in the first team squad. We know we've got to make many more inroads in that area, but that is the most satisfying thing to me.' However, keeper Taylor was indisputably a Premiership winner through accident rather than design, wearing the gloves for nine league matches due to simultaneous injuries to David Seaman and Richard Wright. Needing only one more appearance to qualify for a medal, Arsène Wenger brought him on as a substitute for a few minutes of the final fixture of the season.

Although Brady would not admit to it, economic reality means that the club will be forced to draw more water from their own well. Looking ahead, he is in ebullient mood. "From under-twenty-one down to sixteen-year-old level we have as much talent as Manchester United, if not more. This academy has to exist, you can't have a great football club without having a foundation from the youth. No matter who the manager is that foundation must be really, really strong, and I think that if we keep on doing the right things, and keep on working hard, then the investment the club have put into youth will pay very rich dividends in the years to come. I think that there are hard times ahead for football, and they are here already. I think that clubs are probably going to have to be more dependent on young players. And it'll only be a good side if you're ready when that day comes, with good young players. I'm confident we will be.'

Up till now Arsène Wenger may have shown little inclination to place his faith in young blood, but the groundwork he has helped to lay must provide the input to keep Arsenal healthy whilst awaiting the move to their new home. Finances dictate that 2003–04 will inevitably see the academy forced to show its mettle, as David Dein acknowledges: 'We have to do the best with the players we have, and hopefully bring through some of the younger talent as well. We'll give them the opportunity and see if they're good enough.' And possibly save the club a few million they can ill afford to spend in the process. Ashley Cole and Stuart Taylor are a start, but there has to be more; much more.

Chapter Ten

Attack Is the Best Form of Defence

Shizuoka, Friday 23 June 2002. At 4.30 on a burning hot Japanese afternoon, three exhausted Arsenal players walked in a circle around the pitch applauding the supporters who had travelled from the other side of the world to follow the national side. Vanquished, their tournament was over. According to the seedings this World Cup quarter-final was scheduled to pit Brazil against the holders and therefore it would not have been surprising if the three players were the French trio Thierry Henry, Patrick Vieira and Sylvain Wiltord who had performed leading roles in the acquisition of Arsenal's Premiership and FA Cup double. However, World Cup finals rarely follow expectations and with their far east sojourn lasting less than a fortnight, the holders had packed their bags after a 2–0 defeat in their third and final group game against Denmark. Whilst the Danes travelled to Japan for a knockout match with England, Roger Lemerre's squad returned home chastened and crestfallen, having failed to score a solitary goal in their attempt to retain their crown. So, after dispatching the Danes, it was England that faced the in-form Brazilians, and the defeated Arsenal men on their lap of honour were in fact David Seaman, Sol Campbell and Ashley Cole. Martin Keown looked somewhat less forlorn not having played a single minute of the five matches England contested. His most notable contribution to the finals was the growing of a beard he now sported.

The contest was a high-profile nightmare for David Seaman, as he was blamed for the Brazil winner, a long range free-kick from Ronaldinho which floated over the back-pedalling goalkeeper in a fashion reminiscent of the last gasp goal he conceded as Arsenal lost the 1995 Cup Winners' Cup final to Real Zaragoza. The ponytailed Yorkshireman took it on the chin and accepted responsibility for the goal and England's exit, as he told television viewers back in the UK, 'It is very hard to take but that's just life as a goalkeeper. The main thing is I want to say sorry to the fans and the people I've let down today.' Though in truth, it was the poverty of his team-mates' performance – after taking the lead and only having to face ten men for most of the second half after Seaman's nemesis Ronaldinho was dismissed – that was the main reason England were taking the return flight earlier than expected. Actually standing up and being counted did not prevent an outbreak of finger pointing at Seaman from a footballing nation that looks for scapegoats all too readily.

Arsenal double winner, former television presenter and goalkeeping coach, Bob Wilson had no time for anyone who vilified his friend for England's exit. 'It's an absolute disgrace. How can you not be respectful of a guy who in eight of his first ten seasons at Arsenal had the record of fewest goals conceded? If you meet any of the other goalkeepers or the players who work and train with him, and ask them who is the best goalkeeper in England, they would simply say "The Goalie" meaning David Seaman.' As a goalkeeper, Wilson described himself as a 'chancer' often diving recklessly at opponents' feet, enduring buffeting and bruising in the process, so much so that he was only able to take the field with the aid of cortisone injections for which today he is paying the price with an immobile left shoulder. But despite his bravery, he was unfairly accused by one manager of staying down to get a player sent off, an accusation that was taken up by the media on the grounds, all too common in football, that if there is smoke . . . there must be a fire somewhere. Thirty years on, times have changed for the worse, according to Wilson. 'Whatever I could say about my experience (of trial by media) multiply it by fifty or a hundred and it's somewhere near the level of criticism David Seaman has had to endure. It is to his eternal credit that he has the Yorkshire bloody-mindedness and guts to go out with a smile, wave to the opposing fans and always shake the opposing goalkeeper's hand at the end of every game. I've never seen anybody as prepared in victory or defeat to shake anybody's hand. Only when he has gone will he really be appreciated.'

However, many Arsenal fans did not share Arsène Wenger's

The special relationship – Arsène Wenger and David Dein (Gettyimages)

'We won the league in Manchester . . . ' Vieira, Cole and Campbell exult (Gettyimages)

Thierry Henry scoring one of his goals versus Roma in the Champions League . . .

. . . and even five Leeds defenders can't keep the Footballer of the Year in check
(Tom Jenkins)

Patrick Vieira: 'He came from Senegal, to play for Arsenal . . . ' Fans hope they'll be singing the praises of 'PV4' for years to come (Tom Jenkins)

'We love you Freddie . . .'
Ljungberg celebrates the
second goal against
Chelsea in the 2002 FA
Cup Final win

If only it was bigger . . .

Dennis Bergkamp – the
signing that changed the
club (Gettyimages)

The victor and the vanquished – John Carew, Arsenal's Champions League nemesis with Thierry Henry (Gettyimages)

Sol Campbell – if only there were two of him (Tom Jenkins)

The team that wins
together stays together?

Robert Pires – just passing through? (Tom Jenkins)

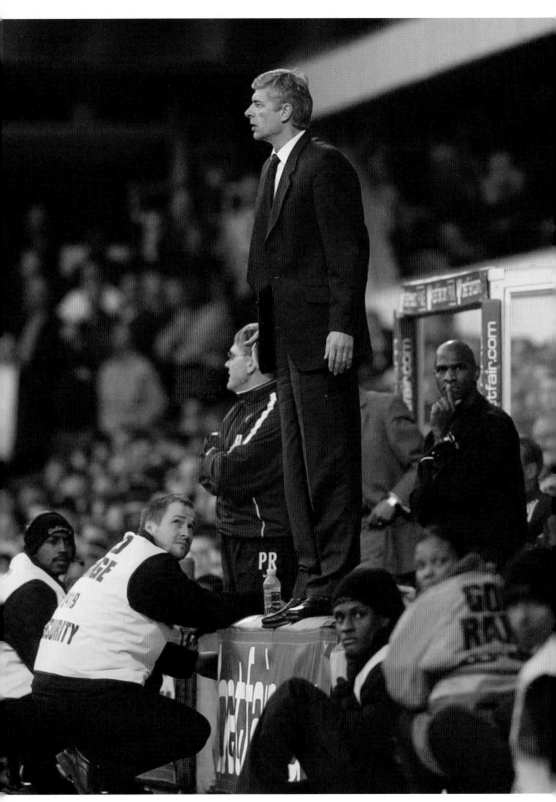

Arsène Wenger – more good times coming over the horizon? (Tom Jenkins)

opinion. At the age of thirty-eight, the player was actually out of contract at the time of the World Cup, although a one-year extension had been put on the table by his employers. As if to confirm the manager's faith in him, Seaman decided against retirement and shortly after signed on for a further twelve months. Arsène Wenger then sold his deputy and perceived short-term replacement Richard Wright to Everton. Wright had never been the number one choice, except for a run out in the FA Cup matches in 2002, until the final in Cardiff, when significantly Seaman was handed the gloves for the match that mattered most. All the same, the prevailing view was not whether he should continue for England, but if he was still up to doing a job week in week out for his club. Some supporters had been agitating for his replacement as far back as 1998 when Alex Manninger kept goal in place of the injured first choice, and did well enough for many to be convinced he should have remained in the team even when the more experienced man was fit.

As Bob Wilson says, 'Sometimes Arsène contradicts himself. He believes in power, pace and youth. Over thirty and you are going to hit a slippery slope, but he has been proved wrong (with the defence) and to his great credit he has admitted as much. But when I have a young goalkeeper of whom I say "this is your best number two", quite clearly he has not always agreed with me and paradoxically has gone for someone who is four or five years older on the basis not that he has more ability but maybe more personality. Stuart Taylor is a very good example of that.' So it appears experience and presence are the attributes the manager looks for in a goalkeeper and although Wilson goes along with that notion as far as David Seaman is concerned, he believes that, 'Stuart Taylor could emulate Ashley Cole by breaking through from the youth academy to become a first-team choice. Technically he's as good a young goalkeeper as I've ever had. He's been at the club with me since he was a kid so it's been a huge disappointment to see certain things occur.

'When Stuart Taylor won a championship medal he performed very creditably if not brilliantly. He had a couple of iffy goals – one against Liverpool and one against Watford in particular – they stay in my memory more than the saves. But when David Seaman got an injury this season Arsène went with Rami Shabaan. It does frustrate me. He could be very close to losing the player (Taylor) and I think that would be catastrophic when there aren't goal-keepers anywhere in the world whom you can put your bottom dollar on. Such is the nature of the position nowadays that when you've got a potentially outstanding young man of twenty-two and you might lose him that is a worry to me.'

He would say that wouldn't he, when Wilson affirms most managers are not capable, do not have the necessary experience to assess a goalkeeper. That may well be so but Arsène Wenger has tried to make good his deficiency. He has thought long and hard about the position and has come to the conclusion that imposing physical specimens are a prerequisite. 'Because the ball moves quicker and quicker, the time to react is less and less. Size gives a goalkeeper an advantage,' he states. 'Small keepers can compensate with their speed of reaction and there are small keepers who read the game well but they cannot reach the highest level.' Hence until this season at any rate, his unwavering support for David Seaman and conversely, though tempted by his agility and experience, Nantes keeper Mickaël Landreau's height of 1.78 metres precluded a move to Highbury due to his lack of inches!

Wilson feels that although Arsène Wenger likes to have spe-cialists on call, he won't always heed what they have to say. 'He doesn't always listen to me, because he is very much his own man. He listens to what everybody says and he is a great man for saying, "Yes, I may be wrong," but not when it comes to the crunch decisions for instance, when I have said, this man is your number two and he clearly deserves to be.' It says a lot for the high regard and affection Wilson has for the Arsenal manager that he finds it difficult to say no to him in spite of the specialist advice he is employed to give being ignored from time to time. So, although he intended to retire from coaching in the summer of 2002, when Wenger asked him to carry on for a further year, Wilson relented.

Bob Wilson also coached the keepers for George Graham, who appreciated that only practitioners of the art could really under-stand the demands of the role. 'George was very much hands-on in his coaching and wanted to do everything,' says Wilson. 'The only person he really allowed to do anything different was myself, specialising with the goalkeepers. George left it to me, "I trust you," he said, "you go and do it." ' It was directly as a result of the close relationship between the former team-mates of the Arsenal double side of 1971 that David Seaman came to the club in the first place. 'George told me "I'm going to change the goalkeeper", and John Lukic was very much a hero after 1989,' recalls Wilson, 'and he asked me about David Seaman. I told him he is the closest I've ever seen to Pat Jennings.'

More than a decade later Wilson is still happy to champion Seaman's cause. 'Of course his reactions coming up to his fortieth birthday aren't as good as they were but you put his experience, know-how, awareness of angles, understanding and reading of the game and usefulness in the dressing room against what he had in the period when his reactions were quicker, and he doesn't suffer by comparison overall. In other words, as a goalkeeper, the older you get, the better you get.' Intriguingly, Seaman's rival at Tottenham and Norway's goalkeeping coach Erik Thorstvedt disagrees. He believes a more accurate indication that age is catching up is the inability to deal with crosses, the confidence to come out and claim those '50/50' balls. Confidence is a fragile commodity and there can be little doubt that this can be affected by a run of injuries, of which Seaman has had more than his share. For the future, there is little doubt that Wilson's preference is for Stuart Taylor. 'Rami Shabaan was brought in on trial as one of three or four goalkeepers. I had him for two or three days and told Arsène, if you can't get the Argentinian Carlos Roa, the best one to have as third choice was Rami Shabaan.'

In fact, one keeper who should have arrived at Highbury after the World Cup was the Uruguayan international Fabian Carini. Unable to oust Gianluigi Buffon at Juventus, the Italian club arranged a loan deal with Arsenal that included an option to purchase the keeper outright after a year. Although only twenty-three, he already had an international reputation, having appeared in all three of his country's matches in the 2002 World Cup finals. It looked a done deal as he appeared twice for the club in pre-season friendlies, but something obviously went awry and his registration was not completed. The official line was that the player could not agree personal terms, but his subsequent move to Standard Liege in Belgium suggested that perhaps it was also a case of once bitten twice shy regarding the validity of South Americans and their passports. Silvinho had left the club under a cloud and besides, there had already been a hiccup in bringing the Brazilian Edu to London. Whatever the reason, Carini didn't join but subsequently Rami Shaaban did. 'It's not my place to argue with Arsène,' says Bob Wilson regarding the Stuart Taylor/Rami Shaaban issue. 'I think he knows how I feel about Stuart Taylor. He is the next-best goalkeeper at Arsenal in my view and I think potentially he would solve the problem of having to find a goalkeeper to replace Seaman but Arsène will make that decision with or without my help.'

In May 2003, Seaman's FA Cup heroics against Sheffield United and Southampton suggested that those who wrote him off did so at their peril. Nevertheless his manager led him to understand that he would no longer be first choice for the coming season. Seaman, believing he had an international future, opted for a move to a club where he would still be the main man, and accepted Kevin Keegan's invitation to replace the retiring (and two months his junior) Peter Schmeichel at Manchester City. It remains to be seen whether Stuart Taylor, in Arsène Wenger's view, has done enough to warrant the goalkeeper's berth or will, once again, see someone brought in above him as happened with both Richard Wright and Rami Shabaan.

A year previously though, there was no debate about Wenger's first choice number one, when he described David Seaman as 'the best goalkeeper in England,' in the days before the thirty-eight-year-old put pen to paper to sign on for a further term, feeling he could not do any better without spending a fortune on a big name import. But even if the manager was content with his keeper, there was unquestionably the need to bolster the back-line, for since the 1997–98 double which saw an impregnable alliance of Lee Dixon, Martin Keown, Tony Adams and Nigel Winterburn protecting 'The Goalie' there was not the same sense of safe hands despite Seaman's appropriating the nomenclature. What's more, in those days, if Adams or Keown were injured, Steve Bould was always a reliable replacement. Now though, with the retirement of Adams and Dixon, (injury had already forced Steve Bould to take the same route after a season with Sunderland) only Keown of the old guard remained. In addition, both Nelson Vivas (in 2001) and Gilles Grimandi had been deemed surplus to requirements. To the charge that he should have brought in new blood, Wenger responds that he didn't because 'I tried to keep a part of the Arsenal spirit in the team and I thought I was always in a position when it would be very critical to lose all the players because they had given something to the team that takes time to get into the other players; the spirit, the resilience, the values which we want to express in the side and in the club.'

Arsène Wenger has been fortunate in inheriting a solid defensive set-up at both his major clubs. In 1987, keeper Jean-Luc Ettori, defenders Patrick Battiston, Manuel Amoros and holding mid-fielder Marcel Dib – all highly experienced in their positions – were already in place when he took charge at Monaco. That Emmanuel Petit was also breaking through meant that he was able to groom the player as a centre-back without needing to enter the transfer market for defenders. For probably the first time in his career, he faced the challenge of building a new defence as the final salutes of the remaining old guard were imminent.

Once upon a time more attention had been paid to his rear-guard. 'At the start of course, when I coached I had weaker teams,' he says, 'so I played more defensively, but even at Monaco I was more defence-oriented than I am now.' The 2002 title had been secured by outscoring the opposition. As a consequence of the possession play that commenced in Arsenal's own half a greater number of goals were conceded simply by dint of the ball being misplaced in the build-up. On the other hand, when the team was on song, defensive lapses were mitigated as they enjoyed so much possession that they invariably created more chances and overawed and outscored their opponents. Even so, were the jewels in Wenger's attack camouflaging fundamental weaknesses in defence? Was the reason Arsenal didn't cut it in Europe that Arsène Wenger had been lulled into a false sense of security by the inferior standard of Premiership opposition incapable of exploiting his rearguard often enough for him to realise top-class reinforcements were needed?

The first choice centre-back partnership of Keown and Campbell was well-regarded, although few pundits would have put any money on the thirty-seven-year-old Keown getting through the season without injury. To give him a standby in the event of Keown's unavailability, Wenger returned home to purchase Pascal Cygan from Lille, for whom he had performed capably in Europe. If on paper, it looked as if the player had been drafted in to help fill the void left by Adams' retirement, the reality was that Wenger should have had no illusions about replacing the irreplaceable. To add to the manager's dilemma, the other back-ups already at Highbury, Matthew Upson and Igors Stepanovs, did not by any stretch of the imagination possess the same authority as either Campbell or Keown. As for the full-backs, Lauren, a converted midfielder still auditioning for the role, and Ashley Cole, had played the majority of the matches the previous season, with Oleg Luzhny available to slot in if needed. Despite Wenger's claim that he had two players for every position, by any criteria the defensive cover appeared vastly inferior to the home-grown and inter-national talent available to Manchester United, Chelsea and Liv-erpool, to say nothing of the likes of Real Madrid, Juventus and Milan. The twenty-six-man squad who posed for the pre-season photo might have been numerically sufficient, but whether the personnel reflected the necessary quality in depth was a moot point.

There was little doubt that if Arsenal were to reprise their *annus mirabilis*, Sol Campbell would have to continue to replicate the authority shown by Adams during the years that the former Spur had plied his trade at the other end of the Seven Sisters Road. Campbell had enjoyed a remarkable first season at Highbury, although the best of him was only seen after he had exorcised his demons on his return to White Hart Lane in November 2001. In the build-up to the fixture, there was widespread belief that the centre-half would be diplomatically rested against the club in whose eyes he had transmuted from hero to villain, but with Tony Adams on the injured list, Wenger chose to partner Campbell and Keown at the back. The atmosphere was hostile and intimidating, much more so than past derbies, with the Arsenal coach – the bus not the man! – coming under assault upon its arrival at the stadium. Despite being booed whenever he touched the ball, after an early intimidating yet perfectly fair tackle on Les Ferdinand, Campbell settled to give a commanding display in a 1–1 draw, and Arsène Wenger enthused he had seen 'the real Sol Campbell, the player I signed in the summer'. Patrick Vieira, his captain was equally complimentary: 'He knew what he was going to get but showed he is a strong man. He never allowed what was going on around the pitch to affect him and showed he is thoroughly committed to us.' The afternoon was the making of the number 23 (his old Tottenham number, deliberately chosen by Campbell to indicate that it belonged to him and not to the past or his old employers) as an Arsenal player. Up until that point it was apparent that he had yet to regain the fitness that had made him an uncontested member of the national team before ironically, an injury suffered against Arsenal in the FA Cup semi-final the previous April curtailed his final season with Tottenham. As Bob Wilson later reflected, 'People's criticism of Sol Campbell absolutely amazes me as he has slotted in to what was a famous back five and I don't even think he took a long time to settle in. He has been a huge presence. Of course there have been times when you think he has had a poor game but he is a major contributor to the success of Arsène Wenger's side.'

With Arsenal's reputation for outstanding central defenders such as Herbie Roberts, Leslie Compton, Frank McLintock, David O'Leary and Tony Adams, Campbell certainly had a lot to live up to by moving to Highbury. With both Adams and Keown nearing the end of their time, the former Tottenham skipper bore a huge responsibility with the prospect of being the senior member in a back-line that would have to stand comparison with the high standards of its predecessors. Physically, no one could argue that Campbell lacked presence. A giant of a man, the concept of a fifty-fifty challenge involving him simply defies belief until the day opposition sides start fielding World Wrestling Federation heavyweights in their forward lines. But to make the short journey from N17 to N5 it took a big man in more ways than one (although many Tottenham fans will never ever forgive him for what they perceive as a traitorous act from 'one of their own'). Both Barcelona and Internazionale were courting the player, and his free transfer status meant that even though he was handsomely rewarded by his new club for choosing to stay in London, he could have made a lot more money by opting for Spain or Italy.

But Campbell was happy in London. There was no need to pack up and move home, and if Arsenal could satisfy the sense of ambition that had been stultified year by year at White Hart Lane he would have the best of all worlds. Now he was the bedrock of a club that could win trophies, and as Adams and Keown missed more and more matches through injury, it was fortunate for Arsenal that they always had at least one commanding centre-back. As the season progressed, Campbell became highly influential, prompting his manager to say, 'In the last fifteen minutes of games that we might have lost last year, he has come out from the back and won some important fights and crucial headers to keep us safe. There is a big pressure on Sol to show his qualities but you tend to see the best of him when you need someone to be a hero.'

It was a brave decision to move to the most detested rivals of his former club. The pain Tottenham fans must have felt was compounded when their former favourite spoke about needing to make the move in order to improve as a footballer. When George Graham took over at White Hart Lane, he wanted Campbell to ape the way that Tony Adams had played for him at Arsenal. Stop the opposition, get rid of the ball and nothing fancy. As a regular England international since 1996, Campbell knew that there was a positive side to his position and his characteristic surges from the back used to drive Graham spare as he contemplated the holes his captain had left behind him. By the time of Glenn Hoddle's arrival the die had been cast. Campbell had already decided he would leave on a free transfer with all the attendant benefits – both for his football and bank balance. The opportunity to play regular Champions League matches as part of a team that revelled in possession football could only develop his game for the better. Campbell later concurred with this view, 'You could be a fantastic player but you've got to have the experience ... it counts for everything.'

Red carded only once and cautioned just seventeen times in over 300 appearances – almost unheard of for a Premiership defender – Campbell was one of two Tottenham players that were coveted by Arsenal fans (the other being right-back Stephen Carr). That he then signed for their club, with no fee exchanging hands, made Gooners feel that they had really put one over their local rivals; the defender was an instant Highbury hero without having to kick a ball. He had given many years to Tottenham with only a

League Cup winner's medal to show for it. Moving was the right thing to do, even if his ultimate destination would inevitably bring the bubbling north London rivalry he was so familiar with to the boil.

For Arsène Wenger, Campbell was one of his easier acquisitions but a vital one. Only a signing-on fee was necessary to attract someone who didn't want to uproot. The way that the player almost fell into his lap was a stroke of good fortune, especially with the club's existing first choice centre-backs being the wrong side of thirty-five. They could not go on indefinitely, and the manager had no track record of paying serious money for a defender. The £4 million for Silvinho was as high as he had gone; the £7 million Lauren was more of a midfielder who out of necessity was pressed into the full-back role. Perusing Arsène Wenger's purchases, it would not be out of order to conclude that someone of Campbell's stature and reputation could only have come to Highbury on a Bosman. His free transfer enabled him to be financially compensated, through his signing-on fee, without the club's wage structure being turned upside down with the risk of sowing dressing-room discontent. More importantly, at the season's end when he had earned the highest honours in the land he could reflect that, 'Working with the players here and playing against top opposition, I think I've improved in all aspects of my game.'

It was just as well, given the question marks about those lining up beside and behind him as Arsenal attempted to retain their title. Naturally, with a manager hell-bent on conducting the beautiful game, it appeared that the more mundane aspects of team-building were not paid the attention they warranted. It was simply optimistic to believe that a combination of scintillating forward play coupled with a dilapidated defence – that despite Campbell was atrophying – could again repel all-comers. Indeed if the now unavailable Tony Adams had not returned for a run of five crucial games late in the Premiership campaign, that saw only a questionable penalty against Tottenham conceded, Arsenal might have finished up as the bridesmaid yet again.

Nevertheless, Wenger could point to the fact that Adams did not play in twenty-eight of the thirty-eight league fixtures, and to compensate for his retirement and to further augment his options he procured a defensive midfielder who had a far more gratifying World Cup than any of Arsenal's contingent. Gilberto Silva, who arrived for £3.5 million from Atletico Mineiro in his native Brazil, was on the field for every minute of his country's victorious campaign in Korea and Japan. Given his anchor role in such an attacking formation, any negligence of his defensive duties would have been quickly exposed, but Gilberto emerged unscathed and with an enhanced reputation good enough for many to believe Arsène Wenger might have picked up the transfer bargain of the summer. Alongside Patrick Vieira in central midfield, it looked as if the hole left by Emmanuel Petit had been filled, so that the defence might receive the necessary cover to compensate for the departures of Adams and Dixon.

The early indications were that there was no undue cause for alarm. Arsenal were opposed by Premiership runners-up Liverpool in the FA's traditional curtain raising Community (formerly Charity) Shield opener in Cardiff. As in the 2001 FA Cup final, Arsenal dominated, but this time, the defence was good enough to hold out. Both sides took the game more seriously than the usual pre-season friendly, possibly in an attempt to score some psychological points for the months ahead. On that basis, Arsenal had little to worry about from England's second best team of the previous season. That the new boy Gilberto scored the winner was an unexpected bonus.

The serious business of the league got underway with three home wins and two away draws – both London derbies. Anything but maximum points at Highbury would have been a major letdown, as by a quirk of the fixture list, the first three sides to visit were those promoted from the First Division – Birmingham, West Brom and Manchester City. Although the defence did not cover themselves in glory by conceding a total of three goals to the newcomers, no one cared as nine were rattled in at the opposite end by Thierry Henry and company, and Arsenal never really looked like needing to get out of second gear to win. Even so, the warning signs were clearly visible. The visit to Upton Park should, by rights, have produced their first Premiership away defeat in over a season, 2–1 down and facing a West Ham penalty, but Freddie Kanoute's effort was easily saved by Seaman and an equaliser two minutes from time earned a point, although psychologically, the boost from remaining unbowed was probably worth more. As Wenger admitted afterwards, 'When you come back from 2–0 down to 2–2, it feels a bit like a victory.'

A similar tale unfolded at Stamford Bridge. Finding themselves 1–0 down after a long range Gianfranco Zola free-kick had sailed past a perplexed David Seaman (the villain rather than hero on this occasion), Arsenal then had to complete the last forty minutes with ten men after Patrick Vieira's somewhat harsh dismissal for a second yellow card. However, they had proved to be Chelsea's bogey team in recent years, and the trend remained intact when Ivory Coast newcomer Kolo Touré headed the equaliser after an hour. It was a spirited recovery and, unlike the draw at West Ham, a thoroughly deserved result, according to Arsène Wenger. 'Playing with ten men and 1–0 down on an away ground, we have shown great, great spirit. We reacted well (to Vieira's dismissal).' And taking his cue from Lauren, who played his international football for Cameroon's 'indomitable lions', the manager enthused, 'Suddenly we were ten lions on the pitch; always coming at them, wanting the ball.' Just before the season kicked off, Wenger had stated, 'We are the defending champions and we really want to be up for it. But we have to do that from the start and then keep the momentum going.' After five matches, Arsenal led the table from neighbours Tottenham.

Before the next match at Charlton, skipper Patrick Vieira complained of fatigue having competed in sixty-six club and international matches the previous season and a shortened summer break due to the World Cup. 'I'm not just tired, I'm cooked,' moaned Vieira. 'I can hardly stand up at times. My back hurts, my legs hurt, I hurt everywhere. I am going to see the manager because he must give me some rest. I don't know when or how, but we have to do it quickly because the Champions League is coming and there will also soon be two international matches with the French team. I know all too well that my performances are up and down.' At least the sending off at Chelsea ensured that he would get some respite to rest his weary limbs. It was not what Arsenal fans wanted to hear, but if the captain was below par, it wasn't noticeable when he turned out at The Valley five days later. Charlton simply didn't have the stamina to resist Arsenal's high tempo pressure. They held out until just before the interval, but Thierry Henry's opening goal broke the resistance and the final whistle saw a 3–0 scoreline.

With Arsenal looking unbeatable in the league, despite the added burden of frequent midweek Champions League commitments, the possibility of holding on to their Premiership crown looked more like a probability, especially with Manchester United already losing twice and sitting six points off the pace after seven matches. There was no question the Highbury outfit were the flavour of the moment and if the hype was contagious Arsène Wenger appeared to have been infected by the virus. Asked about whether or not he felt the treble won by Manchester United in 1999 was a possibility for his team, he responded, 'I think it's strange for a manager to go into a competition and not think he can win it. I am one hundred per cent convinced about my players' quality and attitude. When I see this team playing there are moments when I think that I would pay to watch them.' Fair enough, but he was certainly dicing with fate, believing not only that the Gunners could win all three trophies, but could remain undefeated in the Premiership while doing so. 'It was done by Milan in 1992. I can't see why it's shocking to say that we can do it this season. If we lose, people will turn and say "you have a big mouth" but I can only be honest. If I say I have no confidence in a team that has gone twenty-eight games unbeaten you'd call me a liar. It's everyone's dream to go through a season without losing so let's give it our best shot. If it doesn't happen it's not the end of the world.'

Unsurprisingly Alex Ferguson dismissed the notion as 'impossible' and felt that Arsenal had made unnecessary hostages to fortune of themselves, perhaps mindful that David Beckham had made a similar ill-advised statement the season before. George Graham summed up the view of most pundits when he called the forecast 'unwise to say the least'. Given that no English side in the last century had ever completed a league season unbeaten, it seemed that Arsène Wenger's pride and belief in his team's ability had instilled a measure of delusion. Arsenal were undoubtedly enjoying a purple patch, but so far it was exactly that. Such spells never last an entire campaign; somewhere along the line, even the greatest will suffer a setback.

Possibly as a result of the momentous conclusion to the double triumph – they stormed past the winning post with eighteen straight wins – Arsenal had seemingly slipped seamlessly into a fertile groove. The absence of Pires and Ljungberg notwithstanding (both recovering from operations) the team had remained victorious despite a variety of personnel changes in the starting line-up. The aura of invincibility not only permeated the entire squad but seemed to adversely affect their opponents so that Arsenal now enjoyed the psychological advantage of a fearsome reputation, just as Manchester United had for most of the nineties.

Arsenal's opponents, if not beaten men before a ball was kicked, were certainly apprehensive about what was to befall them and had every right to be. Yet goals, albeit consolation ones, were being conceded which should have rung a few warning bells. When the needle finally slips out of the attacking groove, the defence would be called upon to stand up and be counted in full measure and produce the required clean sheets. However, it looked unlikely that they could be relied upon to the same degree as their colleagues and consequently points would almost certainly be dropped.

In their run of form (Europe too, was producing concurrent wins), the prospect of a trip to Leeds on the last weekend of September should have held no fears. The fixture though had added significance, as Arsenal had the opportunity to create a record for scoring in consecutive league matches. Since a visit to Newcastle for a 0–0 draw, securing second place and automatic Champions League entry in May 2001, they had played forty-six league games without failing to score, in the process remaining undefeated away from home for the entirety of the 2001–02 Premiership season. A goal at Elland Road would break Chesterfield's seventy-two-year-old peerless achievement. It took only nine minutes to reach a new high, courtesy of Kanu. Arsenal looked terrific as after only twenty minutes Kolo Touré, in place of the recuperating Ljungberg, wrapped up three points with a second goal. After playing some breathtaking passing football at a venue where they have not always enjoyed the best of fortune, Arsenal ran out comfortable 4–1 winners.

The club had failed to win the league two years in a row since the 1930s. In 1991 there was a feeling that having won the title with only a solitary defeat they were well placed to emulate Liverpool's consistency, but George Graham had to bow to Alex Ferguson who filled the void created by Liverpool's fall from grace. But he had to wait six years before beginning his collection of championships while Arsène Wenger won the double in his first full year. Now, Arsenal were seemingly once again poised to become the dominant force in English football. Of the display against Leeds, Wenger said, 'It was one of the top performances I have seen during my six years at the club,' but added ominously, 'we can improve in a lot of areas.' Based on this performance, it was difficult to see how.

Against certain opponents, the team could operate on cruise control, such was the gulf in class. The visit of Sunderland to Highbury was a typical example, witnessing a contest effectively over before half-time, as a 2–0 lead established by two Kanu goals never looked in danger of being threatened. Vieira's addition to the total before the interval ensured that the second half could be played at walking pace. It seemed Arsenal could win after coasting for half of the match. Their campaign had begun like a runaway train, and the continued absence of league defeats accompanied by impressive displays in the Champions League made those kill-joys who criticised the defence seem churlish. Sure, playing this way might see the odd notch in the goals against column, but what could go wrong with all the firepower available seemingly able to score at will.

All well and good, but there were bigger hazards lying in wait. Although starting well in the Champions League, the more intense phase of the competition was still to come, and the portents were not favourable for a back-line who might find their lapses resulting in more costly consequences if Milan, rather than Manchester City was the opposition. Having spent his entire Arsenal career seeing his Continental sorties stymied prematurely, Arsène Wenger was now relying on his team's attacking flair to carry them further than ever before.

For those with long memories, the concept of gung-ho Gunners in Europe was not a new phenomenon. With forwards Alan Smith and Kevin Campbell supplemented by Paul Merson and Anders Limpar on the flanks, Arsenal had begun their 1991–92 European Cup assault in style with a 6–2 aggregate win over the Vienna-based FK Austria. Only the Portuguese champions Benfica stood between them and a place in the last eight. After a 1–1 draw in Lisbon manager George Graham was justified in feeling confident as the Sven Goran-Eriksson-coached Benfica arrived at Highbury for the second leg. However, a strangely indisciplined performance was ruthlessly punished and Eriksson's side, by winning 3–1 in extra-time, ensured that Arsenal's Continental sojourn was a short one. Alan Smith recalls how that game affected the tactical approach. 'I think George Graham learned a lot from the Benfica episode. He felt we were too cavalier and naïve. We left ourselves open in the final stages. We were inexperienced. I think we put the experience to good use when we got back into Europe in the Cup Winners' Cup. He set out his team differently. He would play 4–4–2 on the Saturday but for the midweek European game, it would often be 4–3–3. I would play through the middle and two out of Kevin Campbell, Ian Wright or Paul Merson would play either side of me and drop back when we lost the ball so we created a strong reinforced midfield. We were now more tactically aware. We knew what it was all about in 1993.'

In contrast to Wenger, Graham built his sides from the back. Preservation was paramount, as Smith points out. 'We had a strong defence first and foremost. It was a time when we weren't a fantastic attacking side; we didn't play with great width or pose a threat everywhere on the pitch. We were very dependent on Ian Wright but if we got a goal you can bet your bottom dollar we were able to defend the lead. George always knew about our opponents. He was aware of their danger men and would work out how to handle them. Occasionally he would use a man-marker, usually Martin Keown, who was excellent in that role. If you can nullify a vital opponent it can help you a lot, though if you are not careful it can spoil your shape if players drift all over the shop.'

To Graham, discipline was the key. 'He wasn't one of those managers,' Smith recalls, 'who said, "We don't fear anyone, we will concentrate on what we will do rather than think about them."' And it was carried over from the field of play and applied on a personal level. According to Smith, 'Once he'd seen your optimum performance – what he felt was the best you could do – he wanted you to approach that level as often as you could and if you dropped below it and he felt you could do better, he'd let you know what he thought in no uncertain terms.'

Arsenal encountered Eriksson again nine years after the painful Portuguese lesson, when he brought Lazio to London for a Champions League group match in late 2000. Their tactics had gone full circle and this time, the two-goal defeat was handed out to the visitors. Arsène Wenger conceded that 'offence' is his priority. 'We concede more goals than George Graham's team because we go forward more. You have to play differently in Europe today. Now you have to attack because the teams are so good going forward that if you concentrate on defence you will pay the price. You cannot depend on defence because you are under too much pressure and the standard you face is too high. So we try to play as in the Premiership – home and away we try to put our opponents under pressure.'

Yet Graham is not convinced his successor is on the right track. He concedes that Wenger has assembled 'a wonderful bunch of players' but qualifies the praise with the implication that he should do so anyway as his foreign background gave him a head start. The bottom line for Graham is that, 'I can't believe they didn't do better in the Champions League. People say they've been unlucky in Europe but you can't be unlucky for years on the trot. In Wenger's first year in the UEFA Cup they lost to a Greek team who were halfway down the league.' He still believes his way – 'players want to be led' – is the better way. As Alan Smith remarked of his former boss, 'He always used to say it was "hard work playing under me" but at the end you'll have trophies to show and it will be worth it.'

Having served as a goalkeeping coach to both George Graham and Arsène Wenger, Bob Wilson is well placed to bring some perspective to the argument. 'George took a lot from Bertie Mee, the manager of the double-winning side of 1971. He admired Bertie's discipline and attention to detail and his organisational skill. Arsène is more flexible and fluid in his approach. The sides that George Graham created he made into great teams. He made them play to their absolute strengths. What George achieved was nigh on a miracle but the plain fact is that the most beautiful football Arsenal Football Club have ever played in their entire history has been in the time Arsène Wenger has been their manager.'

All the same, in his old-fashioned way, Graham could put his silverware on the table and claim 'I would have won something with them'. But times change. As Alan Smith recalls, 'He set out to rule using a certain amount of fear but you can't really do that now.' Maybe, but what Graham's teams had in abundance was a never-say-die spirit which was exemplified by Arsène Wenger's old stagers – the famous five – whom he inherited from Graham. They surprised him with their longevity but, as their careers wound down, often missing through injury or when fit, marginally slower than in their peak years, they could not be relied upon to carry Arsenal through the toughest Continental encounters in the way that they had under Graham.

Now, with only Seaman and Keown remaining, Wenger's team had evolved to the point where, Campbell and Cole notwithstanding, his most capable performers were undeniably playing ahead of the back-line. But without a genius in the ranks, a Maradona, a Zidane, trophies are rarely won by half a team. If Arsenal were to justify their manager's faith and make a serious assault on the Champions League, the rear Gunners would have to start impressing as much as their more celebrated colleagues. And with the quality of opposition that inevitably lay in wait in Europe, they would certainly get their chance.

Chapter Eleven

'To Travel Hopefully . . .'

Hampden Park, Glasgow, 15 May 2002. As a preamble to the Champions League final, Arsène Wenger stood on the pitch with three other practitioners of the coaching art who had made the journey to Scotland as celebratory guests to witness UEFA's showpiece in the flesh. As the flashbulbs fired, did it occur to the Arsenal manager that maybe he should not be standing alongside his peers on this night of all nights? After all, Fabio Capello, Alex Ferguson and Marcello Lippi had all led their teams to a European Cup triumph. No one could blame *Le Technicien Alsacien* if there was some rueful brooding on 'what might have been'; even jealous thoughts about Vicente del Bosque of Real Madrid and Klaus Topmöller of Bayer Leverkusen, about to issue final instructions to their players. More likely for Arsène it was simply: case closed. On to the next one. And maybe in a year's time, he would be in their shoes.

Like Arsène Wenger, Fabio Capello had coached a side to the league title in both his native country and abroad. All the same, given the resources at his disposal, winning with Milan and Real Madrid was probably easier than winning with Monaco and Arsenal, as Wenger had done. And Capello had also reprised his Italian triumph with Roma, perennial underachievers despite a succession of wealthy presidents. Alex Ferguson had also attained championships in two countries. His accomplishment of a Scottish title and a subsequent European Cup Winners' Cup with Aberdeen, proved his ability to turn up trumps under comparable circumstances to Wenger. Moreover, he had succeeded in Europe where Arsène Wenger, albeit under unfortunate circumstances had failed. If Marcello Lippi had never worked outside of Italy, plenty had failed at Juventus as the club had endured eight years of penury before his arrival in 1994. The booty that followed his two spells, interrupted by a brief unhappy sojourn at Internazionale, established his credentials as a great coach. Reaching three consecutive Champions League finals was a record that only their arch rivals Milan could claim to match. Perhaps it was uncharitable to think that Gérard Houllier had to gatecrash the Glasgow photoshoot, although having managed Liverpool to UEFA Cup glory in 2000, he could at least point to something that still eluded Arsène Wenger: a European prize. It was just as well Otmar Hitzfeld hadn't shown up, having won the Champions League with Borussia Dortmund and Bayern Munich, otherwise the Arsenal manager might have felt he was sharing the spotlight under false pretences.

Undoubtedly, gnawing away at Arsène Wenger was a feeling that a great manager would have at least a Champions League trophy in his cabinet. Certainly he should have a better record, although he would claim mitigation that in their entire history Arsenal, with their annual Champions League appearances, have never basked in the European sunshine as much as they do today. But having built a side he felt was capable of winning the ultimate club prize, he no doubt found it immensely frustrating that so far he had not got anywhere near it. Smaller clubs than Arsenal had made the final in recent years. If Ajax, Valencia and Bayer Leverkusen could do it there should be no earthly reason why Arsenal – in Wenger's belief better equipped to mix it with the big boys – shouldn't be there as well.

Having won the Premiership and established themselves once again as the only English team that could live with Manchester United, now was the time for Arsenal to go on the razzle, consigning their inconsistency to the dustbin of history. The quest for European glory had become an obsession, Arsène Wenger had his fill of flattering to deceive. There must be substance along with the style that was making Arsenal one of the Continent's most popular clubs.

All the same, the failure of both France and England in the 2002 World Cup, with their significant Arsenal representation revealed that despite a season of domestic dominance, the Highbury-based internationals, had been found wanting at the highest level for their countries just as they had been for their club. However, the season to follow was the one in which Arsène Wenger's players were to not only progress further than they had ever managed before in Europe's major club competition, they were going to win it! After all, the manager had said so after their second stage group exit the previous season. In football speak, he set his stall out early doors eschewing the principle of taking one match at a time. Some may have needed more convincing than others, but according to Arsène Wenger: 'What has changed and what people don't realise in England is that Arsenal are seen in Europe as a big team and we are expected to dominate, to play our game, and that is what we try and do. Judging by trophies in Europe you cannot say we are a complete force but in the minds of people we are a big team even if it is not justified yet. So there is a fear factor present that we have to exploit and come out and play our game as naturally as we do at home.'

If he was to justify the bravado, there had to be a sea change. Certainly results on the road would have to improve dramatically, and perhaps their away form in the Premiership, a key factor in their success, may have been a confidence booster. Whether the squad were better equipped was another debate. Gilberto had arrived from Brazil, and the games for his country had given him only a fleeting acquaintance of what would be demanded from him in the Champions League. Yet, on paper he unquestionably improved the midfield. Furthermore, those alongside, and in front of him in Arsenal's attack were a year more experienced with, apart from Dennis Bergkamp, much more to come. Bergkamp himself, despite his travel restrictions, appeared to have been allotted once again a more prominent role by Wenger, who was prepared to play him in Continental fixtures he could easily reach by land and sea. Obviously upset by being discarded, particularly after making the tortuous trip to Leverkusen only to sit on the bench, his exclusion from some of the more accessible ties in the previous two campaigns had done little to aid Arsenal's cause. Arsène Wenger may have felt justified in prioritising consistency in team selection, but ultimately, results indicated that he had suffered as much as his number ten.

So all looked well with the midfield and attack, but could the same be said of the defence? With David Seaman and Martin

Keown inevitably more fallible due to their advancing years, Arsenal were some way from matching the line-up that took them to two successive European finals in the mid-1990s. Sol Campbell could stand comparison in any company as his election to FIFA's all-star line-up for the Korea–Japan World Cup finals proved, and Ashley Cole and Lauren, although comparative novices, were first-choice internationals. But with no Adams or Dixon could they cut it as a unit? And was Arsène Wenger, blinded by the brilliance of his offensive weapons, blithely unaware of the potential liability of his back-line? At the highest level, even if you happen to be Real Madrid, you can't win without a defence worthy of the name.

Real were the holders, and set the benchmark for Arsène Wenger. 'When they have the ball, I can watch them for hours,' he enthuses. 'Because it looks so classy, it's art. When football gets close to art and the communication between the players is right so that everybody does something intelligent when he has the ball, it becomes an art and it's that moment of beauty when you really enjoy to watch.' But that view only reveals half the story. Roberto Carlos may have even more zest for attacking than Ashley Cole, but his defending was good enough to see him flourish at Internazionale before his move to Castilla. If he wasn't up to the mark, Real have the resources to replace him, but have never felt the need. At right back, Michel Salgado is a highly rated Spanish international, as is centre-back Fernando Hierro, though his best years are no doubt behind him, as could be said of his partner Ivan Helguera. (2002–03 would prove a season too far for Hierro, and his manager's failure to drop an iconic player ultimately cost him his job on the same day that his captain's employment at the club was terminated, ironically the day after *la Liga* was secured.) More importantly, the fact that both centre-backs are converted midfielders and are at ease with the ball at their feet enables the team, at their best, to play further forward and pile up pressure on opposition defences accordingly. Sol Campbell may have improved his control under Wenger's tutelage, but he isn't in this company with the ball at his feet and not to denigrate his considerable assets, it goes without saying, neither is Martin Keown.

Arsenal, Real and Manchester United all entered the competition with an old head at the back. Hierro had retired from international football after the World Cup, while United's Laurent Blanc had preceded him after Euro 2000. Although Keown made no comment about his England career, it was generally accepted it was now an academic subject after being passed over in Korea and Japan. Blanc was purchased by Alex Ferguson for his organisational abilities on the field and for his influence on the emerging talent such as Wes Brown and John O'Shea off it, although as it became evident that his lack of pace was becoming a liability, he was phased out as the 2002–03 season wore on. Did Arsène Wenger have the kind of quality offered by United's Brown or O'Shea, or Real's Francisco Pavon to replace ageing stars? Arsenal's nearest equivalent was Matthew Upson, although the decision to send him on a three-month loan spell to Reading indicated he hadn't reached the standard Arsène Wenger had set for him. Thus almost by default, new signing Pascal Cygan would be the man to fill in for the inevitable Keown absence.

It seems Arsène Wenger simply took a gamble. 'I bought Cygan for £2 million because there was no more money available,' he admitted at the end of the player's first season, confirming the club's cashflow problems were impacting team building some time before they became public knowledge. The top Italian and Spanish sides were as good as Arsenal going forward, yet unarguably better in defence. Instead of being seduced by Real Madrid, the manager could have cast his mind back to another Spanish side, one that had beaten Real to the title at the same time as Arsenal had overhauled Manchester United, Arsenal's conquistadors of 2001: Valencia. Target man John Carew notwithstanding, a combative and energetic midfield augmented a fluid attack, with players adept at switching position and drifting into danger areas. Arsenal had something of this flexibility about them, but defensively the two sides were like chalk and cheese; Arsenal as potentially brittle as Valencia were resourceful. It was only the depth of quality of *la Liga*, that consigned Valencia, after appearing in two consecutive Champions League finals, to the UEFA Cup in the 2001–02 season.

As Premiership holders Arsenal were, for the fifth successive season, automatic qualifiers for the first group stage of the Champions League. If the UEFA rankings could be taken as signifying anything beyond ensuring that the top guns from the most successful countries were kept apart, then Arsenal were the seventh ranked club on the continent, just behind Juventus. So on this level, Arsène Wenger was correct in stating that his side was indeed 'a big team' in Europe. Their consistent appearances in the competition were no mean feat, although the time was overdue when qualification was viewed as an end in itself. Arsène Wenger was still as optimistic about his team's chances as he had been after their elimination the previous March. 'I think there's a lot of hypocrisy and superstition attached to football, but I don't go into a competition not to win it,' he said before Arsenal's European opener. 'Everybody else perhaps thinks they will win it but they don't say it. I will say it, because I'm convinced we can win it. The desire is there and the experience is there so we can give it everything and go and win it.'

Arsenal's group opponents were Borussia Dortmund, PSV Eindhoven (winners of the competition during the 90s and 80s respectively) and Auxerre. They started with a rendezvous at home, a novelty after travelling to Lens, Florence, Prague and Mallorca in the preceding four years. Borussia Dortmund were first up. After an unbeaten start to the domestic campaign, it was a confident crowd that made their way to London N5 on a mid-September evening. They were not let down by what followed.

Freddie Ljungberg had suffered a hip injury during the World Cup and had not played for Arsenal since the climax of the previous season. Dortmund was his comeback game and a surprise to many as under Arsène Wenger, convalescents recovering from long-term injuries usually begin their first-team involvement from a place on the bench. It was to be a reunion of sorts for three participants of the World Cup Final in Yokohama at the end of June. Brazil were represented in Arsenal's line-up by Gilberto Silva, whilst Dortmund fielded Torsten Frings and Christoph Metzelder who had started for Germany. Coincidentally, the result was the same, with the Brazilian's side emerging as 2–0 victors. The goalscorers were Bergkamp and Ljungberg.

The former German international Matthias Sammer generously put Arsenal on a higher plane than his own men. 'Arsenal started slowly in the Champions League in the past, and we now have to improve like them. They gave us a lesson. We have to learn from this game if we want to stay in the competition.' Arsenal were certainly up and running despite the absence of Robert Pires, still rehabilitating on the sidelines. No one could claim Dortmund were a soft touch, having won the Bundesliga ahead of Bayer Leverkusen and Bayern Munich, so Wenger's delight was understandable. 'We showed great teamwork, discipline and maturity as we showed patience,' he said. 'It didn't always go our way but we got through the frustration without making any mistakes at the back. It was a real test, not only on the football side but also mentally. We saw a team that has learned a lot.' So far so good, but one swallow does not a summer make, and anything but a home win would have been an upset for a team in such a rich vein of form.

The chief unresolved enigma from the two previous Champions League campaigns was the purgatory of Arsenal's away performances. Beginning in November 2000, a run of eleven matches had seen them glean a solitary victory and draw, a meagre four points out of a possible 33! It was an appalling return for a side with pretensions of challenging for the trophy. The first road trip took them to Holland to face PSV Eindhoven, managed by Guus Hiddink, fresh from guiding South Korea to a World Cup semi-final, and who had begun their own campaign with a 0–0 draw away to Auxerre. Hiddink talked up his opponents in the pre-match build-up. Referring to their two point lead, he said, 'Arsenal are in the driving seat now. They have a very good team of mixed nationalities playing excellent football. They are a strong all-round side. I truly believe that Arsenal and Real Madrid are the two best teams in the world at the moment.' Pressed about the poverty of his team's record on the Continent, Wenger put it all down to caution. 'I'm convinced it was because our attitude was a little restricted at the start of games. We have not been positive enough. If you analyse all the games, the second half was nearly always sixty–forty for us but by then the match was already lost. The players are frustrated at not achieving as much as other English clubs in the Champions League. I think we have shown all the teams who come to Highbury we play good football. Our big problem has been away from home and that is something we have to fix if we want to be successful.'

Dennis Bergkamp began his first Champions League away match since 1999 and was instrumental in a fulminating start, sending Thierry Henry down the wing, from where he crossed to Gilberto Silva to fire Arsenal ahead after a mere twenty seconds had elapsed. So much for being initially overcautious! It beat Alessandro Del Piero's record for the fastest Champions League goal by 0.05 seconds. Martin Keown was substituted early on due to a strained hamstring, and Pascal Cygan entered the fray for his competitive Arsenal debut. It was an acid test for Wenger, but his luck was in as PSV's profligacy let him off.

PSV spurned their chances, and the visitors did not allow them to gain a foothold after the interval, posting a remarkable 4–0 scoreline. It was a stark contrast to the meagre fare Arsenal fans had become accustomed to on their travels and full justification for the manager's optimism. Hiddink's achievements with South Korea in the World Cup Finals may have been based on a sound defence, but faced with Arsenal in full flow, his pre-match pronouncements about the quality of the opposition suddenly had a ring of truth about them. For all the plaudits, a cold hard look at the match revealed that, despite the scoreline, Arsenal were susceptible at the back in the first half. PSV were able to fashion three gilt-edged chances for themselves in David Seaman's goalmouth – two point-blank headers and a one-on-one opportunity – all squandered by Serbian striker Majeta Kezman. The final scoreline was an example of perfection for Arsène Wenger. When asked later if he would prefer to win a match 4–3 or 1–0, he responded, 'I would prefer to win 4–0.' In reality, his ethos, combined with prudence in the market so far as defenders are concerned, dictates that there are more likely to be goals for both sides whenever Arsenal play.

As a variation from the ritual of past seasons, which involved travelling and training the day before the encounter, the ultimate pre-game training session now took place at Arsenal's London Colney base in the morning before an afternoon flight to their destination. The matchday as usual was reserved for rest and relaxation with limbering up exercises and a gentle stroll the sum total of physical activity before kick-off. At their host's stadium, Wenger alluded to this alteration in the itinerary in his post-match press conference. 'Sometimes, psychologically, you try to change things to break habits, but I'm not a witch doctor, I'm just a football coach. That's not the main factor though. The important thing is that my team has class, spirit and soul. They have shown that for more than a year now and they showed it again tonight. I believe we wanted a strong start. I said that the problem we faced last year was that we were always starting slowly and finishing strongly. We started well here by scoring the first goal.' No one could argue with that. Whether or not such a result would have been attained without Dennis Bergkamp was another question. It would be answered soon enough as injury forced his withdrawal and also put paid to his availability for a month.

The next task was a cross-channel journey to Auxerre. The French club were without their star player, twenty-one-year-old Djibril Cissé, the new striking sensation who had appeared alongside some of Arsenal's players in the World Cup Finals. Although Auxerre were currently top of *le league*, they had struggled in their European fixtures, gaining only a solitary point so far. They were coached by the incomparable Guy Roux, who had been in the job since 1961 (apart from a year's absence when he realised à la Ferguson that he was quite unsuited for retirement, and fortunately his employers concurred), transforming an amateur club in a small provincial town into perennial challengers for national honours. As the doyen of European coaches, he was well qualified to pass judgement on his compatriot's team, and commented, 'They are capable of scoring within five seconds of getting possession, that's how good they are. Both individually and collectively, they are the best I have seen. I think they have the potential to be like Real Madrid or Milan, they really are in that category.' Taken at face value, this was high praise indeed, but could there be an element of kidology involved by the coaches concerned? The compliments aside, this was reaffirmation of the club's status abroad, at least in France. Certainly the knockout stages of the Champions League are a foreign territory more often than not, but Arsenal's exposure as one of the leading lights of the most popular league in the world, broadcast live in over 150 countries, had built a reputation that, conversely, the likes of Roma, Lazio and Internazionale enjoy in the UK. None of those sides have come within touching distance of a Champions League final in the last few seasons, but their successful *Serie A* campaigns brought them widespread renown.

* * *

141

There were more good tidings in the run-up to the match as Patrick Vieira announced that he was negotiating a contract extension. 'I can't see any reason why I won't stay,' he stated. 'I've experienced so many things with the club and winning the Champions League with them would be more meaningful than with anyone else. Being captain here fills me with pride.' Was this the same man who was on the point of leaving just over a year ago or the player who had compounded his red card at West Ham in October 1999 by spitting at his provocateur Neil Ruddock? Unsure until reassured by his peers whether he had the stuff of captaincy within him, he could now reflect that it was an asset, that he had 'Improved as a man and technically as a footballer. The captaincy makes me feel more responsible as a player.'

The turn for the better in his side's performances since the summer of 2001 had evidently seduced the newly installed club captain and if there still hadn't been any lavish spending in the transfer market, there hadn't been a recurrence of the opportunistic selling which had so perturbed him. It still nagged him though, that no unnecessary obstacles should be put in the way of the team's prospect of realising what might be. 'There is more to come because we are still a young side. I think it is very important to keep the same team year after year because that will make us improve as we have over the last few years.' For the moment he was 'happy' at Highbury. Equanimity in his occupational and private life, he could dismiss speculation that he might respond to Alex Ferguson's blandishments. 'I've always said that if I have to leave one day I will go abroad. I will never leave Arsenal to go to another English team.' Hopefully for Arsenal fans that day won't dawn.

Without Vieira's pivotal influence the Gunners look depleted. The midfielder's ball-winning ability was there for all to see right from the moment he first stepped on to the Highbury pitch. He seemed to have telescopic legs that allowed him to win balls that he had no right to and that other players wouldn't have got near, and despite his tender years his sheer presence quickly earned him a permanent place in the starting line-up. Arsenal were his third club as a professional. At Cannes, then in the French first division, he was awarded the captaincy despite his being only eighteen years of age. His talent was noticed across the border in

Italy, where he was snapped up by Milan in 1995. There, he spent a season largely on the sidelines, watching Demetrio Albertini and Marcel Desailly occupy the central midfield positions. With the teenage prospect looking unlikely to replace either in the short term, Milan agreed to sell him to Arsenal in the late summer of 1996 for £3.5 million, at the behest of the Gunners' manager-in-waiting, seeing out his time in Japan.

Vieira joined Arsenal at the same time as his much older compatriot Remi Garde, but initially, he could only express himself articulately on the pitch as not surprisingly he had difficulty understanding the English language as expostulated by the likes of Ray Parlour. So much so that an early nickname was 'What', due to his constantly needing to ask what had been said to him. Born in the Senegalese capital of Dakar, Vieira moved to France with his family when he was seven. He describes himself as 'French with a big African heart', which doubtless resulted in mixed feelings when he played for *Les Bleus* against Senegal in the opening match of the 2002 World Cup. As a teenager, he showed enough promise to earn a place at the French academy in Clairefontaine, only to be initially told by under-21s coach Raymond Domenech that he had the wrong physique for the central midfield role. 'He was too big, had no muscles and a weak point with the knee,' Domenech recalls. One wonders if he would have graduated from Arsenal's academy. Fortunately Domenech's opinion was academic as Vieira established himself at Cannes as a teenager.

Ball-winning and midfield dominance aside, the other salient trait of an on-song Vieira is his ability to drive forward in the heat of a highly charged contest. Having won possession, some of his best moments have seen him carry the ball forward shrugging off challenges before laying off a pass to an attacking colleague. When Vieira advances in this manner, he is reminiscent of one of those medieval knights in a bygone Hollywood epic. 'The Black Prince' charges into battle and slays any opponent in his path. In so doing, he lifts the crowd, more so even than when Tony Adams used to try something similar without the same effect. It is as if the heart of the team is working harder, pumping oxygen, invigorating colleagues and supporters alike. One example, from many, of the havoc he can cause was the winning goal against Tottenham in the 2001 FA Cup semi-final. After heading the equaliser, his coruscating run to the edge of the opposition box spreadeagled their defence enabling two of his compatriots to apply the *coup de grâce*. Sylvain Wiltord was fed wide and he crossed for Robert Pires to tap in.

Although 2000–01 was the last season before Vieira was given the captain's armband in Tony Adams' absence, he was already demonstrating that he was Arsène Wenger's true leader on the field. In January of that year, Adams announced his international retirement. Looking ahead to his departure from Arsenal which occurred some eighteen months later, he had no doubt who should take over. 'I'm already trying to mould Patrick into my captain's role,' he said. 'I might have to teach him some things that just came naturally to me, but he has the ability to do it. He is Arsenal through and through and he has the potential to become a great player for the club. He's curbed some of his indiscipline and when he is provoked he just gets on with his game.'

Anarchy was Vieira's Achilles heel. He has picked up eight red cards as an Arsenal player, and because of a tendency to react to provocation, became a target for the opposition, well aware that they would stand a better chance of beating Arsenal if Vieira had first use of the showers. Wisdom and responsibility came with age. If, after his fifth and sixth dismissals in consecutive matches in August 2000, Vieira seriously considered leaving the English game, the two subsequent expulsions found him simply anxious to get his suspension out of the way and return to action as quickly as possible. In the 2002 Community Shield against Liverpool, England international Steven Gerrard's assault on Vieira was punished with a yellow card, although it could easily have been red, but the Arsenal skipper did not seek retribution, rather, he was able to grin and bear it. 'It was a nasty tackle by Gerrard but it was OK,' he said afterwards. 'He didn't do it in a way to hurt me because he's not that kind of player. I like and respect him as a player, but when you're young you make mistakes. I went through that. Captaincy has made me more mature, improving me as a man as well as a player. I'm not a natural leader like Tony Adams, who talked a lot. I contribute to the team through my desire and commitment to fight until the end to win. Maybe the team will be led by my determination.'

Able to reflect on his own complex history he admits, 'I have made some mistakes in the past, but have calmed down because I have a big responsibility on my shoulders; I am captain of Arsenal. I used to react the wrong way after a tackle or an incident with another player, but that wasn't the way to show I was unhappy. I have had to understand that if people do a bad tackle on me or try to wind me up, that's the only way they have to stop me. I take it as a compliment now.'

Gerrard himself has generously expressed admiration for Vieira, not least when speaking in the aftermath of the 2001 FA Cup final that saw a dominant Arsenal finish as unlucky losers to Liverpool. 'I learned an awful lot in that final,' said Gerrard. 'For a start, I realised Vieira was a much better player than I am. It was my intention before the game to take control of the midfield and he just did not allow me to do that. He's such a great player. He's so fit, and he dictates the pace of a game. There are a lot of things you can learn just by watching him.' Gerrard's education went beyond the on-field tussles with his rival. 'I try and watch as many Arsenal games that Vieira is playing in as possible,' he said. 'It's exciting to watch, and I like to see what he does. In many respects he is like a role model to me. Obviously he has the advantage in that he is a few years older than me, and with age comes extra strength. But I need to make sure I do become fitter and stronger, because that is what I need to become as good as him. At least I have the FA Cup winners' medal, though.' Some consolation after ninety minutes in Vieira's shadow.

When Patrick Vieira was made Tony Adams' vice-captain for the season that followed the Cup Final defeat, some fans saw it as a strange kind of reward for someone whom they felt had tried to engineer a transfer for himself a few weeks previously. Yet many others felt it was a belated appointment, with the midfielder so obviously the dominant influence in Adams' absence. Whatever the rights and wrongs of the appointment, Vieira led the side in the vast majority of matches that resulted in the two trophies Arsenal captured in May 2002. His key role was acknowledged by Adams who, after the defeat of Chelsea, lifted the FA Cup in tandem with his deputy.

Following Adams' decision to hang up his boots, Vieira was confirmed as the captain in his stead, and Wenger's comment on the decision looked optimistically to the future. 'Patrick is a natural leader by his example on the pitch. He's only twenty-six but it looks to me like he's already the natural successor to Marcel Desailly as captain of the French national team. And maybe now that Patrick has a privileged position and can communicate with referees, he will be more protected by them.' Not by Andy D'Urso at any rate who gave him two yellow cards at Chelsea four matches into the 2002–03 campaign. When Vieira told D'Urso that he had 'no personality' before leaving the Stamford Bridge pitch, the Football Association was forced to create a charge about 'using insulting words', instead of the standard nomenclature of 'foul and abusive language', when it became apparent that in informing the official that he was not doing his job properly no swear words had been involved. The £25,000 fine, along with the statutory two-game ban, was totally out of proportion to the nature of the offence. As the vice-chairman of the Football Association as well as Arsenal, one hopes that David Dein, at least privately expressed his misgivings to his colleagues and his commiserations to the player. As evidence of his new-found maturity, despite the ludi-crous sentence, Vieira took it on the chin and with the ban out of the way got back to leading his team. His observation – 'I must be the first player to be punished for hurting a referee's feelings' – succinctly summed up the farcical situation.

Often described as the best player in the world in his position, it is little wonder that Vieira is constantly linked with a move to a mega club. Perhaps what keeps him at Highbury is his con-tentment with life in England. 'It is one of the best places in the world to be a footballer,' he says. 'The atmosphere in the stadiums is so good and the football is so fantastic because people here play to win the game; in some countries, they play not to lose the game.' Vieira has set up home with his long-term girlfriend Cheryl in chic Hampstead, north London, the favoured enclave of most of his French team-mates. 'I live a fantastic life,' affirms Vieira. 'London's a very cosmopolitan city and people respect your privacy. I can walk through the streets, go into shops, buy what I want to buy, put it in my car and go home and no one disturbs me. I can go to a movie with my girlfriend and no one disturbs us. I can do anything I want to. English people respect that footballers are normal people as well and they never cross the line. That's why many foreign players come to this country. They know they will enjoy the life here.' The player is all too well aware of the sacrifices he would make in returning to Italy or moving to Spain. Though his bank balance would profit, the cost to his equanimity may be a price he wouldn't countenance.

However, as a World Cup and European Championship winner with France, the glaring omission in his personal honours list is a Champions League medal. If Arsenal did not become serious contenders, it would only be a matter of time before Vieira would succumb to the overtures of someone who could offer him a more likely passage to the winners' podium. For now though, like his manager, Arsenal's captain was focused on bringing European glory to north London, and six points out of six was all he could ask for to start the 2002–03 campaign.

The match in Auxerre witnessed a very different Arsenal to the one that had scored four goals in their previous two games (a win at Leeds was sandwiched by the two European trips). The performance was more reminiscent to that given by the visitors in the same stadium in 1995, shortly after George Graham's dismissal. The result was identical too – one-nil to the Arsenal. With fleet-footed strikers and a mobile midfield, Guy Roux's side of 2002 were the closest Continental version of France's favourite English team and a counter-attacking stalemate was only broken when Gilberto secured the winner shortly after the break, despite the late scare of the hosts hitting the crossbar. It was a disciplined display that showed Arsène Wenger's side had the wherewithal to win matches without having to set the pace or feeling the need to entertain. The manager admitted as much. 'It was more of a tactical game, a little bit like chess but I must give a lot of credit to my team. They have that mental strength to know that sometimes you need to be patient.'

At the halfway stage of the group, Arsenal led with a maximum nine points. With two of the remaining three encounters at home, qualification to the second stage looked a mere formality to a side being touted as favourites, alongside Milan and Real, to lift the trophy next May. The display in Auxerre was, in its way, as reassuring as the trouncing in Eindhoven, as it indicated that if the attack had an off day, the defence, with Cygan in Keown's place, could stand up and be counted. With a minimum of sixteen matches required to reach the final there would inevitably be other days when it would be hoped they were not found wanting. Arsenal had given themselves some breathing space. It was just as well as four consecutive defeats, all coincidentally by a 2–1 margin (two in the Premiership, two in Europe), brought them back to earth with a bump.

The home match to Auxerre fell on the same day as Arsène Wenger's fifty-third birthday, but there were no presents from his players as Guy Roux's team extracted revenge for the defeat three weeks earlier. Having seemingly conquered their travel sickness were Arsenal about to surrender fortress Highbury? Deportivo La Coruna's win the previous March had been the only reverse in nineteen occasions, so for Auxerre to take all three points was a major upset. Moreover there were no complaints as the home side looked out of sorts and unable to deal with the problems presented them by goalscorers Fadiga and Kapo, notwithstanding the continued absence of their star player Djibril Cissé. And David Seaman did nothing with either goal to allay suspicions that his reflexes were on the slide. The England number one was already under scrutiny because of a goal conceded straight from a corner against Macedonia. It turned out to be his final appearance for his country as an Arsenal player. The only positive note to the evening was the reappearance of Robert Pires as a substitute after seven months out of action.

The birthday boy was not panicking. 'There is no reason to be alarmist. You have periods like these in a season,' he said. 'I believe this team is strong mentally and will recover from tonight. It's very important that we bounce back now, that's the biggest thing.' He paid due compliments to Auxerre. 'They started very well, while we had not recovered from the shock of losing on Saturday.' Whether or not a defeat at Everton three days before the visit of Guy Roux's team, when their teenage sensation Wayne Rooney buried Arsenal with an injury-time strike caused post-traumatic disorder, warning bells were ringing regarding the lack of protection afforded a fallible goalkeeper.

The visit to Borussia Dortmund was the final match in the freakish run of 2–1 scorelines. It was the first time in twenty years that Arsenal had lost four consecutive matches. How valuable the three wins from the first three Champions League matchdays now looked. Wenger had said before the Dortmund defeat, 'In chasing

148

the game against Blackburn (the second consecutive league upset) we forgot about some basics in defending and that's what we have to get back.' In suffering another reverse in Germany, his defence still looked vulnerable, and although Dortmund's winner was from the award of a dubious penalty, the German side had the luxury of being able to spurn many good chances.

Arsenal managed to win their first-stage group courtesy of a goalless draw at home to PSV, although the lack of depth at the back was exposed by Kolo Touré's brief appearance in place of the rested Ashley Cole. Maybe a more experienced man should have been lined up against Danish international Dennis Rommedahl, arguably the Dutch side's most dangerous player. Touré's evening stint lasted only until the thirty-fifth minute, by which time the naïve youngster had received his second yellow card for another rash challenge. It was as well his team had already qualified.

Chapter Twelve

'... is a Better Thing Than to Arrive'

Having attained the second group stage, Arsène Wenger could now admit in private, 'I will be very disappointed if I don't get to the final because we have the experience, we have the quality, all that is needed to go through. Of course you go step by step but I can feel how deep it is in the guts of the players. They want to win the Champions League. They want it as well as me.' The desire to fill in those empty spaces on numerous CVs was laudable but fraught with danger; to prioritise a competition – the knockout stage of which they invariably don't reach – would be in all likelihood tempting fate. All the more so when the battleplan was to put the onus on the attack. 'The Champions League has changed the rules in Europe,' explained Arsène Wenger, 'because teams are so good going forward that if you only defend you will not be able to resist. You cannot live only by defence because you are always under pressure and the quality you face is too high.'

Arsenal now had to move up a gear and ready themselves for the stout challenges from Valencia, Ajax and Roma, whom they would face in the second group stage. A 3–2 defeat away to Southampton was not the ideal preparation for their first match in Rome, especially as the defensive frailties shown by the Campbell–Cygan partnership were there for all to see at the St Mary's Stadium. Still, given Roma's feeble strike rate of three goals in their six first stage fixtures, perhaps they were the ideal team to play at this time. More so as the Italians had uncharacteristically also conceded three away to Parma in their last outing. The words of coach Fabio Capello – 'We have to forget this game and the result as quickly as possible. Our defence did not have a good day' – could just as easily have been uttered by his counterpart in England.

The contest heralded a reunion with Gabriel Batistuta, who three years earlier as a Fiorentina player had slammed the door in his opponents' face. 'I still have visions of the goal he scored at Wembley,' Arsène Wenger revealed. 'In terms of the Champions League that is probably my lowest point since I joined Arsenal.' After their previous three European results, Wenger needed a point or three to re-establish momentum right from the outset of the second stage. 'We are going to Rome to win but we would not be unhappy to return with a draw,' he said before the kick-off. A point appeared wishful thinking when after only four minutes his team found themselves a goal behind, thanks to Antonio Cassano turning Sol Campbell inside out before scoring off the post.

But turning a game inside out was Thierry Henry's forte and this was to be his night, as he rattled up a hat-trick, a remarkable feat against an Italian defence at any time, but an even greater accomplishment on Roman soil. And the defence redeemed themselves with Pascal Cygan preventing what looked like a certain goal by clearing off the line with the scores level. As a last throw of Capello's dice substitute Gabriel Batistuta made his entrance. This time he was not to prove Arsenal's nemesis. There was a new sharpshooter in town. To confirm his reputation he set his sights to strike his third goal from a free-kick five yards outside the penalty area.

It was Arsène Wenger's one hundredth European match as a manager, a statistic that probably says as much about the sheer number of fixtures required to progress in the Champions League than it does about his successful longevity at Highbury. The hat-trick hero put matters into perspective after the win: 'The victory shows we had the right attitude from the whole team. We have been looking for this kind of victory. It was not only the way we played but the mentality we had. This win is a good start but we need to be there at the end. That is the most important thing. You can start like that, but then if you are not there at the end it will look a bit sad. I feel we can get better and better but we have to keep our feet on the ground to do that.' Roma had been given a drubbing, but it was only three points. Arsenal had proved on their own patch they were good enough to usually come out on top, but now they needed to show that the pyrotechnics in Rome were not a flash in the pan.

For all that it was a case of two steps forward, one step back. The visit of Valencia before Christmas showed once again that the only consistent facet of Arsenal's European record was their inconsistency. Unable to penetrate the visitors' rearguard, despite sixteen efforts on goal and Valencia finishing with ten men, the 0–0 draw suited Rafael Benítez's side, as Arsenal failed to replicate the result of April 2001. The two-month break that followed allowed Arsenal to focus their efforts on domestic affairs, which they did convincingly. Between the Valencia draw and the visit of Ajax in February, they undertook thirteen matches without defeat, despite visits to Anfield, St James' Park and Old Trafford.

Ajax were coached by former Dutch international Ronald Koeman, whose side was characterised by two aspects of team-building which contrasted significantly with Arsène Wenger's approach – an emphasis on defence, and a preponderance of home-grown young players. The latter was no surprise. Arsenal's Liam Brady had been to visit the much longer established academy in Amsterdam and noted, 'Ajax had the foresight to see that youth was the way forward, as they didn't have the money to go into the transfer market – in fact they're a victim *of* the transfer market, as they can't really keep their players once they become established.' That may have been the case after their last European Cup final appearance in 1996 when the introduction of the Bosman ruling allowed the likes of Edgar Davids, Clarence Seedorf and Patrick Kluivert to up sticks for richer pastures in Italy and Spain. Bereft following the sudden exodus of their stars, Ajax compounded their loss by unsuccessfully using the transfer market as a short-term fix, pushing themselves heavily into debt. Their plight has presented them with Hobson's choice: to revert to the homespun tradition of promoting their own. And, as even the Italian and Spanish giants are nowadays also feeling the financial pinch, there is a good chance that they will be able to hang on to the youthful prodigies such as Rafael van der Vaart and Nigel de Jong, at least for a while. It is no coincidence that Ajax under Koeman, having rediscovered their principles, were making serious headway in the competition for the first time since a semi-final appearance in 1997.

The emphasis on a sound defence was a new though not unexpected concept. Koeman had twice won the European Cup as a centre-back for PSV Eindhoven and Barcelona, as well as the 1988 European Championship for Holland. As a coach, he already had a Dutch double to his name. Tactically, he was showing Europe a different face, acknowledging that the total football of the past was not an option for an inexperienced side.

Arsenal started brightly enough with Ajax old boy Bergkamp teeing up Wiltord for the opening score, but the Dutch side kept their young heads and equalised through Nigel de Jong. Ashley Cole's failure to cut out a cross-field pass allowing the eighteen-year-old midfielder enough time to beat the exposed David Seaman. It was a costly error, as Arsenal failed to add to their score and the moral victors were Ronald Koeman's team. Inability to beat what were in truth a bunch of European novices on home soil hardly pointed to a team who were serious contenders for a final place. Having taken the lead against a defensive side, all Arsenal had to do was keep a clean sheet. Ajax didn't even need to swarm forward in great numbers to score and once level they appeared by far the more composed line-up in their solid 4–5–1 formation. The draw meant not only had four points been dropped at home, but that fortress Highbury suddenly looked to have a hollow ring to it, as the last win had been back at the very start of the competition, against Dortmund. With fixtures coming thick and fast, at least Arsenal had their chance to rectify matters a week later in the return encounter.

Arriving in Amsterdam, Arsène Wenger spoke astonishingly like a man who had already achieved his greatest ambition rather than a pretender, the pinnacle of whose success story so far was a solitary quarter-final place. 'We want to win with a style of play and a way of enjoying the game, to give people watching us something. Teams like Real Madrid, AC Milan and the Ajax are remembered in history not only because of the trophies they won. They were a natural consequence of the football they played. But if you look at a team like Bayern Munich, who won the European Cups three times running, you couldn't say that every time they went out to play they were a great team. Before you can say a team is a great side, let them show they can dominate the championship in their generation and not just one year. Manchester United had that style in the nineties and Liverpool did it in the eighties. I would like to be remembered as the manager who won the European Cup for Arsenal for the first time. If you look at the record books at what we've done over the last fifteen months, that's not been done by anybody in the last fifty years, going over fifty games and scoring in every one and going unbeaten through a season away from home. That's not been done in modern football, nobody's done that.'

Granted, domestically the previous eighteen months had witnessed Arsenal sweep all before them, but when the bar was raised in the Champions League, his side still had plenty to prove. High scoring victories over PSV and Roma were outnumbered by the defeats and draws in which Arsenal had played with anything but panache. It was unlikely that Wenger had time to pop into the Ajax museum at the Amsterdam ArenA, but if he had, the replicas of the four European Cup trophies would have been a clear indication that along with the style, there was considerable substance. Here was a club that had over-achieved in a manner Arsenal could only dream of. Even in the decade before 1995, when Ajax were rarely major participants in the European Cup, they could still produce stars like Marco van Basten, Frank Rijkaard and Dennis Bergkamp and walk away with the UEFA and Cup Winners' Cups.

Home comforts notwithstanding Ronald Koeman's objective was simply to avoid defeat. Often, Continental opponents had sufficient respect for Arsenal that rather than devise a game plan to beat them, they would concentrate on preventing Arsène Wenger's team from winning. They knew that Arsenal could be frustrated if they defended deep, as by denying Thierry Henry the space into which to make his runs, his colleagues would be forced into a long ball game without the necessary target-man for it to have any impact. In the Premiership, such a tactic against Arsenal might be doomed to failure because mistakes are more likely, given both the increased pace of encounters and the lower quality of defenders. Manchester United's greater success on the Continent is partly down to their being able to adapt the best aspects of their Premiership football – especially the pace at which they can play – to a different type of contest, pulverising the kind of teams Arsenal seem to flounder against. In Amsterdam, despite

Arsène Wenger's pronouncements about style, only devotees of tactical football would have extracted any pleasure from the vapid encounter.

When a barman at Schipol airport asked returning Gooners the day after the goalless draw, 'Did you enjoy the chess last night?' he hit the nail squarely on the head. Even so, a surprise consolation for both participants was Valencia succumbing at home to Roma so that if Arsenal and Ajax won their next matches, they would both progress to the quarter-finals.

However, Manchester United were showing their countrymen that if you want something done, it is best to do it yourself as along with Milan they ensured not only their qualification as quarter-finalists, but also as group winners and could now afford to rest their key men in their final two group commitments.

With Roma having only conceded a solitary goal in their previous five Champions League away matches, it was as well that they were forced to seek three points at Highbury, as a draw could see them eliminated in the event of an Ajax victory against Valencia. Although Arsenal had beaten them 3–1, their home form should certainly have imbued Capello with a sense of optimism. His counterpart spelt out in spades what was at stake, when he forecast, 'This could be a moment of truth for us.' It was, but not as he would have wished. It was another case of *déjà vu*: an early goal followed by an equaliser. And into the bargain, shortly after Patrick Vieira's header had given his side the lead, Roma were reduced to ten men after captain Francesco Totti tangled with Martin Keown to earn himself a red card. Nevertheless in spite of the home side enjoying the rub of the green, another defensive lapse cost them dear. With the interval imminent, a floated long ball out of the Roma defence caught Pascal Cygan napping and allowed the sole striker, Antonio Cassano, to put matters all square.

Perhaps the Premiership demands a period of adjustment for an imported player, but this was more familiar territory and anyway there was simply no excuse for someone of Cygan's ability to fail to read and cut out a hopeful punt from the other end of the pitch. With limited funds and reinforcements required, Cygan was bought after being one of the mainstays in Lille's astonishing run from the French second division to the Champions League, and usually took his place in the starting line-up when either Sol Campbell or Martin Keown were absent.

Gone were the days when the reserve man was Martin Keown, Steve Bould or even Gilles Grimandi. When called upon, Matthew Upson had carried out the task efficiently in the double-winning season, but after recovering from a long-term injury he found himself on a three-month loan to Reading at the beginning of the season. On his return, Arsène Wenger spoke in complimentary tones, fielded him for an FA Cup-tie against Oxford and then sold him to Birmingham City for less than half the money spent on Cygan, although the fee could rise in time to £3 million. As Upson could also fill in at left-back, his departure seemed a perplexing decision, especially in the light of Cygan's obvious discomfort in the games he played before Upson's January sale.

The conclusion was obvious. Arsène Wenger could take offensive potential and shape and polish rough diamonds till they shone, but his failure to adequately replace the defence he inherited, or even realise who his best stoppers were, makes one wonder how much more success he could have had if he had paid more attention to his rearguard. To rub the point home while his makeshift back-line was struggling manfully on the biggest stage, Upson, given the first-team run he craved at St Andrews, was guiding his new club to Premiership safety and playing his way into Sven Goran Eriksson's England starting line-up by the season's end.

Although in hindsight Wenger believes perhaps he should have kept Upson at least till the end of the season, he takes a pragmatic view of the issue, 'He could have been injured as well. It is like that. I always say a manager cannot always be relied upon to be right,' and in his mind Upson just didn't measure up to the required standard. 'Well, I always wished him to be at Arsenal, but I think you have to respect, when somebody doesn't play that he has the right to play. I think we have been very patient with Matthew Upson, we have helped him a lot, made him grow and now he expresses his talent elsewhere. Everybody says though, okay, if he was there at Highbury. But he was for five years and he didn't play and we won things, so I'm not convinced that he would have been the solution.'

But it begs the question, was Pascal Cygan and should Arsène

Wenger have done something, anything, when he admitted before the Ajax game, 'I'm worried about the defence. Our defensive record is not good enough. We are conscious of that and we want to improve it. That's our target over the next three months. We feel we have the best attack but sometimes we feel it may be a price to pay because we are an offensive team.'

Still, Arsenal's attackers had forty-five minutes to ensure their Champions League qualification against a ten-man team who needed the three points as much as themselves. Sylvain Wiltord is a busy, bustling player who often gets in the right positions at the right time, although his reputation for frequently being unable to locate a bovine *derrière* with a stringed instrument, was unfortunately growing among the Arsenal fans. He will score enough goals to be a contender, but a tally of his misses tells the sorry tale of someone who should have a collection of Golden Boots on his mantelpiece. Actually he did once finish *en tête du classement des buteurs* (leading scorer) when Bordeaux won the French title in 1999. Against Roma he failed to come up trumps with four clear-cut chances. Yet the final outcome could have been so much worse. The most blatant opportunity of the night came late on when Roma broke to create a clear, unchallenged header for substitute Vicenzo Montella in the Arsenal goalmouth. Hearts were in mouths as Highbury witnessed an unlikely miss. And from a man with a phenomenal *Serie A* record of nearly a goal every other game. In the final analysis, Arsenal got out of jail with a point. Afterwards, even Wenger acknowledged where the blame lay when he admitted, 'We gave a cheap goal away against Ajax and a cheap goal tonight.'

For the third season in a row, Arsène Wenger's men having failed by their own efforts, nevertheless approached their final second-stage group match away from home with qualification for the quarter-finals still on the cards. Once again, the outcome of the other match could aid them, even were they to be vanquished in Valencia. A draw between Ajax and the Spaniards in Amsterdam, and Arsenal's latest deception giving Roma something to play for had set up a situation whereby any of the four teams could still go through. Even if Arsenal lost, a Roma win at home to Ajax would still put them through, but to avoid relying on events beyond their control, a point in Spain would be sufficient.

Two years after Valencia had put paid to Arsenal's hopes at the quarter-final stage, there was a strong sense of foreboding, *plus ça change, plus c'est la même chose*. Patrick Vieira believed otherwise, affirming, 'We are a better side now, we have improved and learned a lot in the past couple of years. We will go there to win the game. Two years ago, it was very frustrating as we felt we were good enough to go through. This time, it will be different as we are a better team, we're very good away from home and our confidence is good.'

As reigning Spanish champions, Valencia had also made headway. Of the outstanding team that had taken them to two successive Champions League finals, Jocelyn Angloma had been replaced by a younger French model – Anthony Reveillère. Gaizka Mendieta had moved on, but the notable strength in depth made light of the departures. Even without the suspended Rubén Baraja and the injured Kily González, they did not look to have a chink in their armour. If only the same could have been said of Arsenal.

A demoralising defeat at Blackburn the weekend before the trip to Spain was hardly ideal preparation. Vieira, Campbell and Cole (at last succumbing to the surgeon's knife for his hernia), were not fit to play and when Martin Keown limped off after eighteen minutes it left Lauren as the only component in the first-choice defensive unit still on the field, Stuart Taylor covering for the injured Seaman in goal. Fans travelling to the Mestalla feared they might be supporting a centre-back pairing of Pascal Cygan and Igors Stepanovs, compounded by a midfield bereft of Vieira, but the full extent of the manager's gamble only became apparent when the teams warmed up before the match. Neither Vieira nor Campbell took part in the standard routines, as each went through their paces accompanied by a member of the training staff. As the goalkeeping coach Bob Wilson had noted, 'Arsène has made them into such finely tuned athletes, if they feel any strain at all or if there is any doubt, Arsène won't play them.' But desperate times meant putting principles to one side. Neither player was one hundred per cent fit, yet Wenger named both in his starting eleven. It flew in the face of his normal policy. In the days leading up to the game, Tony Adams had talked about the manager's philosophy: 'Arsène is what I call a physiological manager. He is more scientific and gets players out there who are at their physical best.' But this was a do or die Champions League night. This was the competition he craved for. Paradoxically Vieira and Campbell were too important *not* to risk, and against a side of Valencia's excellence, the alternatives didn't bear thinking about.

Arsenal were already depleted with Kolo Touré at left back. In Ashley Cole's continued absence Giovanni van Bronckhorst had started against Roma, but hardly acquitted himself satisfactorily, so Kolo Touré was recalled. Cygan remained in central defence, as did Taylor in goal. Departing from his habitual 4–4–2, Wenger aligned five in midfield, with Wiltord played wide right and Ljungberg wide left, and Vieira, Gilberto and Pires (albeit in a more advanced freer role), in the centre leaving Thierry Henry in splendid isolation up front.

Arsenal, positive from the start were unfortunate not to score early on, but Canizares denied Henry (twice) and Ljungberg before Gilberto had a header deflected by Vicente on the goal line on to the woodwork. The tide turned and a Cygan error had dire consequences. As the defender was drawn into midfield trying to gain possession he found John Carew behind him and onside. Once Cygan had failed to win the ball, Pablo Aimar put the unchallenged Valencia striker clear to fire past Stuart Taylor with thirty-three minutes on the clock. It was yet another cheap goal. News filtered through that Ajax had taken the lead in Rome, and the future looked bleak.

All was not lost as Arsenal only needed a goal of their own to put themselves back in the qualifying positions, and shortly after the interval, it duly arrived. Pires fed Henry and that was that. With the required scoreline in the bag it was time to forego the beautiful football favoured by Arsène Wenger, play the Spanish at their own game and apply safety first tactics. Kanu was on the bench, and although a rare starter of late, he was an expert exponent of holding on to possession and tying up at least a couple of defenders. To substitute Wiltord or Pires and revert to a 4–4–2 formation could provide a better balanced unit to hold on to what had been dearly earned.

Wenger had seven minutes to change things around before another costly error effectively put paid to his aspirations. Under pressure, Arsenal cleared the ball out to the right wing where

Sylvain Wiltord failed to get it under control and presented possession to Vicente. A quick cross was converted by John Carew, who moments earlier had seen Taylor save a similar effort, as he made good his boast that he would repeat the knockout blow of two years ago. Arsenal were down and out, left waiting for glad tidings from Rome which never came. Ajax managed a draw and accompanied Valencia into the quarter-finals.

Valencia did exactly what Arsenal needed to do with the score at 1–1. Remove any sense of flow, or momentum from the opposition's football. Later in the season, Arsenal began to take the ball to the corner flag in the dying minutes of matches as they learned that absorbing time is a perfectly legitimate tactic. A lesson learned too late. For all Wenger's insistence on winning with style, the history books do not record how trophies were won – just who wins them.

The night was the culmination of the annual *Las Fallas* festival in Valencia. The day before the game Peter Hill-Wood, in thanking the Valencia directors for their hospitality told them in that dry, humorous way of his, 'I didn't realise you were so keen on fireworks. I awoke in the night and thought I was in Baghdad' (the first attacks against Saddam Hussein having just been launched). After five days and nights of firecrackers, fireworks and processions, hundreds of giant effigies built in the middle of the streets at intersections of the city's grid system were to be set alight at midnight. Unfortunately, at the Mestalla Stadium Arsène Wenger had already seen his hopes go up in smoke, a bonfire of the vanities.

In 2001 Dixon, Keown, Adams and Cole did their best to protect David Seaman and took Arsenal to within fifteen minutes of a Champions League semi-final. Two years on, the combination of Lauren, a half-fit Campbell, Cygan and Touré in front of Stuart Taylor was ample demonstration that Arsenal had regressed.

As an independent observer, Trevor Brooking made the point on BBC Radio 5 Live that there was, 'a shortage in the back four, particularly when you get to this stage in the Champions League. Any side who wants to pass and play football as we want to watch it must remember it all starts with the back four.' This view was confirmed by the two clubs with the best back-lines – Milan and

Juventus – being the ones who contested the competition's final in late May at Manchester United's Old Trafford stadium.

Neither Arsenal's first-choice back-line nor their replacements were simply not good enough. The team were too reliant on a number of key players: Sol Campbell, Patrick Vieira, Robert Pires and Thierry Henry; and too much was expected of Vieira and Henry. Dennis Bergkamp was absent when needed most and none of Vieira's deputies were capable of helping him take a game by the scruff of its neck. Injuries to Cole and Keown left huge gaps that were never plugged.

Perhaps Arsène Wenger could have lined up Ray Parlour and Freddie Ljungberg at the wide points in a diamond shape, with Vieira holding and Pires the one midfielder given a free role; and one of Kanu, Wiltord or Francis Jeffers partnering Thierry Henry. Such a formation could have contained Valencia better, compensating for the weakened defence while looking more compact than the 4–4–1–1 selection fielded at the Mestalla. Such speculation would be academic had the manager addressed the issue of his defence in the first instance. Not only had he seemingly neglected it, with hindsight the sale of Matthew Upson aggravated the situation. He could argue that Arsenal were flying high at the time, but the danger signs were clear for all to see.

In the run-up to Manchester United's quarter-final with Real Madrid, Wenger claimed that Arsenal could beat the Spanish giants. It was a strange thing to say, given they could not even beat Valencia. And as shaky as Real's Hierro-led defence may have been, did he seriously believe he had the players to contain Ronaldo, Raul, Zidane and Figo? More to the point, in the unlikely event that Arsenal could beat Real, were they good enough to overcome Juventus or Milan?

It may have been Arsenal's first defeat in the group, but they should have been able to go to Spain, as Manchester United had done the night before against Deportivo La Coruna, and field half the youth team. The haul of three points from the nine available at Highbury was ultimately the real reason they found themselves once again in their customary position of being forced to salvage their season in the domestic competitions.

Attempting to rationalise his disappointment, Arsène Wenger pointed out that, 'We have had more Champions League games in the last five years than in the whole history of the club.' And reviewing what might have been he said, 'We always have this controversial situation. Does Dennis Bergkamp travel or not? It is always a big thing and affects the whole preparation for the game. And then I think maybe away from home we were a little too positive, but we didn't lose the qualification away from home, we lost it *at* home.' Reflecting on the influence of domestic concerns, he admitted, 'What I would have done differently is (how I handled) the FA Cup. We lost too much strength (in beating Manchester United). In England it is difficult because the FA Cup is very big. Even from my own players, there was pressure to play a strong team.'

Yet, a harsh critic might think that maybe Wenger doth protest too much. Bergkamp's refusal to board a plane was known from day one and anyway the manager apparently had come to the decision that whenever feasible he would select his number ten. Accordingly, he rested him along with others – most notably Henry – from the FA Cup. At the time of the crucial encounter at Old Trafford Bergkamp had his feet up at home in readiness for the forthcoming reunion with his former Dutch employers while Henry was a late second-half substitute with the result effectively done and dusted. Furthermore when Arsène Wenger said, 'You cannot win by defence alone', he may have been strictly accurate but if you don't have one of sufficient quality as both Arsenal and Real Madrid showed you will almost certainly lose and fail to achieve your target. Perhaps the spellbinding entertainment provided by Real Madrid obscured the compact solid formations which supported the supreme strikers of both Juventus and Milan, who paradoxically ended up contesting a goalless final.

At least Arsenal's continued Premiership consistency meant that they would get another chance to mix it with the big boys. Arsène Wenger issued his customary words of defiance as he swept away the bitter ashes of defeat. 'I am absolutely sure that one day we will win the Champions League. That is the one thing I have not won. But I am sure that every year we have got better and we want to do it next season. What I will say is that we had absolutely no luck this season in Europe. If you look at the number of shots we had on goal in the six matches in the second phase and the number of shots against, it is amazing.' And with a touch of revisionist thinking thrown in for good measure, he added, 'At the start of every season, for me the Premiership is the priority. And we still have that to play for as well as the FA Cup so they are two huge trophies. Naturally the players feel down and I will have to lift them. There is so much still to play for.'

In retrospect Arsenal never got to grips with the Champions League format. It is a hybrid – both league and cup – and requires a different approach at different times. Moreover, the situation is exacerbated by the staccato nature of the competition. No sooner had Arsenal got themselves into a group-stage groove than along came the winter break and they never really found the same rhythm again.

With the Champions League exit, domestic bragging rights were conveniently still up for grabs. Resting players ahead of Champions League action, and risking Vieira and Campbell in Spain revealed the expediency behind the manager's words. But the stark reality was that Arsenal, in Wenger's own words, still had much to play for: the chance to make history by becoming the first English club to accumulate consecutive league and cup doubles. If they were not up to the mark against their Continental cousins, at least they knew their way around back home, and what it took to win trophies there.

Chapter Thirteen

Slipping and Sliding

They formed a huge circle in the corner of the Old Trafford pitch nearest the away supporters and jumped up and down in celebration. Nine months after winning the title on Manchester United's home turf, the Arsenal players were once again dancing in delight after defeating their deadliest rivals. This time, they had just dumped Alex Ferguson's side out of the FA Cup, after yesterday's hero Ryan Giggs became today's villain by contriving to squander an open goal with the match scoreless. Behind closed doors Ferguson's frustration at the inept display he had been forced to endure was such that in a freak accident a boot kicked in anger split David Beckham's eyebrow. All this after their failure to come out on top in the Manchester derby the preceding weekend. Everything looked to be going the way of the north London club.

Awaiting the FA Cup draw, fans of clubs like Arsenal have two wishes uppermost in their thoughts – a home draw and avoidance of other big shots. In February 2003 their hopes were dashed on both counts as the first tie drawn out for the fifth round sent their team to Old Trafford, where they had already tasted defeat earlier in the season, in December. On that occasion United had a point to prove, not least after surrendering their title at home earlier in the year, and set about their task in the same aggressive manner which had been their undoing the last time around but on this occasion proved to be the right tactic. Even if there was a clear handball in the build-up to the first United goal in their 2–0 victory, no one from Highbury could begrudge them their superiority on the day. Even Arsène Wenger admitted, 'We cannot complain as they were more aggressive, wanted it more and won more fifty–

fifty balls.' This reverse was Arsenal's fourth league defeat, already one more than they incurred in the entire title winning campaign of 2001–02. Having smashed the records for remaining undefeated on the road and scoring in consecutive matches, as autumn turned into winter – in spite, of their manager's confident pronouncement a few weeks before that he could complete an entire league season unbowed – his team had to face up to the stark reality that they were far from invincible.

The great Liverpool team of the late 1970s and early 1980s used to say 'four and no more' in reference to the number of league defeats that could be allowed if they were to win the title. Four down already, despite not having fulfilled even half of their league fixtures, only a timely run of twelve games after the United reverse saw Arsenal remain at the top from late November until late March. Such was their consistency that one bookmaker was persuaded, with only twenty-nine of the thirty-eight fixtures completed, to pay out to those punters who had backed them to become champions. The fact that Sol Campbell had partnered Martin Keown in all but one of the twelve matches told Arsène Wenger that all was well when he could select his first-choice central defensive partnership.

Then, with the FA Cup success it appeared that a turning point in the season had been successfully negotiated. Wrong.

Although the cup exit was certainly painful (more so for Beckham), it provided the incentive for United to bounce back and restore their wounded pride, putting tremendous pressure on the leaders. Certainly when Arsenal were eight points clear of United (albeit having played an extra game) after defeating Charlton 2–0 at the beginning of March, there was some breathing space, but if they thought they had seen the back of United just because they had sent them packing from the cup they were in for a rude awakening. Alex Ferguson's side bounced back from their fifth-round defeat to secure twenty-nine Premiership points from the thirty-three available.

Arsenal had got into the habit of conceding costly goals, going in front only to see the boys at the back fail to hold on to the three points as draws were snatched from the jaws of victory. Although normally a point would have been an acceptable return from trips to St James' Park and Anfield, Arsenal were ahead and coasting before defensive errors sent jitters throughout the whole team. It was only a matter of time before the draws turned into losses.

Against Blackburn at Ewood Park, Arsène Wenger was forced to field a weakened side: Seaman, Campbell, Cole and Vieira were all missing. To add insult to this casualty list, Martin Keown lasted only eighteen minutes, leaving a back-line of Lauren, Cygan, Silva, and van Bronckhorst to protect Stuart Taylor as Arsenal turned in their worst performance of the season and Blackburn's 2–0 victory consigned them to a fifth league defeat.

Wenger might have got away with rotating his midfield and attacking options in the FA Cup. Ray Parlour would usually start on the right side of midfield while Francis Jeffers often replaced Thierry Henry up front, and Gilberto Silva gave way to his countryman Edu, but if his first-choice defenders were available, they always started. A pairing of Campbell and Keown offered solidity, but if one or other was absent, the team was handicapped before a ball had been kicked. The previous season Tony Adams, Lee Dixon and Gilles Grimandi were all on the staff. Now there were just insufficient alternatives and the defensive chickens were coming home to roost.

Despite Kolo Touré's immaturity and Giovanni van Bronckhorst's poor form, Wenger was forced into deploying one or other in the left-back role in the place of the injured Cole. Sadly, van Bronckhorst scarcely resembled the Dutch international he is, nor the player who sparkled for Rangers before his injury, which should have alerted Arsène Wenger to the likelihood that his exorbitant transfer fee of £8.5 million might not represent the best value for money. As for Pascal Cygan, he simply looked out of his depth. Wenger would surely have used the international defender he had up his sleeve to save Cygan further ignominy ... if the man in question was not Igors Stepanovs, who had been tried and found wanting. When, after the Blackburn drubbing, Wenger admitted, 'We were not completely reassuring defensively,' anyone who had travelled to watch his team could justifiably accuse the manager of understating the obvious.

The Champions League may have been in the manager's heart but the Premiership was the club's soul, its *raison d'être*. At boardroom level, there were no illusions about where the club's priorities should lie. For the directors it was a case of concentrate on the Boltons and the Barcelonas will take care of themselves. 'You have to be very careful you don't get carried away with Europe,' vice-chairman David Dein admonished. 'Europe is a cup competition. The Premiership is thirty-eight games,' and switching into culinary mode to underline his point: 'Europe must be seen as the icing on the cake. It is not the main course. The Premiership is the fans' bread and butter and you take the fans for granted at your peril. Our fans want to beat their rivals. Geographically Spurs are our closest rivals, but our hottest rivals in football terms are the contenders for the Premiership title namely, Manchester United, Liverpool, Newcastle, Chelsea. I think you start off the season wanting to be top of the domestic pile or to be precise qualify for the Champions League. The next objective is probably to win the Premiership and the third one is to go as far as you can in Europe. I always feel I want to be champions of England. If we can be champions of Europe as well, yes that's great, but not at the expense of the Premiership.'

Really? If Arsenal won the Champions League and yet finished mid-table, they would still be able to defend their title the following season as Real Madrid did in 2002–03. The Spanish giants showed where their priorities lay, by only fortuitously winning *la Liga* on the final day of the season to compensate for not being able to successfully defend their Champions League crown. But with five consecutive top two finishes, could Arsène Wenger possibly be excused for taking domestic success for granted? If he did, David Dein would understand. 'To the manager, to the coaches, to some of the players, it (the Champions League) may mean more, but I'd be amazed if Arsène said the European Cup is more important than the Premiership.' Even after two doubles? 'We want the third, the fourth, the fifth.'

A keen student of history, well Arsenal history at least, Dein knew that a prerequisite to dominating your era and creating a dynasty was the retention of your title at least. Aston Villa at the turn of the century, Arsenal under the visionary Herbert Chapman in the 1930s, and, in recent times, Liverpool and Manchester United had done so. However to win the league in consecutive seasons had proved beyond Arsenal since the Chapman era. Success at home over a nine-month campaign was arguably, and certainly according to David Dein, the true test of greatness, because over the course of a Premiership season, there is no luck of the draw, unlike Cup competitions, which is what the Champions League ultimately becomes.

The 2002–03 season presented Arsène Wenger with the opportunity to demonstrate that the triumphs of the previous season were not a blip on the radar of Old Trafford sovereignty, as the 1997–98 double had turned out to be. It was the chance to break the pattern of near misses that the Highbury public were all too familiar with.

In 2002, Arsenal had reacted to the termination of their European adventure by sustaining their impressive domestic form. A year on, and the two matches that followed the Champions League exit again saw Arsenal at their battling best, as if they were determined to prove they were still made of the right stuff. With an international weekend imminent, they were forced to play an FA Cup quarter-final replay at Chelsea only two days after entertaining Everton in the league.

The 2–1 win against Everton looked in jeopardy at one stage, as a 1–0 lead was carelessly lost. Fortunately Patrick Vieira was there to take the game by the scruff of the neck and show exactly why he was so badly missed at Blackburn. Fittingly, he scored the winner after sixty-four minutes to put his team back at the top of the table. Not far behind was the display of a substitute who at once picked up the tempo of the contest with his aggressive, wholehearted approach. That Ray Parlour entered the fray would have met with the unconditional approval of Tony Adams, and not before time he might have added.

Ten days before the Everton match, Adams expressed the view that his former room-mate should no longer be ignored. 'You need players with his grit and determination to win vital games and this is a time when Arsène will really earn his money as manager. If it was me I would certainly bring Ray Parlour in.' He felt the make-up of the midfield quartet was not complementary. 'Robert Pires and Freddie Ljungberg do not fit into the same side away from home, unless Ljungberg is playing in the Dennis Bergkamp role, as he did sometimes when he first came to Highbury. Better a man like Ray Parlour, who improves the balance of the team.'

The concept of sacrificing skill for guts and determination (and balance) poses no dilemma for Arsène Wenger. He simply won't do it unless he has to. He tends to fill the wide positions with two from Pires, Ljungberg and Wiltord. Parlour seemingly only getting a look-in if the game is not at the top of the manager's agenda, or if there are a spate of injuries. Wenger is prepared to take a chance that creativity can compensate for his dodgy defence but there appears to be no Plan B when the fancy stuff isn't working and Arsenal do not remotely resemble the solid outfit of Wenger's first double season (in which Parlour habitually appeared). In his new model, with two attacking widemen in front of full-backs who also like to advance, the bulwark is concentrated in the middle of the formation, making them vulnerable to quick breaks down the flanks.

In the past, Arsenal have had a number of hard-working midfield players such as George Armstrong, David Rocastle and Brian Marwood, who all played a key role in title wins through their willingness to work the length of the touchline in tandem with their full-backs. Although Freddie Ljungberg could perform a similar function, his tendency to drift infield, which undeniably adds to his goal threat, means he does not undertake the requisite defensive duties – Wiltord and Pires are even more dilatory – that Parlour could be relied upon to carry out.

'I like Ray Parlour,' said Wenger when quizzed at the end of the 2002–03 season about the player's limited usage. 'If you look at the number of games he missed last year, you would see that's down to injury. He was injured from September until December, and had a recurrence in January and was out nearly the whole season. That's why he didn't play so many times.' With Parlour regular selection in the FA Cup from January's fourth round onwards, the manager's words put a gloss on the harsh truth. The preferred line-ups were customarily those fielded for the Champions League, in which Parlour made a mere two entrances as a substitute.

Patrick Vieira may be a hard-working ball winner in midfield and Gilberto Silva's reliability means that possession is not often lost, but Parlour is a different type of player. No one would argue that the man possesses the finesse of some of his colleagues, but his sheer will to win is not replicated by many whose touch is surer. Occasionally, although a component in the sophisticated build-up play Arsenal often indulge in, the number 15 can look like a weak link, but his presence is justified precisely because he offers an alternative to the fantasy football, on days when the fluidity isn't coming off.

Despite his preference for vigour, George Graham was also ambivalent about Parlour. After his debut in 1992, the 'Pele from Romford' – as a former team-mate sarcastically referred to him – managed to rack up a high number of appearances, largely as a utility midfield player brought in when a preferred starter was on the treatment table. Arsène Wenger's arrival in 1996, at the same time as Tony Adams' decision to stop frequenting public houses, undoubtedly provided Parlour with the chance to shape up or be shipped out, like many of his team-mates who didn't conform to the higher standards now insisted upon, on and off the pitch.

He had his share of scandal while George Graham was in charge, with reported incidents such as letting off a fire extinguisher in a pizza restaurant. Later he admitted, 'I was probably getting in the wrong end of the papers, the front end rather than the back. Sometimes it was my own fault, going to the wrong places at the wrong time. I still enjoy socialising, but at the right time. I've got a couple of kids now. That's settled me down.' No doubt if Parlour had not curbed his ways, he would have followed the likes of John Hartson out of the door. As Wenger warned, 'You can't survive today at the top level with the physical demands if you don't have a healthy lifestyle.'

Parlour was shrewd enough to realise his career was at a cross-roads. 'When he (Wenger) came to Arsenal, he made it quite clear that everyone had a chance. He gave me encouragement. I thought, "Well, this is my last chance" because I had been in and out of the team. Some people were getting fed up with me not doing the business, saying that I wasn't good enough for a big club like Arsenal. It was up to me to prove them wrong.'

Reward for his recently acquired conscientiousness came in the summer of 1997, when the departure of Paul Merson, allied to the arrival of Marc Overmars and a switch to a 4–4–2 formation, ensured Parlour a coveted and undisputed starting spot. His potency was undoubtedly aided by his midfield colleagues. The balance of the 1997–98 midfield composition was just about perfect. Centrally, Emmanuel Petit provided both invention and forcefulness to complement the physical presence of Vieira, while the willing Parlour, wide right, enabled a better balance to be struck.

Parlour's progress led to international recognition. Having played his way into Glenn Hoddle's England squad, he (reputedly) scuppered his chances when during a session with the national coach's faith-healing guru Eileen Drewery, he requested a 'short back and sides' when her hands made contact with his head. Understandably, for Parlour who socialised with fellow-Essex lad Tony Adams in bygone days, the journey from bottled spirits to spirituality was a step too far. Happily, when Kevin Keegan succeeded Hoddle, the slate was wiped clean and he went on to represent his country on ten occasions.

When Marc Overmars left in 2000, the arrivals of Robert Pires and Sylvain Wiltord, combined with Freddie Ljungberg, and subsequently Gilberto Silva presented Arsène Wenger with other midfield options. Despite being marginalised, the 'Romford Rocket' has never publicly complained about his treatment, although the fans have often taken the manager to task on his behalf.

Parlour's popularity is largely down to his never-say-die attitude. The chant of 'Ooh Aah Ray Parlour' doesn't usually do him justice as a more accurate reflection of Parlour's style should be an 'ouch' as no quarter is given when he goes into a challenge. His aim in front of goal is inconsistent to say the least, but he has scored a few long-range belters in his time, even recording a couple of hat-tricks. His perceived lack of ability to threaten the opposition goalkeeper was turned on its head during the 2002 FA Cup final against Chelsea. Sky Sports broadcast the match with a 'Fanzone' commentary option for digital subscribers. Two celebrity fans had the microphones, and Soccer AM's Tim Lovejoy represented the Stamford Bridge side. With no score, Parlour was in possession in the Chelsea half and heading goalward. 'It's only Ray Parlour,' said Lovejoy expressing his lack of concern at the prospect of danger. A second later a blistering strike was unleashed into the top corner of the goal that astonished Arsenal fans as much as the crestfallen Lovejoy, whose words have come back to haunt him as he now has to endure the taunting of Arsenal fans whenever their paths cross.

Arsenal's strength through the middle has rarely allowed the uncomplaining team man to play his favoured role. 'I would prefer to be playing in the middle (where he began his professional career) because I think that's my best position,' he says. 'I can do a job on the right but, ideally, that is not where I would want to be. You can find yourself missing a lot of the match out there and I prefer the constant pressure of being in the middle, fighting for the ball. It keeps you sharp.' Whether covering for a wide right or central position, if Ray is only to be used as a reserve, at least the helping hand he offers is more reliable than the ones available for any other position. In a sense, Parlour's plight personifies the area where the manager is most often criticised: neglecting home-grown talent and English players in general. In 2002–03, men from that background were way down the pecking order behind the overseas personnel.

Probed about his preference for overseas talent, Arsène Wenger claims, 'I favour skill. I don't look at the passport. Because there are as many players who want to win in France as in England. Just look at what England wins and what France wins and you see that France wants to win as much. When did England last win something?' Which explains why he finds the quality he seeks on his travels and the evidence of his predilections points to a lack of belief in his British options with the notable exceptions of Seaman, Campbell and Cole. Unlike Parlour, Francis Jeffers, Matthew Upson, Stuart Taylor and Jermaine Pennant, players such as Sylvain Wiltord, Pascal Cygan, Rami Shabaan and Kolo Touré all enjoyed extended runs during the course of the season, despite their form sometimes not warranting selection.

Soon after arriving at Highbury in 1996, Wenger confronted the economic issue that was encroaching on his freedom of choice. 'The danger is that foreign players will outnumber the English,' he warned. 'Every manager in the league will tell you that a Continental player costs half an English player and the salaries are the same. If you project ten years into the future, the best teams in England will play with seven or eight foreign players. That means English football will suffer.' Yet he did buy British – Jeffers, Upson and Pennant – presumably in the belief that he was getting value for money. Which destroys the theory that he has to justify his Continental purchases by picking them, yet leaves

173

the question unanswered: why doesn't he do likewise with his Brits?

Two days after Everton were overcome, more of the same fighting spirit was needed in the quarter-final replay away to Chelsea, and for once, the squad rotation was fully justified considering the short timeframe between the fixtures. All the cup regulars – Parlour, Jeffers, Edu and Kolo Touré – along with Sylvain Wiltord were there. Strangely, despite carrying an injury, Patrick Vieira was not rested, and his contribution was immense, a *tour de force*, as Arsenal stormed to the semi-finals with a performance that mixed skill and aggression in equal measure. Even being reduced to ten men with Cygan's dismissal for two yellow cards did not unduly disturb their serenity.

The Champions League had ended in disaster, but within a week, it seemed as if they were back on course to repeat their double triumph of the year before. The Everton and Chelsea matches had pointed to the reality that the early season pretty play would have to be liberally spiced with extra doses of grit and determination. But the two wins could not hide the fact that the captain was carrying an injury, Parlour was not an automatic choice, and the defence was still suspect.

On the same day Arsenal had been overwhelmed at Blackburn, Manchester United had stolen away from Villa Park with a 1–0 victory in their pocket. No one covered themselves in glory, but a solitary goal was sufficient. United battled their way in front and held on to the bitter end. Three weeks later, Arsenal also took the lead against Villa, but unlike United conceded a soft own goal by left-back Kolo Touré, who sliced what should have been a routine goal-line clearance. Ashley Cole's six-week absence was coming to an end and he was on the bench. Arsène Wenger must have wished he was on the pitch. At the end of the campaign, Wenger surmised, 'I thought we were weaker this year on the left-back position than in the centre-back position, because when Cole was out, we lost the Champions League and we lost points in the championship, especially in games like Blackburn with no left-back.' A case of no Cole, no cover. Yet the recently departed left-footed Upson had played in Cole's position three times in the preceding Premiership campaign, never looking the liability that both van Bronckhorst and Kolo

Touré appeared to be. Moreover, Wenger had even fielded Upson in pre-season friendlies while Cole enjoyed an extended post-World Cup break, so he was in theory well aware of the player's versatility, but had deemed him expendable and now the cupboard was bare.

The following weekend Arsenal again played poorly in edging out Sheffield United at Old Trafford in the FA Cup semi-final. The confrontation was a battle, ugly on the eye, although with the first-choice back five, allied to the staunchness shown by Vieira, Parlour and Ljungberg in midfield, the day was carried ... just. Seaman pulled off a wonder save to preserve the 1–0 lead and remind his critics that he was still capable of match-saving deeds on his day.

In the Premiership however, Arsenal were like a stalled car watching the vehicle in the next lane inevitably overtake them before they could get going once again. Having clawed back an eight-point deficit courtesy of winning a game in hand and seeing the holders drop five points at Blackburn and Villa, as Arsenal were pre-occupied with their semi-final, United took a three-point lead, annihilating Newcastle 6–2 at St James' Park. It was a remarkable display, an emphatic reaction to their 3–1 Champions League first leg quarter-final setback in Madrid.

Next up, as the season was coming inexorably to a climax, was a head-to-head clash that set up United's visit to Highbury as a potential title decider. It was a mere two months since the Arsenal players had performed their jigs of joy at Old Trafford in the aftermath of their cup win, and yet so much had changed. Having delivered what at the time appeared to be a knockout blow to the chief obstacle to retaining their trophies, Arsène Wenger's side were now playing catch-up. Reversing the early season scenario, Arsenal were now stuttering while United were swaggering.

Yet, three points at home would allow them the luxury of drawing one of their remaining five matches even if United took the maximum available points. For once, Arsène Wenger was able to field a full complement of outfield players (Stuart Taylor was in goal), but Patrick Vieira only lasted thirty-four minutes. It was to be his final appearance of the season as his injured knee could take no more. By the time he limped off, obviously having been limited in the extent of his contribution, the visitors were one up courtesy of a virtuoso strike from van Nistelrooy capitalising on a Campbell slip.

After the interval, Arsenal refused to lie down and exploited the rub of the green with a brace of Henry goals. The first, a fortunate deflection from an Ashley Cole strike, and the second after racing through from an offside position to a pass from Gilberto Silva. One-nil down, 2–1 up, a throwback to the typical resilience of the Graham era, so much so that the scoreline gave its name to a (now defunct) fanzine. But times change. The seconds that followed were a microcosm of Arsenal's season. They thought all the hard work had been done. Still buzzing with elation they relaxed and allowed Ole Gunnar Solskjaer to cross into the heart of their penalty area. Only Martin Keown had stayed focused during the celebration of Henry's goal, but his pleas to his team-mates to concentrate went unheeded and Ryan Giggs rose unchallenged to head home the equaliser.

Although not out of the race, the opportunity to put themselves back in the lead had been frittered away. But the bad news didn't stop there. Bringing the ball out of defence, Sol Campbell flung an arm out to ward off Solskjaer's challenge and caught the United forward in the face. Although replays showed minimal contact, the sighting the match officials had of the incident looked conclusive enough for Campbell to be issued with an immediate red card (the forty-ninth of Wenger's reign). It meant a four-match ban (the consequence of his second dismissal of the season) that would prevent the defender, along with Vieira from lining up for the concluding league matches *and* the FA Cup final. When Alex Ferguson celebrated on the Highbury pitch at the conclusion of proceedings he had good cause. Arsenal complained bitterly about the sending-off, yet the bottom line was that the decision was right. If a West Brom player had committed the offence there would have been no controversy. Campbell's fame and the ensuing repercussions made it into a major issue.

Campbell's dismissal had been the fifth that had befallen Arsenal in 2002–03. In the four previous seasons, the campaign that had witnessed the greatest number of sendings off (twelve in 2001–02) was also the only one that had seen Wenger's team win any prizes. The red cards perhaps give a clue as to the greater determination and attitude of the players, and without the edge (and accompanying desire to beat the odds with their backs to the wall) provided by being reduced to ten men, maybe something was missing from Arsenal's make-up. It was almost as if they needed kick-starting by the officials. Accordingly, Campbell's exit against United spurred his colleagues to have the best remaining chance in the contest, although Henry's snap shot was saved by Fabien Barthez.

The result left Arsenal with absolutely no leeway and the stakes were upped. Yet despite United's apparently easier run-in, Wenger refused to be downcast, telling himself 'you must recover from disappointments.' His words were tested right away and the team came up trumps by going to Middlesbrough, who boasted an impressive home record, and walking away with a 2–0 win. A week later at Bolton, another day, another must-win situation looked to be at hand as after the interval Arsenal stormed into a 2–0 lead with goals from Wiltord and Pires. It looked like a replication of events almost exactly a year previously when they carried the day by the same scoreline to put them within touching distance of the championship. This time though, there was a sting in the tale. In 2002 Bolton were safe from relegation, now it was a case of desperate times and desperate challenges which cost Arsenal dear. Injuries suffered by Ljungberg, Cygan and Lauren in a short spell in the second half resulted in a succession of defensive permutations which destroyed the equilibrium of the side. And Arsenal pressed the panic button. Bolton's first goal came from Oleg Luzhny's careless clearance after needlessly conceding a corner. The fall guy for the equaliser was Martin Keown, who had only just entered the fray, and got his head in the way of a Yuri Djorkaeff free-kick to deflect the ball past David Seaman with just six minutes remaining.

Arsène Wenger was incandescent with rage on the touchline as another two points slid away. Some weeks afterwards, he explained his anger, saying, 'They slaughtered Ljungberg without the referee reacting. For me it was a disgrace. We lost three players in five minutes at Bolton where we basically lost the championship. It was the decisive moment (in the league campaign).' No could really disagree.

Tony Adams reflected on the situation his old club faced as Bolton strained every last sinew in search of a point. 'I really wished I could have been in the thick of it, defending a one-goal lead, I always loved that,' he said. 'Of course my knees and ankles wouldn't have been up to it – it's a struggle to jog fifty yards these days – but the spirit was there.' In 2002, Adams was there in spirit and body as the defence held firm in one tough battle after another to bring Arsenal the double. Now he was watching on television. By the time Arsenal played again, United were eight points clear with one match remaining, leaving them needing three wins out of three and hoping United failed to beat Everton at Goodison Park on the final day.

While United had enjoyed strolls in the sunshine to defeat Tottenham and Charlton, two teams with only the not to be neglected Premiership prize money of £503,000 per place to play for, Arsenal were pitted against Leeds, surprising relegation candidates after months of self-imposed turmoil. The Gunners' misfortune in conceding three goals (one following a blatant handball, while the winner two minutes from time was probably offside) was compounded by hitting the woodwork several times in the 3–2 defeat. It simply wasn't their day. They made a fist of it though, despite being undermined by injuries and suspensions with Vieira, Lauren and Campbell all absent and spiritedly twice coming from behind to draw level. But the indiscipline in defence was alarming, underlining the missing magnitude of Campbell, now beginning his four-match suspension. Either side could have added to the total, and a marvellously dramatic afternoon ended with Arsenal, despite Arsène Wenger insisting otherwise, confirmed as the second-best team in the country. All that remained was the possible consolation of an FA Cup final to ensure they didn't finish entirely empty handed.

Since being eight points clear at the top at the beginning of March, Arsenal had gleaned a negligible nine Premiership points from a possible twenty-one. Over the season they threw away sixteen by losing or drawing games in which they took the lead with any number of culprits to shoulder the blame. The same carelessness against Ajax, Roma and Valencia put paid to their European hopes. Wenger later reflected, 'I think there were two reasons we lost the championship. We dropped our level a little bit in the second phase after we went out of the Champions League because it was a big blow, and it is always more difficult mentally when you see somebody's coming back. And I think as well we have been badly done in the last ten games – it was everything against us.' Certainly, the loss of Patrick Vieira and key defenders – all of the first-choice back four were casualties or suspended at one time or other – meant that from February onwards, only once was the same line-up fielded in successive matches. Unfamiliarity breeding disharmony amongst the ranks.

'One–nil to the Arsenal' became less of a chant of celebration, more a cause for concern, an invitation to opponents to exploit the rearguard collywobbles! On the other hand it seemed far-fetched to blame the European exit. A year ago Arsenal bounced back from their early elimination (and by now they'd surely become accustomed to it) and, anyway, the two matches that immediately followed the Valencia debacle showed they were still on-track to retain their trophies. In citing Europe, the crestfallen manager in fact betrayed his own obsession, which perhaps trans-mitted itself to the players.

The defensive deficiencies of Arsenal's style were camouflaged in the 2002 double win because the squad had enough quality in depth to compensate for injuries and suspensions. The retirements of the summer and Wenger's limited spending power changed all that. Gilberto Silva was bought to stiffen the midfield but further back (Campbell's salary excepted) there was the distinct feeling of looking for bargain basement buys, with the most expensive defensive purchase of the current squad being the £2 million Pascal Cygan. Then there was the folly of selling Matthew Upson, although in mitigation Wenger says, 'You know when you make these kind of decisions, that there is a financial involvement first of all.' What wasn't appreciated at the time was the paltry budget, due to the voracious demands of the new stadium, that the manager had to play with.

Arsenal finished ten points clear of Manchester United in 2002. A year later they trailed them by five points. Wenger admitted that, 'in the last ten, eleven games nerves played a part.' It is no wonder when players are fielded who cannot be relied upon to do the job asked of them. Belatedly the manager is facing up to his problems, 'The art is to have a balanced team that is always dangerous offensively and can defend well. The teams who can do both are great teams, but it's very difficult to find and very difficult to get tuned in because we scored this season eighty-five goals and conceded forty-two. That's ten too many.' Already, he is looking ahead, 'Our number-one priority is to come back stronger and that means we want to defend better as a team. It could be that we sign one or two defenders but there's no revolution needed.'

The centre-back crisis threatened to sabotage the cup final against Southampton too. With Campbell suspended, Cygan definitely out injured, and Keown and Luzhny on the treatment table, Igors Stepanovs was given the last two Premiership matches to attempt to establish some kind of match fitness as insurance, while the fans scoured the squad to come up with permutations involving Stathis Tavlaridis, Kolo Touré or Gilberto Silva lining up alongside Stepanovs. Fortunately, Keown and Luzhny were passed fit on the day, and both turned in heroic performances – Luzhny in what transpired to be his final appearance in an Arsenal shirt. Psychologically, the cup took on huge significance, as to finish the season empty-handed would have been scant reward for the marvellous entertainment provided. A victory would also put an end to the abortive seasons after being crowned champions, a pattern that stretched all the way back to the Herbert Chapman era.

Arsenal dominated the match, with the winner coming from Robert Pires after a build-up featuring Henry, Bergkamp and Ljungberg. Once again they failed to kill off the opposition and had to thank Ashley Cole's late goal-line clearance for preventing extra-time. The celebrations at the end were indicative of the importance the trophy had assumed; the besuited Campbell and Vieira jumping around as if they had just secured their first ever medal. It proved to be stand-in skipper David Seaman's last game for Arsenal, and it was fitting that he and club captain Vieira raised the trophy together.

It was apt that Pires should score the winning goal, having missed the last year's bonanza due to his convalescence from cruciate ligament surgery. The following week he flew to London from the Côte d'Azur to participate in the Premiership title ceremony. His contribution was acknowledged by a 'we are not worthy' bow from his colleagues as he took his turn to lift the trophy. It was a special tribute that showed how highly Pires was rated by his peers.

Arsenal's starting line-up against Southampton featured both Ray Parlour and Robert Pires. The performance was proof that their two very different styles could be complementary, although Arsène Wenger would admit it is Pires that represents everything he would want from an attacking midfield player and he returns the appreciation by committing himself to the manager. But there is no deep bond with Arsenal. He is happy at Highbury, but it is only a job and unlike Ashley Cole and the famous five, Pires is just passing through. He has not made the same effort to integrate into the English way unlike Thierry Henry and Patrick Vieira who have more reason to stay around, having established long-term relationships with partners met on these shores, and whose command of the language is far better. Pires prefers to conduct his interviews in his native tongue, despite living in London for three years.

There is no illusion about the man's love for Arsenal. Arsène Wenger's presence in the manager's office is above all a key to his remaining at the club. 'If we French players are here, it is because Arsène Wenger came and got us,' he says, 'and knowing that we will be coached by a French coach is an immediate advantage. If Arsène Wenger left Arsenal tomorrow, I think I'd probably do the same thing because he brought me to the club. If another coach follows with a different culture, a different way of playing, the French players certainly wouldn't like it. The style cannot be changed. The others might stay, but I think we French players wouldn't go along with it.'

Pires is frank and honest. He is friendly and accessible and his opinions are widely canvassed back home without any of the ballyhoo of the British media. Unfortunately, when the tabloids get hold of this material, he is painted as a stirrer, trying to rock the boat, and can come across as disloyal and self-serving when he is simply voicing his views without pretence, speaking from the heart, although he has not declared his love for Arsenal in the way that Henry and Vieira have. Any unfavourable impression the media might have conveyed would be contradicted in an instant by meeting him.

In his *Times* column, comedian Frank Skinner relayed his

encounter with Pires. A car stopped to allow him to traverse a zebra crossing. Realising the man behind the wheel was Robert Pires, Skinner gave him a thumbs-up greeting. Pires looked at him quizzically for an instant, before returning the gesture. It is unlikely the Arsenal man had any notion of who he was signalling to, but rather than be aloof he acknowledged a friendly moment. Despite never having spoken to him, Skinner now considers Pires 'my mate'.

A more pertinent example of his willingness to send out the right signals was a book-signing he undertook at Sportspages bookshop to promote his autobiography, *Footballeur*. Scheduled to sign for an hour, Pires stayed late into the night, to ensure that those in the queue which snaked some distance down the Charing Cross Road had not waited in vain. However, there were still copies to be signed for people who had not been able to make the event in person, so he agreed to sign another batch and one of the bookshop's staff brought them to his favourite coffee house in Hampstead.

If the man with the trademark goatee strip (which he reputedly cannot shave off until a certain sponsorship contract expires), does choose to remain at Highbury, one of the reasons might be his contentment with his lifestyle in London. His home in Regent's Park is close enough to his Hampstead-based colleagues Vieira, Henry and Wiltord for him to see them socially and he often shares a nosh with Henry at an unostentatious local noodle bar. 'I choose to live in the centre of town because everything is accessible,' he explains. 'I can go shopping at Selfridges and Harvey Nichols without being molested. People recognise me but leave me in peace.' Although Tottenham fans might have good reason to be antagonistic towards someone who frequently scores against them, he says, 'I have met them and they have been okay. They admit Arsenal are better than Tottenham, and there is respect for me as an individual.' No wonder, for Pires is exactly the type of 'flair player' Spurs fans have not been able to cheer since David Ginola said *adieu*. When he says, 'There are lots of things to discover in London, but with games every three or four days I have to prioritise football,' it could be his manager speaking.

Initially he didn't find it easy to settle. It took him a few months on the field to reveal his full potential; while off it, he was relieved to be amongst friends. 'What saved me on arriving was that Thierry, Patrick and Gilles (Grimandi) helped me to adapt.' Although it helped him acclimatise, the large Gallic contingent at Highbury is probably the reason he has not tried too hard to learn English. It would be a mistake though to interpret this as any lack of intelligence. He broadcasts a weekly radio show in France from his London base, often featuring guests from outside football, and discussing matters cultural and political as well as sporting. He keeps informed of events back home via the French channels he can pick up on satellite, although *Jour De Foot*, Canal Plus' weekly review programme is the only football he watches regularly on television. 'Football is nothing compared to the world situation,' he states. 'Real news is not football.'

Along with other entertainers, Pires spoke out against political right-winger Jean-Marie Le Pen because he feels, 'a country which has freedom of expression cannot be governed by the extreme right.' He continues: 'It was the natural thing to do. In 1998 (when a French team of diverse ethnic origins won the World Cup) there was much emotion, good images of people mixing, with sport the catalyst. Four years later, people have quickly forgotten.' Pires' status in France was reflected by a phone call from Prime Minister Lionel Jospin to wish him well after his cruciate ligament injury forced him to withdraw from the 2002 World Cup Finals. His wife Nathalie took the call, and believed it to be a set-up when the voice on the other end informed her it was the Prime Minister's office. Nevertheless she passed the number on to her husband, who subsequently chatted with Jospin. He also received a telegram from President Jacques Chirac wishing him well.

His laborious recovery has so far prevented him touching the heights he reached in the double season. Although, despite featuring less, he notched sixteen goals, three more than in 2001–02. If Pires is not at Highbury for the long haul, one consolation for the fans may be that the team was most effective early on while awaiting his return. Although a guaranteed starter, perhaps the number seven is not as vital as Vieira or Henry to Wenger's plans, however easy on the eye he might be. The word that best describes Pires in possession is 'elegant'. Despite the skill required to beat players, he makes it look effortless, the mark of a great player.

He is not an orthodox winger in the sense that Marc Overmars is. Although his gait can be deceptive – his shuffling run belies his speed – he rarely takes the ball down the line in the way that Thierry Henry does before cutting in. Pires prefers to drift inward and link up with his forwards using sharp one-touch passing. His value to the side, like Henry's is measured not only in goals, but assists. His minus points are his evident petulance and willingness to become involved in on-field feuds, allied to an occasional propensity to lose his footing rather too easily in an attempt to win penalties and free-kicks (and because he is from foreign parts in a successful team dominated by his compatriots, he is labelled a 'diver' by the British media whereas the likes of Michael Owen or Alan Shearer are never accused in the same way).

When David Dein enters the dressing room before matches to wish every player good luck, it brings back memories to Pires of his time at Metz. There, the president Carlo Molinari would ritually shake every player by the hand and tell them all, '*Si on veut, on peut*' (if you want it, you can do it). 'That phrase summarises many things,' Pires reflects. 'The attitude, the solidarity of a group, its force of character. In terms of Arsenal, that's what we are trying to do and David Dein does the same thing.'

It is a testimony to Pires' commitment that although he has expressed the importance of playing for Wenger and gives him his wholehearted support, he had no compunction about carrying out his job in the same way for Rolland Courbis, whose approach was far more akin to that of Alex Ferguson's than Arsène Wenger. 'Rolland Courbis could coach an English team because he knows and loves his job, and has lots of ideas. He loves the players and is the first to defend them. I got on with him okay and he made me captain at Marseille. We had a good relationship and still do today even though he is not my coach.'

Pires is an unusual man, refusing to shift blame for a drop in his standards – along with a number of high-profile colleagues he underperformed at the Stade Velodrome – seemingly bearing no grudges and not on a personal ego trip. So when he said at the end of April, 'I would like to know what are the ambitions of the club for the next season and the season after because the way we played in the Champions League showed we need two more players,' perhaps it was less of a signal that he sought a move than a hint to the board that they were not going to achieve success without some serious investment.

To be sure, the Champions League matters as much to Pires as it does to his coach. Not being a one-club man, or having grown up in the English game he is less concerned with shifts in the balance of power in his adopted country than adding a European Cup winner's medal to his already impressive collection. And if Arsenal are not in a position to be serious contenders, there are certainly others who are and make no secret of coveting the player. Maybe, deep down, Pires regrets choosing Highbury over Real Madrid in the summer of 2000, although he may not have flourished in the same way at the Bernabeu, without Wenger's touch and, consequently, may not even have held down a starting place. In querying the transfer policy as a consequence of European deception, Pires was echoing the disquieting words Patrick Vieira had uttered two years before in similar circumstances. On one level, unhappily, it appeared nothing had changed.

But on another, so much had; and for the worse. Arsenal's financial state was now a lot more precarious with far less spending power. A £25 million annual profit had been turned into a £20 million loss during the double season. Could the miracle worker make bricks without straw? Apart from persuading Vieira and Pires to sign contract extensions, he needs funds to be able to strengthen the squad so that the errors of 2002–03 are not repeated. The question was, could the directors afford to back him?

Chapter Fourteen

Money, Money, Money

As Arsenal's 2002–03 season reached its anticlimax, a stone's throw from their Highbury headquarters, all was quiet. Whereas a few weeks earlier construction workers had been 'busy bees' preparing the foundations at Ashburton Grove for a new 60,000-seater stadium, now tools had been downed and no one expected to see any more activity for a few months. Overtaken by Manchester United on the field, home games saw Arsenal slipping further and further behind their *bête noire* to the tune of over a million pounds each matchday. More than the difference in cost over the course of a season, between a Rio Ferdinand and a Pascal Cygan. Arsène Wenger had already performed over and above the call of duty in his six-and-a-half-years tenure. Until Arsenal can move into their new home, he will be asked to raise his sights . . . again.

Football was already in the process of mutation when the new Arsenal coach arrived in England in 1996. In the ensuing years the transformation from sport to business has accelerated with no hint of a brake pedal in sight. Although recently admitted to the G14 group of European super clubs (described by David Dein as 'a talking shop which acts as a pressure point on UEFA and FIFA'), the real elite Arsenal want to join are the seven mega clubs – Manchester United, Real Madrid, Barcelona, Juventus, Milan, Internazionale and Bayern Munich. A magnificent seven with whom they are simply unable to compete with in terms of existing wealth and earning potential.

In the days when chairman Peter Hill-Wood's father Denis ruled the boardroom, football was purely a sport. Clubs were often owned by family concerns and chairmen were only household names in their own home unless they became leading lights of the Football Association or the Football League. Although the removal of the maximum wage back in the 1960s gave the players a comfortable lifestyle comparable to their white-collar executives, the only financial aspects that really raised an eyebrow were transfer fees.

In 2003, Peter Hill-Wood is overseeing a very different club to the one he inherited from his father in the early 1980s. The annual turnover of the twenty Premiership clubs is over £1 billion. And yet in the latest six-month figures released, covering the period up to the turn of the year 2002–03, only Manchester United, Newcastle and Birmingham City were making any real money. Although in Birmingham's attempt to retain its Premiership status, this may only be a temporary state of affairs for the Midlands club. Football is now very much a business and in most cases a very badly run business. The combined pre-tax losses for over half their number were around £100 million. Arsenal lost nearly £10 million in half a season despite a substantial rise in turnover producing £44 million in income. Why?

Cost control is evidently an alien concept to most football club directors, the current malaise indicative of the financial imprudence by those in charge. Everyone in the Premiership budgets for success, only the interpretation is different. For four clubs – Arsenal, Manchester United, Chelsea and Liverpool – Champions League qualification is a must; for Aston Villa and Tottenham a UEFA Cup place is the height of their ambition; while for Bolton and Fulham relegation is to be avoided at all cost. And there is the rub. The answer is the same for everyone: spend money on players' salaries and transfers.

With many clubs desperately searching for their own version of success, overheads have spiralled out of control. Wages to turnover ratios of more than 70 per cent are not sustainable. Unless there is philanthropic backing from multimillionaires such as Mohammed Al-Fayed at Fulham; Blackburn's Jack Walker, whose trust fund has continued to bankroll the club since his death; and most recently Roman Abramovich, who wiped out Chelsea's debts instantaneously. For example, Wimbledon, in a futile attempt to avoid relegation in 2000, actually had a larger wage bill than their entire income.

The downside of spending so much on the players is that there is an element of speculation involved. With Premiership prize money increasing by £503,000 per position in 2003, the difference between eighth and thirteenth place in the table might only be a couple of points, but is in effect worth £3 million in income! Enough to pay the annual salaries of three international footballers.

Everyone is gambling and the problems faced by Leeds United show what can happen if Macbeth-like ambition takes hold. Significant sums were spent on financing a strong squad as the club saw themselves as regular diners at Europe's top table. With Manchester United and Arsenal consistently outperforming the competition, there was only one, or, from 2002 two further Champions League places up for grabs. This meant that Leeds were tempting providence by assuming they could finish above Liverpool, Newcastle and Chelsea on a regular basis.

As they overspent with no commensurate success after their 2001 exploits when they reached the Champions League semi-final, their subsequent hubris ensured debts mounted at such an alarming rate that a fire sale of players – their only disposable assets – looked to be their only means of survival. The annual turnover of an average Premier League club is more than £55 million, that of a Division One club is under £15 million. How the mighty might have fallen if they had not pipped Arsenal at the eleventh hour and earned themselves a stay of execution.

The lesson of Leeds is that clubs should be aware of their station in life and keep the dream factor within bounds. In the financial pecking order, Arsenal are below Liverpool, Newcastle and Chelsea, yet they consistently outperform them, mainly because Arsène Wenger is their manager. The championships, cup wins and Champions League places have all been achieved for less than the price Alex Ferguson paid for Rio Ferdinand. It is not Wenger's fault Arsenal are now facing a whopping debt.

Arsenal's turnover is derived from three key sources. Television may provide nearly half of their annual income for 2003–04. The current Premiership television contract is in its third and final year, and the deals for live matches, pay-per-view games and highlights, last season brought the club nearly £40 million from their league outings in domestic and overseas rights sales. Additionally, television payments from UEFA should increase this amount to around £50 million. And all the money comes with no strings attached. No overheads, it goes straight to the bottom line and the temptation is to send it straight out again in the quest for success.

The second source of revenue are commercial contracts comprising sponsorship, advertising and merchandising. The club have done good deals with Nike, O_2 and Granada in this light, although the joint venture with Granada of £20 million for new media rights and the sale of a 5% stake in the club's equity, subsequently increased to 9.9%, for a total of more than £70 million indicates that Arsenal know their price rather than their true value.

Though Arsenal may have received more money for their media partnership with Granada than anybody else bar Manchester United, by so doing they may have been guided more by the need for short-term cash rather than sticking to a long-term strategy. While Manchester United can justifiably claim that they are 'not just a football club ... a global brand', Arsenal can look on only with dismay as United conclude a ground-breaking deal which sees Arsenal's kit supplier Nike take control of their rivals' worldwide merchandising operation in a guaranteed £303 million thirteen-year deal, outdistancing their own £130 million ten-year accord. Furthermore, so far, Arsenal have not been able to benefit in the same manner as Manchester United, who have made arrangements with a number of sponsors, such as Pepsi and Ladbrokes who are the official soft drinks supplier and betting partner respectively.

Striking a number of secondary partnerships have permitted United the luxury of foregoing the temptation of selling the naming rights to their stadium, to their credit and long-term marketing advantage. 'The Theatre of Dreams' has become an integral part of their brand. If they played in the 'Nike Stadium' they would be guilty of shortchanging themselves, undermining their own value.

Unfortunately, Arsenal may not have the luxury of being able to decline a million-pound offer to sell their birthright. Highbury is Arsenal and Arsenal is Highbury. The chances of Ashburton Grove contributing in like manner to a regenerated brand will be circumscribed if someone else has got their name on the new home at the reported cost of only £2.5 million per year.

Arsenal might just as well play at Wembley and save themselves a fortune, for all the contribution the 'Something' Ashburton Grove will make to their long-term brand value. Moreover, Arsenal's cashflow is not helped by additional income from Granada being contingent on the doors of the new stadium being thrown open. By the terms of the agreement, Arsenal may have shared their brand identity with a third party who may not share their values when they try to recoup much of their outlay. One result is that Granada have a cut of licensing revenue.

So, when the DVD and VHS *Centurions* that celebrates the 100 goals scored for the club by Thierry Henry and Dennis Bergkamp had still not been released some six months after the event it purports to celebrate – both players achieving the feat early in 2003 – someone has not been keeping their eye on the commercial ball, With Bergkamp's contract negotiations not going smoothly in the summer, there was even the possibility that one of the video's co-stars might have left the staff by the time of its release.

Another lost opportunity concerns the demand for new replica kits not being adequately catered for. Initially the kits are rarely on sale until the end of the summer, when a more astute move would see them available at the end of the season. What better opportunity to launch the new model than at the cup final when more people watch Arsenal than at any other time, Champions League included. And then finally, once they are available, the most popular sizes often sell out. Anyone wanting to buy an adult-sized shirt between January and the end of the season will often be disappointed. Would the same situation exist if Arsenal employed Manchester United's former director of merchandising, Edward Freedman, who in the nineties increased the club's annual turn-over in merchandising from £2 million to over £23 million?

A product is made in a factory. A brand is bought by the consumer – the customer. Football clubs have high potential as brands because fans are different from customers. A customer can take his business elsewhere but most fans remain loyal to 'the product' even when it fails them and performs disastrously, in the most extreme case suffering relegation. A commitment any commercial organisation would give their right arm for. Arsenal director Daniel Fiszman maintains, 'We are conscious we have to look after the brand.' But their custody gives cause for concern.

A successful team is a *sine qua non* to a successful brand. By any but the highest criterion Arsenal fulfil that requirement.

However, expectations have been raised and have not been fulfilled on and off the field. Champions League failures and running second to Manchester United may on any objective criteria be overperforming, but the customer does not use rational measures to evaluate his level of satisfaction in this industry. More and more loyal users of the brand are failing to be accommodated and those that are, are being asked to fork out an increasingly high price for the privilege. And if they don't like it then unfortunately it's just too bad, the club need the money and there are plenty waiting outside prepared to pay.

In the meantime, it is debatable whether, despite the quality of the entertainment on offer, the club are giving their customers optimum value for money. Are they being asked to put up with too much and pay too much?

Matchday income – gate receipts, season tickets, corporate hospitality, programmes and catering – provides the third source of revenue. The potential earnings are obviously drastically limited by the capacity of Highbury. Over the six months ending 30 November 2002 for Arsenal, and 31 January 2003 for United, the latter took a massive £43 million from matchday revenue alone, a mere £600,000 less than Arsenal's *total* turnover. The lack of corporate hospitality is especially costly as this type of spectator is predictably by far the biggest spender. The current stadium has fifty-six hospitality boxes and executive seats accommodating 1,100 people, compared with United's 5,765. The plans for Ashburton Grove will see the numbers swell to 7,000. Initial ideas to increase the capacity at Highbury by redeveloping the Clock End and filling in the corners (45,000 seats was the projected target), were dropped due to a combination of local opposition, the realisation that 45,000 would still not cater for the demand, and the knowledge that only a limited amount of additional corporate places could be made available.

Vice-chairman David Dein confesses, 'Staying at Highbury wasn't an option because we have to get at least 60,000 people to generate the revenue we need and give more fans a chance to see the team.' The use of Wembley for Champions League matches in the late 1990s clearly established that the club had outgrown their home, with every one of their six fixtures undertaken a sellout. 'When we were at Wembley and played AIK Solna – who brought a man and a dog with them – there were 73,000 Arsenal fans in the stadium,' Dein recalls. 'Why? Because we had 20,000 seats at £10. We simply have to have a bigger stadium.' There is little doubt that supporters would fill a new stadium in the same way, even if the tickets were twice the price.

The site at Ashburton Grove only came to light after some fans, looking at plans of the area in the course of their work, alerted the club to the possibilities: sufficient available land, with no residential housing in the immediate vicinity encroaching on it. However, although the green light for a 60,000-seat stadium was given by Islington Council in December 2001, the move-in date has been put back twice, and currently stands at August 2006. By the time the stadium is up and running Arsenal will have fallen behind Manchester United a further £200 million in terms of matchday revenue alone.

Moreover, the cost of the project has already risen to a whopping £450 million (almost four times the cost of the Millennium Stadium in Cardiff), however, as inflation is apparently covered by the constructors, at least this figure is unlikely to rise significantly. The enormous sum involved is because it is not just a case of building a stadium, but also the acquisition of light industrial premises and the construction of a new waste transfer station (replacing the current facility at Ashburton Grove), plus residential apartments on three sites (including Highbury).

Some £125 million has already been spent without a single brick of the new stadium having been laid. Before this can happen, the new waste transfer station must be operational and leaseholders relocated, and some have no desire to budge until the due processes of the law have been exhausted. Some malcontents are prepared to oppose compulsory purchase orders on the grounds that the project is not in the public interest. They argue that businesses have to move because of the interests of a private company; whereas the local authority regards the regeneration of the area as justifying their support for the scheme.

The amount of money swallowed up by Ashburton Grove is the reason, that, in spite of the increased turnover, Arsenal are now trading at a loss. In fact, some members of the board may have privately allowed themselves a sigh of relief when the team finished as Premiership runners-up in 2003. Although earning £500,000 less than the champions, actually retaining the title would have cost the club considerably more in bonus payments. Automatic qualification for the Champions League was the (temporary) salvation to the club's precarious financial position – failure to do so would have had far greater repercussions than allowing Manchester United to usurp their crown. The twin importance of Premiership success guaranteeing a Champions League place on an annual basis cannot be understated. In this respect the club could be accused of going down the same road as Leeds United.

To state, as Basil Fawlty would say, 'the bleeding obvious', Arsenal's cashflow problems would evaporate if they were able to secure a loan to cover the cost of the new stadium. Their preferred option appears to be the Royal Bank of Scotland (RBS), who have been doing the rounds of the city's financial institutions to try to obtain the necessary backing. However, with many millions required, RBS are not willing to undertake the loan unless they can share a proportion of the risk and finding willing partners is proving hard work. It could be argued that after another potential backer, the French bank Societé Général, dropped out Arsenal could have made a greater effort themselves to look further afield to find alternative saviours, rather than rely on the solitary British choice. For example, the loan for the new Wembley stadium is being funded by the WestLB bank in Germany, while the Portuguese Banco Espirito (who are involved in financing Coventry City's new stadium) have reportedly now come to the fore as an institution willing to consider taking on a significant proportion of the loan.

In an attempt to squeeze every available penny to allow the club to continue operating without incurring unmanageable debt (the interest payments on the estimated millions borrowed already being fairly substantial), several drastic measures have been taken. With all available assets mortgaged – the current stadium, the training centre at London Colney and the land at Ashburton Grove – the supporters have also been asked to play their part. Season-ticket prices predictably rise each summer way in excess of the rate of inflation, a move the club can get away with for the

194

time being because demand far outstrips supply. Arsenal are close to pricing out even the diehards, and fans who decide that they cannot afford to attend regularly may not return at all.

David Dein is well aware of the club's quandary, and admits to his fears for the future. 'We want the next generation of fans to be able to see the team. Today's kids can't get in and we have a waiting list of 25,000 for season tickets. What we are doing now at Highbury, if we are not careful, is gentrifying the audience, because we keep putting up prices in order to try and meet overheads and you end up with a different profile and in my opinion that is not right.' Dein now feels that the atmosphere at Highbury has been diluted with the inevitable demise of standing behind both goals and the concomitant escalation in prices, something he did not foresee when he launched the original North Bank bond scheme in the early 1990s.

Now he is more concerned about the working man, realising that more affluent customers do not get behind the team in the same vocal way. Because of his integral part in luring Arsène Wenger to Highbury, the perception of Dein amongst supporters has changed since the days when he spearheaded the 1991 bond scheme marketing. Now that his remit is dealing with the playing staff rather than stadium development, he is accepted as a football man, the highest possible praise a director can anticipate from the paying customers.

As if existing customers aren't already being charged enough, additional funding measures include a new policy towards 'away season-ticket holders', a scheme whereby members are automatically allocated tickets for every domestic away match with the money being directly debited from their bank accounts. Although in theory it saves work for the box office at the same time as rewarding the most loyal fans, a £20 per annum charge for this service was introduced in the 2003 close season. Further, for ticket registration members (who get first option on the limited number of home-match tickets before they go on general sale), the £20 fee paid each season was previously refunded via a £1 reduction on each Premiership ticket booked – so those who attended regularly were able to claw back most of the fee. However, that saving has now gone out of the window too. On top of an average 12 per cent rise in prices, the membership fee goes straight into the club coffers. In what other business could a commercial organisation treat its customers with such impunity and expect to retain their fidelity?

Ten years after the bonds were issued to finance the construction of the North Bank stand (whose 4,000 bondholders' inflation-proof season-ticket prices have now lapsed and they face swinge-ing price increases – although to be fair they knew at the time of purchase when their subsidy would run out – the £317 price of an upper-tier season ticket rising to £1,220) a similar scheme is being introduced in the hope of raising at least £15 million. With 3,000 customers willing to pay between £3,500 and £5,000 simply to jump the season-ticket waiting list and buy the newly issued bond it shows how times have changed and mores with them.

Ten years ago David Dein fronted the original bond scheme. With the inevitable move from terrace to all-seater stands as prescribed in the Taylor report, in the aftermath of the Hills-borough tragedy, a lot of fans feared they were going to be dis-enfranchised. 'About a week after the launch,' Dein recalls, 'I stopped at a bus stop in Bounds Green and wound down my car window and asked a guy, "Do you know where Myddleton Road is?" (Dein was looking for the Vrisaki Greek restaurant.) The next thing I see is a finger right next to my nose and the bloke says, "I know who you are and I don't like what you're doing." I replied, "I understand that, but do you know where Myddleton Road is?" Anyway he didn't tell me, but I found it. When I got back to my car the back window had been smashed in.'

This time around there wasn't the same sense of outrage from supporters, more an air of fatalistic resignation, in the forlorn hope that the money would be used for team-building rather than consumed by the voracious stadium project.

That is why Arsène Wenger is heaven-sent. People are prepared to part with such an inordinate amount because they are eager to be entertained by scintillating football. Should the leader leave the club though, sooner rather than later the big names will follow, and Arsenal will be left with a run-of-the-mill line-up that might not entice money from bank accounts quite so easily. With few alternatives open to the board, the new bond issue was conceived as yet another money making scheme to help offset the escalating stadium costs.

The inescapable conclusion is that the club have got themselves into a real predicament, so much so that they are having to raise short-term funds in order to continue operating. Until the stadium finance is sorted, nothing much is going to change, except that the reserves will inevitably dry up (£30 million was borrowed for cashflow purposes). So, on the basis that there are only half a dozen board meetings a year, unless in Ken Friar's words 'there is a crisis' in which case they hold five, pretty soon there will be no need for them to convene at all, whereas in reality they have been getting together far too often for everyone's liking. If Arsenal were 'a club in crisis' in 1996, as David Dein described it, could the situation in 2003 be potentially more catastrophic, with the spectre of administration hovering in the background?

The difficulty of balancing team-building needs while the new stadium is proving such a drain on resources has forced the board to be more flexible in their views. Remaining at Highbury is not an option, with its sale – for housing – used to secure loans. Plan A is to go ahead with the existing state-of-the-art design for Ashburton Grove on the basis that the required capital can be raised. 'We're taking a gamble,' admits the chairman. 'It's a brave decision and we're going to achieve it. If we get the finance there will be no worries.' But what if they don't?

An alternative might be to downsize a little – not in capacity, but in ambition. If the original plan is analogous to the Stade de France in Paris, what savings could be made with more of a Parc des Princes design? Does it really matter if it won't win any architectural awards? At its most complicated, a stadium has to consist of four stands, a series of corporate boxes and executive seats and a top notch rectangle of grass in the middle. QED. The artisan approach can still deliver the capacity and the perfect sight lines at a much more favourable cost: revenue ratio, but Hill-Wood is defiant. 'In making it cheaper there is no real gain. There is not a lot of additional cost for the planned version.' It is a stance that is not universally supported in or out of the boardroom.

So far as David Dein is concerned, the sooner that Arsenal can move, the better. 'We could have sold out Cardiff (against Southampton in the FA Cup final) comfortably. When we go to Old Trafford we are at a disadvantage. They've got over sixty thousand of their own fans behind them. People want to see us.

Now is the time to do it (move to a bigger stadium) and we are hot to trot.'

As the director in charge of team affairs, Dein is not primarily interested in bricks and mortar, but football and footballers. Although there is no doubt that the club has outgrown Highbury, he cannot fathom the need to build their own ground at such a prohibitive cost. Although Arsenal are historically linked with Islington, before 1913 they were a south-east London club (and still are to many embittered Tottenham fans). Time moves on. Dein believes that, on the evidence of the Champions League experiment, fans will travel to Wembley to watch the team. And such a move will not leave the club in hock for the foreseeable future, thereby fulfilling his mantra, 'Every morning when I look in the mirror to shave, I see the words written on my forehead: GET A WINNING TEAM.' He refuses to count out any option that would give the club the sought-after capacity increase.

Although the Wembley option could mean some of the millions spent so far on Ashburton Grove might not be recovered, despite some of the residential property deals already effected, the national stadium will be ready before 2006, with work now very much underway. The sum of £120 million would repay the lottery grant allocated to the project (which precludes tenancy) and allow Arsenal (and Tottenham if need be) to be accommodated. The three potential obstacles to the move would be: the need for the FA's approval (although as the owners face financial difficulties of their own this should be a formality); resistance from other Premiership clubs; and the need for Brent Council to allow matches to be held at Wembley on a far more frequent basis than previously – doubtless in the face of opposition from local residents. So with these conditions attached and the attendant obstacles to overcome, such a plan is by no means cut and dried, even if the overall cost of moving would be substantially less.

Peter Hill-Wood's reaction to the idea – 'over my dead body' – leaves little room for misinterpretation. And to send the chairman completely over the top there is of course the heretical suggestion that Tottenham Hotspur Football Club come to Ashburton Grove, not as tenants but as partners in a joint company that would own and control the stadium. The clubs have been down this road before in the eighties – a shared stadium at Alexandra Palace in north London being the proposed site – which of course, hindsight being a wonderful asset, would have solved everybody's problems.

It is still not too late for common sense to prevail. Both clubs need more capacity and both are in the red at the moment. There would be no need to cut any quality corners as additional and munificent revenue streams would be guaranteed. To begin with there would be twice the number of matchdays, half the overheads and no objections for marketing reasons not to sell the naming rights, for both clubs to reside in the Nike, McDonald's or whatever stadium.

While the concept of either ground sharing or renting does not sit well with those pushing for Ashburton Grove, Arsenal's embarrassment stems from the fact that they are a football club, who have got themselves caught up in the property and construction business, through the tangled web created by the three sites. With so much more to consider (to say nothing of the time-delaying planning and legal issues), money is being siphoned from the football side. Stephen Schechter, who has experience in raising finance for Leeds, Newcastle and Southampton through securitisation said, 'Ashburton Grove is three developments in one: a property development at Highbury, one at Ashburton Grove and then the stadium itself. Had it just been the stadium, it would have had fewer problems, but the two property developments make it very complicated.'

The club stand at a crossroads. In one sense, their grandiose plan reflects the approach of Arsène Wenger, the supreme optimist, who has not penalised his employers on the balance sheet. Quite the contrary in fact, with titles, cups and Champions League qualification all acquired at a net annual cost of less than £5 million which has been more than covered by income from the Champions League alone. The millions spent on Ashburton Grove, with so far nothing to show for it, is greater than the club's annual turnover in 2001, the same year Leeds United were the second biggest club in the country. Their turnover was over £32 million more than Arsenal's. Two years later they have accumulated debts of more than £70 million and consider themselves fortunate to be facing any future at all, however bleak it appears. If the Premier League applied the same stringent financial criteria – notably an assessment of assets and liabilities and a consideration of trading deficit – practised abroad, then Arsenal, along with several other clubs, might be facing the prospect of relegation. In 2003 Monaco, Arsène Wenger's old club, despite having finished runners-up in both the league and cup, were relegated to the second division and only reinstated after financial guarantees were put in place. All the same they are very much on probation, their ability to use the transfer market subject to specific permission being granted.

Having just won the double in 2002, Arsenal's plight was already grave enough to curtail the squad reinforcements in the aftermath of the World Cup finals – traditionally a time that sees plenty of transfer activity. Arguably only the disposal of goalkeeper Richard Wright, to Everton, after just one season enabled Arsène Wenger to purchase Gilberto Silva and Pascal Cygan for a combined total of £5.5 million. Although someone of the calibre of an Ayala or a Pellegrino was required in central defence, the budget didn't stretch to it.

Arsène Wenger admitted in September 2002 that the new stadium 'will put the club in a little bit of trouble financially and we are struggling to cope with it.' At the Annual General Meeting that autumn, the board presented a somewhat rosy face to the club's shareholders, despite their knowledge of the problems. When three separate questioners expressed their doubts about how the club could afford to fund the huge sums necessitated by the new stadium, Peter Hill-Wood expressed his confidence that the money could be raised, although he could not give precise details. The truth is probably that, at that point, even if he didn't know, he had reasonable grounds for optimism. By the time of the 2004 AGM, the facts will be out and the board could be in for a rough ride. Whether a few quips from the chairman – and the timely use of 'Would anyone like to hear a few words from the manager?' – will get the board off the hook remains to be seen.

The situation can only deteriorate unless one of two things happen. One, is that the Royal Bank of Scotland would have to get lucky and find enough support to be able to spread the risk of the much needed £250-million-plus loan. For that to happen there needs to be an economic revival, resulting in a greater willingness by the banking sector to lend money over the long term. The other possible source of salvation is an increase in television revenue. As this already accounts for nearly half of the club's income, the impact of new television deals on the horizon cannot be understated. The rights to screen Premiership matches are up for tender; a deal which would come into effect in August 2004. The European Commission has looked into the current arrangement (whereby all live matches are screened by BSkyB) and objected on three grounds. First, there is a restriction on the number of matches that are shown (currently 106 of the 380 played). Second, the exclusive nature of the coverage; and, finally, it feels uneasy regarding central selling and feels clubs should be allowed the opportunity to control the rights to some of their live games themselves.

The Premier League have responded by making more matches available over a number of different platforms, hoping that free-to-air broadcasters – BBC, ITV, Channel 4 and Channel Five – might be tempted along with their long-time pay TV partner BSkyB to bid. More matches could mean more money, even if BSkyB are permitted by the EC to retain their exclusivity, they will have to pay a premium in order to do so. However, if the price to the other broadcasters is simply too high then BSkyB may get away with not only scooping the jackpot, but at a lower fee than they paid last time around.

Nevertheless, prime properties such as the Premier League should be able to buck the downward trend in the rights market as recent deals for the US rights for the Olympic Games and the UK rights for the Champions League illustrate. This deal could represent more good news for Arsenal as BSkyB have come into the picture, for the first time, to increase the UK rights fee to the benefit of the participating English clubs who share a percentage of the amount paid. If Arsenal perform to the same standard as last year, they should comfortably exceed the £15 million they earned from the Champions League.

The possibility of a number of live Premiership matches on non-subscription television for the first time will have a consequential effect above and beyond an incremental fee. The highest audience for a match on subscription television was the 3.4 million who watched Arsenal versus Manchester United on Sky Sports in April 2003. Although to be fair, the number of people who watched in pubs would have greatly boosted this figure. Nonetheless, audiences for live action on terrestrial channels are invariably much larger. The BBC routinely had over five million viewers for its live UEFA Cup ties involving Liverpool and Celtic, while audiences for Champions League matches on ITV sometimes touch the ten million mark. If some Premiership football was screened free-to-air on a regular basis, the deals that Arsenal, who would doubtless be one of the main attractions, could strike with commercial suppliers and sponsors would inevitably net them greater rewards due to the increased exposure. Arsenal would also profit if matches which were not covered by the arrangements with the broadcasters were made available to the clubs themselves. Along with Granada, they might be able to put some real substance into their broadband venture and show games in their entirety on the internet, and charge accordingly.

However, the advent of Roman Abramovich – Chelsea's saviour – has created another watershed in the life of the Premiership, as significant as BSkyB's initial television deal. If Jack Walker could buy a title for £100 million, what price a Russian billionaire who has money to spare to indulge a new found passion to make Chelsea into an amalgam of Manchester United and Real Madrid. In fact Manchester United are answerable to their shareholders, Florentino Perez is answerable to his members, but Abramovich is merely answerable to himself. Along with David Beckham's transfer to Real Madrid, football, at the highest level, has left business behind to throw itself headlong into the wacky world of showbiz.

Fifty million for Thierry Henry? No problem. It may be the furthest thought in David Dein's mind but he may not be able to ignore the kind of offer he can't refuse. Before the new stadium led to debts of millions of pounds there was no need to go fully public as that might mean diluting the control of the small, independently wealthy board. Now, however, their personal fortunes are comparatively minuscule in this new world. Arsenal need money, a lot of it and quickly – so they could be at the mercy of a voracious predator. Putting the interests of the club foremost, the directors could be secretly hoping that it may be a small step from troubles to roubles, or similar currency. And in one mighty bound they would be free, or at least, the object of their affections would be.

So, although the club may be in a quandary, even without the emergence of a wealthy benefactor, there is some light at the end of the tunnel. It is astonishing to think that they are now scrambling around for every pound (even refunds due to season-ticket holders, who did not wish to take up their seats for the Highbury 'away' FA Cup-tie against Farnborough in January 2003, were not sent out until the season was over). From a position of pre-eminence and profit, the 'Bank of England' club are now in danger of finding themselves a 'Carey Street' outfit. When a football finance expert recently asked Arsène Wenger if there was anything he could do for him, in return for a favour, the Arsenal manager replied, 'If you can find four hundred million pounds for me you are really an expert.' The gallows humour reflecting the reality of the situation. If salvation means either Ashburton Grove with fewer bells and whistles, or giving up on the project altogether and groundsharing at Wembley, then so be it. Because, ultimately, if the board are unable to support Arsène Wenger in the way he deserves, he will be forced to go elsewhere and find someone who can. And there will be no shortage of offers. A disastrous chain reaction will be set off. The stars will follow the manager out of the door and the club will slump into decline.

Chapter Fifteen

Always and Forever?

'It's like going into a boxing ring with your hands tied behind your back.' When Arsenal vice-chairman David Dein uses such language to describe the challenge ahead of Arsène Wenger as he makes his plans for the 2003–04 season, there can be no doubt that the short-term future does not bode well. Even with the manager's talent for, as Dein puts it, 'digging diamonds out of the dust', it seems as if he will not even be provided with a spade by his directors until they can extricate the club out of the hole they have dug themselves into.

With the future under a cloud, nobody should have been surprised that, on Friday 23 May, a meeting between Arsène Wenger, Real Madrid president Florentino Perez and his director of football, Jorge Valdano, took place in the Plaza Athenée Hotel on Paris' Avenue Montaigne. Less than a month later, the day after Real Madrid won *la Liga* on the final Sunday of the season, coach Vicente del Bosque's employment was brusquely terminated, his contract having run its course, after bringing the club two Champions League trophies and two league titles in four seasons.

That his replacement was Carlos Queiroz, Alex Ferguson's number two at Old Trafford (rather than Arsène Wenger, as the media had speculated) may have raised a few eyebrows, but not because of the link between the two men – Wenger being instrumental in Queiroz's appointment as his successor at Grampus Eight, before his departure for Arsenal in 1996.

With Queiroz' contract with Real coincidentally expiring in 2005, as does Wenger's with Arsenal, will it be Queiroz who moves on this time? Wenger has stated that he will not leave before then, although the club's financial health over the ensuing two years will inevitably influence his future. Although mischievous minds might believe the intention of the Paris rendezvous with Real was to reach an understanding, to keep the Bernabeu bench warm for him, David Dein is hopeful that his friend will remain beyond his current commitment, commenting, 'The chemistry remains very good between us, but the stadium (resolution) is our greatest test.'

If, privately, the Arsenal manager must be a very frustrated man, with his ambition to build an all-conquering team so undermined by money problems not of his own making, he is far too discreet to give any indication of his disquiet. Additionally, he retains some humour when the subject of his budget limitations arises with Dein. The vice-chairman reveals, 'I went to see the club president of a target I had identified on the Continent and, after about an hour of jousting over what sort of fee they would accept, he then wrote down a stream of figures – based upon appearances, and the like, to increase the final amount – on a very small piece of paper. When I got back to London, I went to see Arsène and said, "They are a seller, but I think they're being hugely optimistic in their value of the player", and I showed him this little piece of paper. He said, "Well, it's a little bit of paper, but they're very big figures!" '

Wenger himself has no illusions as to the magnitude of the move from Highbury. Although, his refusal to face financial facts indicates that his optimism is not tempered by any element of doubt, or perhaps even reality. Asked recently about his decision to re-sign for a further three-year spell in the autumn of 2001, in preference to coaching Barcelona, he said he chose to remain because, 'I want to win the European Cup with this club and I want to achieve more. I want to make this club the biggest club in the world. I really believe (I can achieve) it.' When it was pointed out that Manchester United, for one, will always be bigger than Arsenal, he refused to accept the notion. 'I think if we achieve the 60,000-seater, we will make more gate income than Manchester United.' Maybe, but United have a head start with the, as yet, untapped potential of a worldwide fanbase to come. And David Dein admits that, 'we don't want to be saddled with an enormous repayment schedule that puts us behind Manchester

United, Real Madrid and other clubs who don't have (such arrangements). That is a personal worry for me.' Yet, even in the best case scenario of securing a loan, carrying a huge debt is unavoidable.

The manager talks naïvely, but touchingly, of his vision, and denies his heart is ruling his head. 'I came here to bring my football way of thinking to this club, to win things, and make this club bigger step by step,' he says. 'The first step was to have a training ground, where the club can improve and I think we have done that remarkably well. It's not finished because there's a lot still to build there. The club now is respected in Europe for what we have achieved there. It is a step. We want to win in Europe and we'll do it. We are recognised and respected in Europe for the way we play football. And what I want as well – another step – is to put this club to a level where we have a sixty-thousand-seater and if the manager or the board takes the right decision, can compete with everybody in the world. At the moment, if Milan or Manchester United or Real Madrid are (interested in) the same player, I say "Thank you very much, I'll go somewhere else". And I want that one day the manager – if it's me or somebody else – can say, "Okay, how much is it? I can compete". And that gives you a guarantee, but at the moment if we are wrong in the buys, we cannot compete. If (I get) one or two buys wrong, we are dead. In the big clubs the difference (is that they can say) okay this year, we were wrong. We'll put £50 million in again and we'll be right next time.'

If only. Perhaps the board are guilty of complacency so far as their manager is concerned, realising that he is an honourable man, he is under contract for at least two more years and there is little likelihood of a mass exodus of stars while the man who brought them to Highbury in the first place remains at the helm. For his part, Wenger discounts his influence over the playing staff. 'It would be too big a responsibility for me to go and think that everybody just wants to go (as well),' he says. 'I think there's something more than just me that brought the players in. They love the club as well because there's a special atmosphere at Highbury and (there's) a love for the shirt because they feel part of it.' Perhaps there is something extraordinary about Arsenal football club, which imbues loyalty that only those on the inside can truly testify to. As Bob Wilson says, 'Virtually every Arsenal player who had to leave the club for whatever reason (has told me) when I've met them afterwards, something along the lines of, "Yep. I'm enjoying it, it's a nice little club, but it's not the same ... it's not Arsenal." '

Even so, the inability to pay the going rate when contract renewal comes around could show that loyalty commands a price that cannot be afforded. Although Thierry Henry's matter-of-fact decision to sign up until 2007 (at a salary far less than he could command in Spain, Italy or indeed from one or two employers in England) is reassuring and refreshing, both Patrick Vieira and Robert Pires have not yet committed themselves in a similar way.

Prolonged contract talks have stretched over months, and in March 2003, chairman Peter Hill-Wood went public on the matter, expressing his irritation. 'Players generally will have to get real and realise that wages are no longer going to move out of control. It is possible that players like Vieira and Pires will leave, unless they face facts. We cannot possibly sanction a massive increase in the wage bill. It has been steadily increasing, but in recent years it has escalated by twenty to twenty-five per cent. That is no longer sustainable. The wage bill will have to be more in line with inflation, and that's how it should be.' The one ray of light for fans who feared the worst was the rider, 'Of course, we would make an exception for an exceptional player, and Patrick Vieira is an exceptional player. We want them (Vieira and Pires) to sign new deals, but there is a limit to how much we can offer them – and that's it.'

Confronting the players in this way was dangerous brinkmanship as, naturally, neither appreciated the chairman's statement and Patrick Vieira responded in kind at the season's end. 'Mr Hill-Wood continues to make comments which I am not happy about at all. He said that if I wasn't content with the money I was earning, then I could leave. But he always seems to wait until I am out of the country playing for France before saying anything. It is a total lack of respect and I really do not appreciate it. If Arsenal come and say to me "Madrid want you and they are going to give us the money we need," I am going to go. I know Madrid wanted me and you have to think about it when a club like that comes for you. If Arsenal tell me they are ready to let me go then something is broken between me and the club, which means I will go. It would hurt me to accept it although I would go where I wanted to, not where they told me to go.' For all Vieira's outward displays of affection, there is more chance of him realising his remaining football ambitions elsewhere, and knowing he could walk into the starting line-up (with a commensurately higher salary) of any team on the planet gives him all the aces.

Fortunately, David Dein will probably be the one who decides how the club's hand will be played and he may be more aware than the chairman of when to fold, knowing that Vieira can't be allowed to leave as a free agent in a year's time. It wouldn't be surprising if Messrs Dein and Wenger told the board that if they couldn't persuade Vieira to re-sign, he must be sold forthwith. Neither would contemplate sitting on their hands, as Tottenham did with Sol Campbell, enabling him to leave as a free agent.

Vieira is of course – as one of the best holding midfielders in the world – exactly what Manchester United, Real Madrid and nouveau riche Chelsea want and are currently lacking and although the player has said if he leaves Arsenal, it would only be to move abroad, harsh reality dictates that he could end up opposing them in a Manchester United or Chelsea shirt. Under these circumstances, Arsenal's best option may be to sell him to Real Madrid to get their pound of flesh and persuade them to lease him back for the remaining year of his contract.

David Dein has called the Wenger years, 'A seamless revolution.' Over ninety player movements – out with the journeymen, in with the virtuosos – has seen the image and status of the club transformed. But the sound of money talking is drowning out the manager's persuasive powers. There is little indication that the coffers at Highbury hold enough, with so many millions already diverted to the cause of the new stadium. Wenger believes the money will come, but how long will he have to wait? Everything points to the fact that he will have to sell in order to buy, a reprise of the situation in 2002 with Richard Wright's surprise departure. Or, persuade existing squad members to become part of a player exchange deal.

The board may have promised him a £10 million transfer kitty, but is that on the proviso that he raises the money first through player sales? Already David Seaman and Oleg Luzhny have been released at the end of their contracts. There was doubt as to whether Dennis Bergkamp would be re-signed, whilst Kanu has been offered a reputed £1 million to walk out the door two years ahead of time. Add to this the names raised as either available for sale or possible makeweights for transfer targets (including Sylvain Wiltord, Ray Parlour, Francis Jeffers, Edu and Jermaine Pennant), and it looks clear that the first-team squad will either be lesser in number or feature a higher quota of more modestly rewarded youth team players. However, the stage has not been reached where any player is available at the right price, a situation that has decimated Leeds United's roster.

Although the new Chelsea owner's favourite player might be Thierry Henry, David Dein is adamant that he is not for sale. He says, 'The only pleasure I get in all the political shenanigans is watching world-class players in an Arsenal shirt.' To allow men of the number 14's ilk to be sold would be to undermine everything the manager has strived to achieve. David Dein is forthright about the circumstances. 'We have to sell players to balance the books. Our salaries are in the top three or four in the Premiership, and have to be. You're not going to keep world-class players unless you pay them good money. Otherwise they'll leave,' he admits. 'It's catch-22, in order for us to continue paying big salaries, we have to get the income. We cannot (continue on the same basis) because Thierry Henry and Patrick Vieira get the same salary whether we're playing in front of 38,000 people or 138,000, so we need a bigger stadium to generate more income. Unfortunately, the project that we embarked upon has become so big and so costly that at the moment, particularly with the wages as they are, until we find a way to increase our overall turnover, it's a major balancing act. You have to have both (the team and the new stadium development). We're hoping to sell players but at the moment the market is very thin. If we do move out three or four players, then it's a different story as it opens up the budget again, but we have to be prudent.'

But Wenger's glass is always half full. And he makes a virtue out of necessity. 'It just makes my buying easier because I will have to strengthen my squad while being sensible,' he claims. 'If you are asking me whether I would rather spend fifty million pounds than two million then I would say "Of course". But I believe that I already have a very good team and that I will be sharp enough to strengthen it, where it is needed, with the money I have available.' Not only this, but he feels he will be spoiled for choice. 'There are so many players who want to join us that sometimes we will have good opportunities, especially at the moment when the market is really flat. I know who I want to go for and I know that the money will be available for what I want to do. There are so many clubs who struggle just to pay the wages that they are happy to give away even big players.' All the same, will his headaches be compounded by ignoring the lessons of the past? He admits to palpable errors, such as not giving himself more defensive options but says he is seeking three new faces, 'a goalkeeper, central defender and an attacker'. Yet the back-line warrants serious attention. The purchase of a partner for Sol Campbell will not cover any absence at full-back, especially with Luzhny no longer available. Contrarily, a target-man alongside Thierry Henry might improve an already scintillating attack, which will see his team through and make good any defensive deficiencies, a strategy that has already been revealed as threadbare.

Wenger's desire to go on the offensive does not bring bouquets when the teamwork is not clicking like clockwork. Claiming that Arsenal were the number one team in the 2002–03 Premiership despite finishing five points behind the winners, Wenger missed the point. Manchester United were the best team because, although they may not have played the best football, they played the more effective football. Until league points are awarded for style, the champions will invariably demonstrate a mix of grace and grit, as Arsenal themselves did in Wenger's two title-winning seasons. In a series comprising thirty-eight episodes, there are bound to be some mundane performances, but the real trouper keeps right on to the end. Arsenal could have been more obdurate.

Eventually, at the eleventh hour, too late as far as the league title was concerned, the frustration of too many lost leads led to them killing the FA Cup final as a spectacle as the second half wore on in a successful manoeuvre to preserve their lead. In Arsène Wenger's mind it didn't appear that the end justified the means and in due course the players worked out things for themselves. But should he have held the view that 'what we have we hold' and instructed his players accordingly? (Gérard Houllier failed to take France to the 1994 World Cup Finals because David Ginola continued to play in a carefree manner in the 89th minute and Bulgaria took possession and scored on the counterattack. When France hosted the finals four years later under the more mundane Aimé Jaquet, their progress was marked by method and application compensating for an ineffective attack, without Ginola or Eric Cantona playing any part in the proceedings despite their success in the Premiership.)

If George Graham had been in charge, Arsenal themselves would have instigated the fad for taking the ball to the corner flag in the dying minutes. If one eavesdropped on pre-season training, one could imagine Graham bellowing to a bemused Houston, 'Forget the ******* cones today Stewart, and plant a few corner flags!' Then Graham would get the ball at the flag, and shield it by sticking his ample backside out to prevent dispossession, declaring to his pupils, 'Watch and learn, this is how it's done!' Not content with that piece of gamesmanship, the manager would then proceed to rope together the flabbergasted famous five, minus Seaman (it was beyond even his creative powers to tie in the goalkeeper as well), in order to get them to move in unison. One can imagine Graham falling about with laughter as on the sound of the whistle, Winterburn went forwards and Dixon went backwards, bringing everybody crashing to the ground. It is improbable that, given his penchant for conservation – 'I love 1–0 victories,' he told Tottenham director Douglas Alexiou – Arsenal would have surrendered leads in the way they did were he still in charge. Of course, whether they would have got their noses in front in the first place was highly questionable.

Paradoxically, the conservative Graham was more adroit in his use of substitutes than his successor. Often when in front, Wenger will replace an attacker with a defender. This would be understandable if he was beckoning a reliable reinforcement into the back-line, which with the initiative surrendered invariably becomes increasingly beleaguered. Also, when the need arises to add fresh impetus to the attack, Kanu appears too late when his skill at holding up play, if employed earlier, could preclude the necessity to sling on any defender. At least Wenger appears to have learned that if Dennis Bergkamp can't go for the full ninety minutes then he is a far better starter than substitute, as he finds it difficult to adjust to the pace of the game when it is not his passing ability that is the priority.

One factor that hampered Arsenal last season, and for which Arsène Wenger cannot be blamed, was the state of the pitch at Highbury after Christmas. Following a torrential downpour, the Chelsea league match on New Year's Day went ahead, much to the surprise of the attending Sven Goran Eriksson who felt, as he arrived shortly before kick-off, that he had made a wasted journey. All groundsman Steve Braddock's good work up to that point was ruined, and the surface never truly recovered. Apart from impairing any chance of being awarded his customary 'grounds-man of the year' accolade, the ravages of the weather resulted, according to Bob Wilson, in a proliferation of missed chances due to the unevenness of the surface, littered with bobbles. One such opportunity amongst many that stood out was a Pires effort against Roma which, had the simple chance been converted instead of sailing over the bar, could have taken his colleagues into the quarter-finals. Perhaps fatalists might argue that Arsène Wenger is simply not a lucky manager, and that if Napoleon were choosing a general, he would have been far more inclined to select Sir Alex Ferguson.

The rivalry between the two has defined the history of the Premiership since Arsène Wenger first alighted on these shores in 1996. It was clear right away that Wenger got under Ferguson's skin, prompting the dismissive outburst, 'He has come from Japan and now he is telling us how to organise our football. He should keep his mouth shut.' Unlike Kevin Keegan though, Wenger doesn't rise to Ferguson's jibes with any self-destructing gestures, his cool patronising response – 'When they won the treble, they seemed to have somebody upstairs who decided to give them all three' – only seems to redouble Ferguson's fury. Yet, while their respective backgrounds determine they will never be soulmates, they do share common interests. The self-educated son of a ship-worker and the economics graduate both enjoy cerebral pursuits such as heavyweight political and biographical tomes. But, above all, what binds them together is their passion for the day job. Workaholics both, 'I think there is a common link,' says Wenger. 'We want to win and we are passionately determined to win. He's lasted a long time, I've lasted a few years. To survive in this job you need a big passion because you need to recover from disappointments.'

Recognised for their achievements, one knighted and the other awarded an OBE by his adopted country to accompany his *Légion d'honneur*, they arrived at the summit after overcoming many pitfalls along the way, not least their shortcomings as players. If Ferguson appears obsessed by Wenger perhaps it is because, set for retirement last year, he could not bear to relinquish the reins with the thought that his adversary was set to usurp his domain, the prospect that the Arsenal double was the harbinger of a dynastic upheaval was unbearable. Losing the title on their own patch was a shock to the system. Although there was a real hunger to right wrongs, with Ferguson feeling that the joys of retirement had not been foregone for him to finish second best – especially when he could see his horse Rock of Gibraltar leaving everybody trailing in its wake.

Autumn injuries cut his side's momentum but a coruscating run since Boxing Day took United past Arsenal at a gallop. Helped by fate (the temptation to select Juan Sebastian Veron was removed by the midfielder's injury) and stung by the FA Cup exit at the hands of Arsenal – that game marked the beginning of the end for Arsenal – United's superior resources took them first past the winning post. The difference highlighted by the way Ferguson restructured his defence. Initially he threw money at the problem, with the purchase of Rio Ferdinand, and then when it was obvious that for all his inspirational qualities Laurent Blanc was off the pace, he was able to promote from within in the form of Wes Brown and John O'Shea.

If Ferguson had been at Highbury, although he might have extracted more from the youth system, it is arguable whether he could have matched Wenger's accomplishments. The sheer lack of funds would have curtailed his ability to augment his best kids. And while Wenger has been able to unearth gems from abroad and hone their potential, Ferguson might not have been able to do this because of his initial lack of knowledge of the worldwide market. Quite simply, to supplement the class of '92 (Giggs, Beckham, Butt, Scholes and the Nevilles) money has come to Ferguson's rescue through an amalgam of effective big buys (Andy Cole, Jaap Stam, Dwight Yorke, Ruud van Nistelrooy and Rio

Ferdinand) and the wherewithal to pay the high salaries that enable him to keep them under lock and key and prevent the Spanish and Italian giants picking them off until *he* decides it is time for them to go. Would Anelka, Overmars and Petit have been offloaded by United? Unlikely, because they are never short of cash and even paying top dollar, the salary bill is only half their turnover. But then would they have found them in the first place? In a situation of make do and mend, the strategic omission of restructuring the defence aside, it is doubtful if Ferguson could have emulated Wenger's deeds.

On the other hand, when it initially appeared that Alex Ferguson was going to retire at the end of 2001–02, there was a great deal of speculation about the possibility of Arsène Wenger being lined up as a replacement. If that had come to pass, perhaps he might have coasted to the title and made good his belief that he could overcome Real Madrid. With a transfer war chest at his disposal he wouldn't have to accept the compromise of a moderate defence – 'I would have liked to have signed Rio Ferdinand but for ten million less,' he said – as the price of his scintillating attack.

Further, he wouldn't have to gamble on his buys becoming overnight sensations. He would have more leeway and would simply buy better. And his lack of confidence in home-grown youth, if not restored by the crop at Carrington (United's academy) could be compensated for by the expanded cherry-picking of promising Continental youngsters, such as Phillipe Senderos – whom he has impressed enough to persuade him to select Arsenal above more glamorous suitors. Wenger's own assessment, made when it appeared Ferguson was on the way out, rings true: 'His club has such potential they will continue to be tough no matter who comes in after him ... they have the money to buy a good manager, the money to buy good players. It will go on.'

'You don't ever want to lose a person like this,' said David Dein of Arsène Wenger in 2001. With the wheel having gone full circle and Arsenal's fortunes suddenly in decline through no fault of the manager, two years on and that view is even more pertinent. Asked in June by French station TF1's *Telefoot* programme why his players adored him, he responded, 'There is reciprocity in the respect and confidence. I also have the advantage of being able to select the players myself. If I choose somebody it is obviously a good base for being able to work together.' There is a strong sense of perspective that he finds may be lacking elsewhere. After Milan won the Champions League in May 2003, Wenger commented, 'I've seen people at Milan. They told me two months ago, inside the club was all doom and gloom. And today there is euphoria. That's why the club for me should be stronger than that, because there must be a philosophy of how you see the game, of how you conduct the club.' It is difficult to envisage Wenger obtaining the same degree of job satisfaction in Spain or Italy where the club president takes charge of the transfer policy. Thus, the only scenario under which he would go to Real Madrid would be if he is asked by Arsenal to make too many financial sacrifices.

Arsenal must be perilously close to this position if David Seaman was asked to take a drop in salary and Dennis Bergkamp, despite offering to do likewise in return for a one-year contract, was initially put to one side and not regarded as a priority until the manager knew what few shekels he had to play with. The treatment of Bergkamp – a pivotal figure in the turnaround of the club's fortunes since his arrival in 1995 – is nothing short of myopia for a genuinely world-class player who has previously demonstrated great loyalty. Against such a background, the attraction for Wenger grows of having an all-star squad provided for him in Spain, with the very real chance it offers of adding a Champions League trophy to his CV. He is also sufficiently sanguine to accept that such a post is likely to be of short-term duration, after which he can indulge himself with the less onerous task of managing the French, German or Japanese national team and enjoy his favoured hobby of watching football – free from day-to-day pressures.

The legacy he will leave behind, when finally he does depart will be akin to that of Herbert Chapman – the bountiful memories of a golden era. He has moved the club forward in a way that neither Bertie Mee nor George Graham could. Those two title-winning bosses gave Arsenal a spell in the sun, but they provided short summers, which soon clouded over. With Wenger, there has been sunshine every year.

It is only because the bar has been raised so high that there is deception when the target is not reached and those fans who are overcritical have amnesia. For all that, no one is as deflated as the manager himself when Arsenal fail. But because of his cheerful expectation, introspection does not last long and he is back with a spring in his step. Whether declaring his intent to win the Champions League next time around, after failing to make the knockout stage last time out, or, wishing the 2003–04 season could start straight away as soon as the title loss was confirmed by losing to Leeds.

'You must be an optimist in this job,' he says. 'In effect, a coach is somebody who puts his future in his players' hands. You believe in others, you have to keep a form of optimism. The fact that you have to depend on others can make you aggressive, suspicious or even paranoid. That's why to keep stress at bay you have to have an optimistic vision.'

So the future is all important – the past a different country. So what if, at the moment, Arsenal seem to take two steps forward and one step back each season, at least they are moving inexorably upwards. And with Wenger at the helm, there is always the tantalising prospect of three giant strides.

After enjoying a week's summer break in Sardinia with his family, Wenger travelled to France to join the TF1 commentary team who were covering the 2003 Confederations Cup. With the Real rendezvous still fresh in the mind, he was asked by the doyen of French sports broadcasters, Thierry Roland, during the transmission of the France v Colombia match, 'You're Arsenal forever?'

Wenger answered, 'Yes, yes, yes.'

'You're not going to Real?'

'*Presque jamais*,' came the reply. Almost never.

Index